GENDER AND SOCIAL HIERARCHIES

Gender and Social Hierarchies offers a fresh and coherent picture of applied research from within social psychology on the intricate relationship between gender and social status. It comprises a collection of innovative approaches which seek to understand the pervasiveness of status asymmetry between gender categories. Drawing upon recent theoretical advances in gender psychology, the book provides tools for developing practical and political recommendations to address and resolve status inequality today.

Each chapter examines a different aspect of the impact that gender-based social hierarchies have on people's lives. Part One explores the consequences of gender stereotypes in school, higher education, and in professional settings. The struggles faced by women in the workplace are discussed in Part Two, featuring topics such as work-life balance, the 'glass cliff', and the lack of support for affirmative action. Part Three is devoted to the antecedents and consequences of gender-based forms of prejudice, such as discrimination against gay men, and against women within cultural minorities. The book concludes with some practical suggestions for working towards lasting and beneficial change.

Gender and Social Hierarchies will appeal to scholars and students across the social sciences and offers important insights to practitioners and policy-makers.

Klea Faniko is Senior Researcher, Faculty of Psychology and Educational Sciences, University of Geneva, Switzerland.

Fabio Lorenzi-Cioldi is Full Professor of Social Psychology, Faculty of Psychology and Educational Sciences, University of Geneva, Switzerland.

Oriane Sarrasin is Postdoctoral Researcher, NCCR LIVES, Institute of Social Sciences, Faculty of Social and Political Sciences, University of Lausanne, Switzerland

Eric May :cturer, Institute of Work and Organizatic châtel, Switzerland.

GENDER AND SOCIAL HIERARCHIES

Perspectives from social psychology

Edited by Klea Faniko, Fabio Lorenzi-Cioldi,
Oriane Sarrasin, and Eric Mayor

Routledge
Taylor & Francis Group

LONDON AND NEW YORK

First published 2016
by Routledge
2 Park Square, Milton Park, Abingdon, Oxon OX14 4RN

and by Routledge
711 Third Avenue, New York, NY 10017

Routledge is an imprint of the Taylor & Francis Group, an informa business

© 2016 Klea Faniko, Fabio Lorenzi-Cioldi, Oriane Sarrasin, and
Eric Mayor

The right of the editors to be identified as the authors of the
editorial material, and of the authors for their individual chapters,
has been asserted in accordance with sections 77 and 78 of the
Copyright, Designs and Patents Act 1988.

British Library Cataloguing in Publication Data
A catalogue record for this book is available from the British Library

Library of Congress Cataloging in Publication Data
Gender and social hierarchies : perspectives from social psychology /
edited by Klea Faniko, Fabio Lorenzi-Cioldi, Oriane Sarrasin and
Eric Mayor.
    pages cm
    1. Sex discrimination. 2. Social status. 3. Social stratification.
    4. Sex role. 5. Equality. I. Faniko, Klea, editor.
    HQ1237.G427 2016
    305.3–dc23   2015016585

ISBN: 978-1-138-93809-0 (hbk)
ISBN: 978-1-138-93811-3 (pbk)
ISBN: 978-1-315-67587-9 (ebk)

Typeset in Bembo
by HWA Text and Data Management, London
Printed in Great Britain by Ashford Colour Press Ltd,
Gosport, Hants

CONTENTS

FIGURES

TABLES

CONTRIBUTORS

Jacques Berent University of Geneva, Switzerland

Virginie Bonnot University of Paris Descartes, France

Valérie Carrard University of Lausanne, Switzerland

Aïna Chalabaev University of Grenoble Alpes, France

Julien Chanal University of Geneva & Distance Learning University, Brig, Switzerland

Boris Cheval University of Geneva, Switzerland

Marion Chipeaux University of Geneva, Switzerland

Céline Darnon University of Clermont Auvergne & University of Blaise Pascal, France

Belle Derks University of Utrecht, the Netherlands

Joerg Dietz University of Lausanne, Switzerland

Benoît Dompnier University of Lausanne, Switzerland

Naomi Ellemers Leiden University, the Netherlands

Juan M. Falomir-Pichastor University of Geneva, Switzerland

Klea Faniko University of Geneva, Switzerland

Nicole Fasel University of Lausanne, Switzerland

Paolo Ghisletta University of Geneva, Switzerland

Lavinia Gianettoni University of Lausanne, Switzerland

Eva G. T. Green University of Lausanne, Switzerland

Edith Guilley Educational Research Unit (SRED), Department of Public Instruction, Culture and Sport of the Canton of Geneva, Switzerland

Pascal M. Gygax University of Fribourg, Switzerland

Vincenzo Iacoviello University of Geneva, Switzerland

Claire Johnston University of Lausanne, Switzerland

Emmanuelle P. Kleinlogel University of Clermont Auvergne & University of Blaise Pascal, France

Clara Kulich University of Geneva, Switzerland

Ioana Latu Rutgers University, Camden, USA

Fabio Lorenzi-Cioldi University of Geneva, Switzerland

Christian Maggiori School of Social Work, Fribourg & University of Lausanne, Switzerland

Brigitte Mantilleri University of Geneva, Switzerland

Erjona Manushi University of Geneva, Switzerland

Delphine Martinot University of Clermont Auvergne & University of Blaise Pascal, France

Shékina Rochat University of Lausanne, Switzerland

Jérôme Rossier University of Lausanne, Switzerland

Oriane Sarrasin University of Lausanne, Switzerland

Marianne Schmid Mast University of Lausanne, Switzerland

Fiorela Shalsi UN Women, Albania

Siri Øyslebø Sørensen Norwegian University of Science and Technology, Norway

Sarah D. Stauffer University of Lausanne, Switzerland

Catherine Verniers University of Clermont Auvergne & University of Blaise Pascal, France

Regula Zimmermann University of Fribourg, Switzerland

ACKNOWLEDGEMENTS

First of all, we wish to express our appreciation to all the authors for their valuable contributions to the book. We wish to express our heartfelt thanks to the Schmidheiny foundation, the Fonds General, and the Dean's Office of the Faculty of Psychology and Educational Science (University of Geneva), for their financial support for this project. Our sincere gratitude goes to Routledge, especially to Michael Strang, publisher, and Libby Volke, assistant editor, for making this book happen. We thank our colleagues who provided us with insightful feedback when we prepared the book proposal: Joël Anderson, Till Burckhardt, Marie Besse, Natasha Frederic, François Grin, Gabriel Mugny, Ashley Riggs and Violeta Seretan. We also thank our colleagues at the University of Geneva and elsewhere who made it possible to organize the "Men and women in social hierarchies" symposium that preceded the publication of this book: Pascal Zesiger, Sabine Sczesny, Brigitte Mantilleri, Juliette Labarthe, Olivia Och, Caroline Schneeberger, Marion Chipeaux, Laura Folly, and Justine Mudde. Finally, our deepest gratitude goes to Naomi Ellemers and Belle Derks for their enthusiasm, unending encouragement, and generous support.

All chapters were reviewed by experts in the field, that we thank for their priceless contributions and constructive suggestions: Alberta Contarello, University of Padova, Italy; Alice H. Eagly, University of Northwestern, USA, Amy Eshleman, Wagner College, USA; Andrew Caswell, University of Gannon, USA; Christian Staerklé, University of Lausanne, Switzerland, Claudine Burton-Jeangros, University of Geneva, Switzerland; Clementine Bry, University of Savoie, France; Crystal Hoyt, University of Richmond, USA; Edwin W. H. Poppe, Utrecht University, the Netherlands; Elisa Puvia, Free University of Brussels, Belgium; Fabrice Gabarrot, University of Bourgogne, France; Frederique Autin, University of Lausanne, Switzerland; Gabrielle Poeschl, University of Porto, Portugal; Hanneke Hendriks, Leiden University, the Netherlands; Ilka Wolter, University of Bamberg, Germany; Janine Bosak, Dublin City University, Ireland; Joelle Mezza, National Institute for Research on Work and Professional Orientation, France; Jojanneke van der Toorn, Leiden University, the Netherlands; Jolanda Vandernoll, University of Louvain, Belgium; Judith A. Hall, University of Northeastern, USA; Kimberly Kahn, Portland State University, USA; Léan O'brien, University of Canberra, Australia; Maks Banens, University of Lyon 2, France; Matt Hammond, University of Auckland, New Zealand; Michel Bozon, National Institute for Demographic Studies, France; Michele Kaufmann, University of Bern, Switzerland; Haoua Mouni Kouidri, University of Reims Champagne-Ardenne, France; Nadia Monacelli, University of Parma, Italy; Nicky LeFeuvre, University of Lausanne, Switzerland; Nicolas Margas, University of Caen Basse-Normandie, France; Peter Hegarty, University of Surrey, United Kingdom; Rodrigue Ozenne, National Institute for Research on Work and Professional Orientation, France; Romy van der Lee, Leiden University, the Netherlands; Serge Guimond, University of Blaise Pascal, France; Soledad de Lemus Martín, University of Granada, Spain; Susanne Bruckmüller, University of Koblenz-Landau, Germany; Vincent Pillaud, University of Toronto, Canada.

GENDER AND SOCIAL HIERARCHIES

Introduction and overview

Belle Derks and Naomi Ellemers

Although abundant research on women in the workplace reveals that men and women equal each other in terms of ambition, commitment and competence (Hyde, 2014), women still receive lower pay than their male counterparts and are underrepresented at higher organizational levels. In the United States women receive on average 76.5 per cent of men's earnings, and make up only 19.2 per cent of the boards of stock index companies (Catalyst, 2014; 2015). In Europe the situation is comparable with a gender pay gap that varies from below 10 per cent (in Belgium, Hungary and Norway) to around 20 per cent (in Finland, Germany, Switzerland and the UK; OECD, 2013), and only 20.2 per cent female board members in the largest publicly listed companies. Not only does this state of affairs reflect the inequality in opportunities for men and women in society; the absence of women at higher levels also means that society misses out on the talent and diversity that is available in the work force (Emrich & Shyamsunder, 2014).

Social psychological research suggests that part of the disparities in work outcomes are due to gender stereotyping and discrimination (Agars, 2004; Schein, 2001). Women who aspire to achieve positions of power have to contend with negative gender stereotypes suggesting that women have lower leadership ability, career commitment and emotional stability (Eagly, Makhijani, & Klonsky, 1992; Heilman, 2001). Effects of gender stereotypes are not only visible in women's struggles to climb the organizational ladder, they have their impact much earlier in life, for instance in secondary and higher education where girls drop out of stereotypically masculine academic domains such as science, technology, engineering and mathematics (STEM) (Diekman, Brown, Johnston, & Clark, 2010; OECD, 2012). Moreover, gender roles not only affect women's career opportunities through negative perceptions of their work-related abilities, they also result in women doing double the amount of housework as men do, creating a higher workload for women than for men (Coltrane, 2000; Hochschild & Machung, 2012).

The past 40 years have witnessed a wealth of research and theoretical developments focusing on the differential experiences of men and women in social hierarchies. Although the representation of women in the workplace seems better now than it was 40 years ago, still their presence is mainly visible at lower job levels and in less valued – but stereotypically female – job types and professions. Thus, systematic gender differences in career development and remuneration remain. What has shifted are the psychological processes sustaining these differences against the tide of relevant societal and political developments. With the introduction of equal opportunity legislation, blatant statements of sexist views have been replaced with a range of more subtle and implicit expressions of gender bias (Barreto & Ellemers, 2015). Whereas initially the main concern was to secure equal access to education, equal employment rights, and equal legal status for women, over time it has become clear that these necessary conditions in and of themselves are not sufficient to secure gender equality. Indeed, there is by now broad agreement that there is no single barrier preventing men and women from achieving equal outcomes. Instead, the perpetuation of gender differences stems from the steady accumulation of small disadvantages, due to which slight initial differences develop into larger discrepancies, that perpetuate and reinforce traditional labour divisions between men and women (Ellemers, 2014). As a result of these developments, many people nowadays suffer from a discrepancy between their preferred self-views as being unbiased and social realities in which they too contribute to the persistence of gender differences. This elicits all manner of self-justifying and system-legitimizing explanations, that impede the recognition of gender bias, and attribute visible differences to "free choices" of the individuals concerned (Ellemers, Rink, Derks, & Ryan, 2012).

This book reflects these developments. The range of topics addressed provides a comprehensive overview and engaging snapshot of the latest theoretical and methodological approaches in this rich and vibrant research field, demonstrating the different ways in which the gender hierarchy affects the lives of women and men, and the processes that keep this hierarchy firmly in its place.

The collection of chapters in this volume highlights three important aspects of men and women's roles in social hierarchies. First, the work presented in this volume underlines how the social hierarchy affects men and women *throughout their life-course*. Beginning at an early age, the first three chapters show how gender stereotypes affect the behavior of 8-year old girls in physical education classes (Chapter 3 by Cheval, Chalabaev and Chanal), the vocational aspirations of young adolescents (13–15 years; Chapter 1 by Gianettoni and Guilley), and the academic career paths of male and female students (Chapter 2 by Verniers, Bonnot, Darnon, Dompnier and Martinot). Other chapters focus on later life stages, revealing effects of gender inequality in the life of men and women who are building their careers (Chapter 4 by Carrard and Schmid Mast; Chapter 5 by Latu and Schmid Mast; Chapter 6 by Faniko and colleagues; Chapter 7 by Kulich, Iacoviello and Lorenzi-Cioldi), and women who are combining their career with a family (Chapter 8 by Stauffer, Maggiori, Johnston, Rochat and Rossier). Collectively, the chapters in the volume paint a comprehensive picture of the different life phases and settings in which the social roles ascribed to men and women impinge upon their choices, behaviours and opportunities, and illustrate how seemingly small differences accumulate across the life-span to result in clearly divergent career patterns.

Second, the volume provides a valuable resource reviewing the various *mechanisms* that protect the advantaged position of men over women, and limit opportunities for social change. Apart from the effects of gender stereotypes, which are discussed in the first part of the volume (Chapters 1–4), several chapters accentuate the system-legitimizing dynamics that help to preserve the social hierarchy in which women receive lower outcomes than men. For example, in Chapter 2, Verniers and colleagues discuss how school-related achievement traits ascribed to girls (compliant) and boys (intelligent) contribute to the perpetuation of the gender gap in higher education. Moreover, in Chapter 9, Kleinlogel and Dietz combine two existing perspectives (the justification-suppression model and social dominance theory) to provide a better understanding of the perseverance of gender inequality.

Fascinatingly, several chapters reveal that system-legitimizing forces sometimes come in unexpected forms. For example, Kulich and colleagues (Chapter 7) discuss how the promotion of women into leadership positions with a high risk of failure ('glass cliff positions') can help to confirm negative stereotypes about women and leadership. Additionally, the social hierarchy is not only enforced by men who aim to protect their advantaged position and male identity (Chapter 12 by Berent, Falomir-Pichastor and Chipeaux), but also endorsed and supported by women who behave in ways that protect and perpetuate gender inequality. This is demonstrated by Zimmermann and Gygax (Chapter 10) who reveal why women are likely to endorse sexist beliefs, and Faniko and colleagues (Chapter 6) who present new data demonstrating that women who might be in the position to make important changes actually oppose affirmative action policies aimed at improving gender equality. Finally, as discussed by Sarrasin, Fasel and Green (Chapter 11) pro gender equality arguments are sometimes misused to legitimize other aspects of the social hierarchy, for example when anti-headscarf attitudes which aim to restrict the freedom of women to make their own choices in dress styles are legitimized with the argument that this religious practice is a symbol of patriarchal oppression.

Third, this volume clarifies which *policies* can be implemented to improve gender equality in society, as well as detailing the psychological processes that should be taken into account in order for these strategies to be successful. For example, in their review of the effects of role models on women's leadership ambitions, Latu and Schmid Mast (Chapter 5) specify the boundary conditions under which role models inspire rather than threaten the aspirations of successful women. Similarly, Faniko and colleagues (Chapter 6) discuss the conditions under which quota policies aimed to improve access of women to decision-making positions are more likely to be accepted by men as well as the women who are supposed to benefit from them. Finally, the model proposed by Kleinlogel and Dietz (Chapter 9) facilitates the development of successful interventions: Their analysis of the different levels at which hierarchy-enhancing and hierarchy-attenuating forces have their effects (individual, group, institution) helps to determine at which level interventions are most likely to be effective (and why).

We think that the theoretical insights, up-to-date research reviews, and cutting-edge data brought together in this volume will be a valuable resource for students and researchers from fields such as social psychology, organizational psychology, political psychology, and organizational behaviour and human resource management. Moreover, the diversity of topics, the discussions of research implications as well as the accessible language, will also allow policy makers working on ways to improve equality between men and women in society to benefit from this book.

Organization of the book

Part I of the book, *the Consequences of Gender Stereotypes* contains four chapters. In Chapter 1, Lavinia Gianettoni and Edith Guilley focus on the gendering of vocational aspirations of young adolescents, showing how these are influenced by growing up in a sexist environment. They present a study performed among a large sample of 13- to 15-year-old boys and girls and find that adolescents aspire to more gender-typical career options to the degree that their parents report sexist beliefs. Continuing with the gender hierarchy in higher education, in Chapter 2 Catherine Verniers, Virginie Bonnot, Céline Darnon, Benoît Dompnier and Delphine Martinot discuss the role of gender stereotypes in maintaining existing gender disparities in students' career paths. They propose that gender stereotypes that depict women as compliant and men as assertive and intelligent may have developed in order to legitimize a system in which women are underrepresented in the most prestigious academic fields (science, technology, engineering and mathematics) and at higher ranks. Moreover, they review research showing that system-justification motives can induce women and men to show stereotype consistent self-perceptions. Boris Cheval, Aïna Chalabaev and Julien Chanal (Chapter 3) present new data showing that 8-year-old girls already underperform relative to boys in physical education classes. Interestingly, rather than concentrating on biological sex differences that are often called upon to explain differences in the physical abilities of boys and girls, the authors offer a psychological analysis based on sex-typing of sports domains. The data presented show that the underperformance of girls relative to boys is specific to sports domains that are considered masculine (e.g. rugby) rather than gender neutral (e.g. volleyball) or feminine (e.g. gymnastics). In Chapter 4 Valérie Carrard and Marianne Schmid Mast review research concerning the effects of gender differences and stereotypes on the interactions between female physicians and their patients. In addition to gender differences in how male and female physicians behave, gender stereotypes cause patients to expect different behaviours from their female and male physicians. As a result, whereas male physicians are seen as going out of their way when showing a patient-centered interaction style, female physicians receive no such credit for showing this typically feminine behaviour; they only risk being penalized when behaving in a more masculine way.

Part II, *Women's Struggles in the Workplace*, contains four chapters. Ioana Latu and Marianne Schmid Mast (Chapter 5) focus on the threat that women can experience in the leadership domain. Not only are leadership traits more strongly correlated with masculine than feminine traits, women are even penalized for showing leadership behavior. The chapter discusses how stereotypes impact women's leadership ambitions and performance, and reviews how counter stereotypic role models can improve but also harm women's leadership aspirations. In Chapter 6, Klea Faniko, Fabio Lorenzi-Cioldi, Paolo Ghisletta, Siri Øyslebø Sørensen, Erjona Manushi, Fiorela Shalsi and Marion Chipeaux present new research showing that highly educated women, just like highly educated men, oppose affirmative action policies aimed to improve gender equality. They reveal the important role of amplified meritocratic beliefs among highly educated individuals in this effect, and discuss important policy implications of these findings. Clara Kulich, Vincenzo Iacoviello and Fabio Lorenzi-Cioldi (Chapter 7) review work on the glass cliff phenomenon, whereby women are selected for leadership positions under more precarious circumstances than men. The chapter proposes that stereotypes about women's communal leadership style may lead to the perception that women are uniquely capable to lead companies in times of crisis. The recent studies reviewed here challenge the idea that women are offered glass cliff positions out of hostile intentions, but instead propose that women are chosen for leadership in tough times because their non-prototypical leadership style seems to best serve the goal of achieving organizational change. Finally, Sarah Stauffer, Christian Maggiori, Claire Johnston, Shékina Rochat and Jérôme Rossier (Chapter 8) present results from a large study among working women in Switzerland examining how women achieve work-life balance and the role that social support plays in buffering effects of job strain on professional well-being.

Part III, *Gender-Related Prejudice*, includes the final four chapters. In Chapter 9, Emmanuelle Kleinlogel and Joerg Dietz provide an enhanced understanding of the perseverance of gender inequality by combining two existing perspectives: the justification-suppression model and social dominance theory. Whereas the former helps to explain when and why sexism is expressed (i.e. depending on factors that suppress or justify expression of sexist views), the latter sheds light on why inequality is self-perpetuating and difficult to eradicate. What results is a multi-level understanding of the factors that attenuate and enhance gender inequalities at the institutional level, group level, and individual level, revealing that the dominance of hierarchy-enhancing over hierarchy-attenuating forces produce a self-reinforcing spiral. Regula Zimmermann and Pascal Gygax (Chapter 10) present data that reveals how women contribute to gender inequality by personally endorsing hostile sexist beliefs when they concern other women ('women are too easily offended'), while rejecting these beliefs when they apply to themselves ('but I am not'). By distancing themselves from other women, they can defend the legitimacy of the system, while simultaneously minimizing ego threat. In Chapter 11 Oriane Sarrasin, Nicole Fasel and Eva Green discuss how gender equality beliefs may even be misused to cover up negative attitudes towards ethnic minorities. Their study shows that, whereas negative attitudes towards the Muslim headscarf tend to be legitimized with the argument that this religious practice is a symbol of patriarchal oppression, gender equality beliefs actually relate positively to acceptance of the headscarf. This is because both attitudes are related to left-wing ideology. Furthermore, even though women are more in favour of gender equality than men are, women are more supportive of the right to wear a headscarf due to their stronger left-wing political ideology. Lastly, in Chapter 12, Jacques Berent, Juan Falomir-Pichastor and Marion Chipeaux explain how men's motivation to preserve clear gender distinctions may also translate into prejudice against homosexual men and behaviours aimed at affirming a heterosexual identity.

References

Agars, M. D. (2004). Reconsidering the impact of gender stereotypes on the advancement of women in organizations. *Psychology of Women Quarterly, 28*, 103–111. doi:10.1111/j.1471-6402.2004.00127.x

Barreto, M., & Ellemers, N. (2015). Detecting and experiencing prejudice: New answers to old questions. *Advances in Experimental Social Psychology*, 52, 139–219. doi: 10.1016/bs.aesp.2015.02.001

Catalyst (2014). *Catalyst Quick Take: Women's Earnings and Income*. New York: Catalyst.

Catalyst (2015). *2014 Catalyst Census: Women Board Directors*. New York: Catalyst.

Coltrane, S. (2000). Research on household labor: Modeling and measuring the social embeddedness of routine family work. *Journal of Marriage and Family, 62*, 1208–1233.

Diekman, A. B., Brown, E. R., Johnston, A. M., & Clark, E. K. (2010). Seeking congruity between goals and roles. *Psychological Science, 21*, 1051–1057. doi: 10.1177/0956797610377342

Eagly, A. H., Makhijani, M. G., & Klonsky, B. G. (1992). Gender and the evaluation of leaders: A meta-analysis. *Psychological Bulletin, 111*, 3–22. doi: http://dx.doi.org/10.1037/1089-2699.1.1.98

Ellemers, N. (2014). Women at work: How organizational features impact career development. *Policy Insights from Behavioral and Brain Sciences, 1*, 46–54. doi: 10.1177/2372732214549327

Ellemers, N., Rink, F., Derks, B., & Ryan, M. (2012). Women in high places: When and why promoting women into top positions can harm them individually or as a group (and how to prevent this). *Research in Organizational Behavior, 32*, 163–187. doi:10.1016/j.riob.2012.10.003

Emrich, C. & Shyamsunder, A. (2014). *High potential women in Europe: Underutilized talent.* Retrieved from: http://www.catalyst.org/system/files/high_potential_women_in_europe_print.pdf

European Commission (2014). *Report on equality between women and men 2014.* Retrieved from: http://ec.europa.eu/justice/genderequality/files/annual_reports/150304_annual_report_2014_web_en.pdf

Eagly, A. H., Makhijani, M. G., & Klonsky, B. G. (1992). Gender and the evaluation of leaders: A meta-analysis. *Psychological Bulletin, 111*, 3–22. doi: http://dx.doi.org/10.1037/1089-2699.1.1.98

Heilman, M. E. (2001). Description and prescription: How gender stereotypes prevent women's ascent up the organizational ladder. *Journal of Social Issues, 57*, 657–674. doi: 10.1111/0022-4537.00234

Hochschild, A. & Machung, A. (2012). *The Second Shift.* Avon Books: New York.

Hyde, J. S. (2014). Gender similarities and differences. *Annual Review of Psychology, 65*, 373–398. doi: 10.1146/annurev-psych-010213-115057

OECD (2012). *The ABC of Gender Equality in Education: Aptitude, behaviour, confidence.* Paris: OECD Publishing.

OECD (2013). Jobs and wages: Gender wage gap. *OECD Factbook 2013: Economic, Environmental and Social Statistics.* Paris: OECD Publishing.

Schein, V. E. (2001). A global look at psychological barriers to women's progress in management. *Journal of Social Issues, 57*, 675–688. doi: 10.1111/0022-4537.00235

PART I

The consequences of gender stereotypes

1

SEXISM AND THE GENDERING OF PROFESSIONAL ASPIRATIONS

Lavinia Gianettoni and Edith Guilley

Introduction

Despite political incentives for the diversification of girl's professional aspirations and career choices, taking a course predominantly followed by the opposite sex remains a relatively minor phenomenon in Switzerland (Grossenbacher, 2006, Gianettoni, Simon-Vermot and Gauthier, 2010), as in other European countries (see for example Baudelot and Establet, 2001; Francis, 1996; Lightbody and Durndell, 1996).

This "sexual division of professional orientation" (Vouillot, 2007) is at the heart of the construction of gender inequalities because it lays the foundations for horizontal and vertical segregation of the labour market. The horizontal segregation refers to the fact that many occupations are strongly gendered (i.e. occupied by a clear majority of men, like in technical occupations, or of women, like in caring occupations). The vertical segregation refers to the fact that men are very often at the top of occupational hierarchies (directors, etc.) while women are very often subordinate (Farmer, 1997). These segregations illustrate well the principles of division and hierarchy of the sexes that structure the gender system (Delphy, 2001). The principle of division corresponds to the widespread idea that there are "men's occupations" and "women's occupations". The principle of hierarchy corresponds to the idea that "a man's work is worth more than a woman's work". It is reflected in the lower salaries associated with highly feminized occupations (Olsen & Walby, 2004; England, Allison, & Wu, 2007) and in the clear underrepresentation of women in senior executive or equivalent positions (e.g. university professors; Farmer, 1997). To summarize, women are concentrated in certain areas of competence and cannot easily reach the most prestigious and best remunerated positions. This has obvious repercussions for the career possibilities open to women, and especially to women living in a heterosexual couple with children: They are more likely to reduce their occupational activity once they have children (Vondracek, Lerner, & Schulenberg, 1986), for reasons that are both ideological ("it's a mother's job to look after the children") and institutional (because women generally earn less than their partners). This withdrawal from the labour market, even if only partially, damages their subsequent chances of pursuing a career. Already in adolescence, young girls anticipate their future roles and make a "choice of compromise" for less prestigious occupations that will facilitate the reconciliation between their career and their private life (Duru-Bellat, 2004).

Studying current professional aspirations of young people aged 13–15 years old is important in a life-course perspective since they correlate to subsequent careers once these youngsters reach adulthood. Indeed, occupational aspirations of adolescents are formed with a relatively realistic assessment of future opportunities and difficulties in realizing personal goals (Gottfredson, 1981). They are predictive of subsequent career choices since ambitious occupational plans were shown to be good predictors of high status attainment in early adulthood (Cochran, Wang, Stevenson, Johnson, & Crews, 2011; Sikora & Saha, 2011). This is the case even after youth educational plans and performance are all taken into account.

Professional aspirations: impact of sexist ideologies and family context

Several studies have shown that family structure has an influence on the gendering of young people's aspirations (for an overview see Guichard-Claudic et al., 2008). In particular, girls who have grown up in a family in which the mother's occupational status is equal to or higher than that of her partner choose professional sectors in a less gender-stereotyped way. But in terms of adolescents' professional aspirations, much of the research has focused on parental support and parental expectations (for a review, see Whiston & Keller, 2004). While the influence of the family structure or support is relatively well documented, few studies have explicitly addressed the impact of adherence to sexist ideologies by young people and their parents on the gendering of professional aspirations. To our knowledge, only one recent study showed that the internalization of gender stereotypes by young people (i.e. the use of gender stereotypes to define self-competence) predicted their career intentions (Plante, de la Sablonnière, Aronson, & Théorêt, 2013).

What we know from our own research (Gianettoni et al., 2010; Gauthier & Gianettoni, 2013) is that young adults who express a strong adhesion to traditional gender roles tend to have gender-typical occupations. Indeed, we showed that women who at age 23 occupy very gender-conforming occupational positions give more importance to their family compared to their career. By contrast, women who occupy atypical positions do not relegate their career to the background. We deduced from these findings that occupational activities that are gender-typical reinforce the two basic postulates underlying the gender system (division and hierarchy). In those studies we did not, however, test to what extent gender-typical aspirations are underpinned by a more or less strong adherence to the ideologies that legitimate the gender system. This was because in those studies, based on secondary analyses of TREE data (Transition from Education to Employment, TREE 2013), we did not have measurements of the perceived legitimacy of the gender system (i.e. measurement of sexism).

To fill this gap, the study described in the present chapter explored the role played by sexist ideologies in the gendering of young people's aspirations. To this end, we used the old-fashioned and modern sexism scales developed by Janet Swim and colleagues (Swim, Aikin, Hall, & Hunter, 1995). This scale distinguishes a form of explicit sexism called "old-fashioned sexism" from a more subtle form, called "modern sexism." Old-fashioned sexism refers to gendered stereotypes according to which women are less competent and women and men should expect to be treated differently. Modern sexism is characterized by non-recognition of the sexist discrimination that persists in our society, hostility towards demands for equality of opportunity, and a lack of support for policies designed to promote gender equality (for example, in education or work). Our hypothesis is that, for girls, atypical professional aspirations require not only a degree of self-confidence on their part (see Gauthier & Gianettoni, 2013; Lemarchant, 2008) but also a distancing from the norms of the gender system. We, therefore, hypothesize that modern and old-fashioned sexism, and legitimate gendered roles and gender system, have to be rejected by girls in order for them to be able to aspire to occupations mainly occupied by men (further named as "masculine" occupations). For the boys, we put forward a comparable hypothesis: atypical aspirations on their part also imply a distancing from the socially valued masculine norms, and thus we expect the rejection of sexism again to be a necessary condition for their gender-atypical professional aspirations.

Concerning the link between parent's ideologies and youth aspirations, some authors explore the influence of parent's sexist ideologies on their children's ideologies (Eccles, Jacobs and Harold, 2010), or on children's interests (Barak, Feldman and Noy, 1991). To our knowledge, no study has explicitly analysed the impact of parent ideologies on child occupational aspirations. We nevertheless hypothesize that parents' degree of sexism will have an influence on their children's professional aspirations: the more sexist the ideological context where young people are socialized, the more they will aspire to gender-typical occupations.

Our survey

Our survey was financed by the National Research Program (NRP 60) "Gender Equality" of the Swiss National Science Foundation. For a detailed overview of this study, see Guilley et al. 2014. We questioned 3,179 pupils at or approaching the end of their compulsory schooling in various schools in five Swiss cantons, as well as their parents. The selection of cantons and schools for the survey was made with a view to best fulfilling the principle of representativeness (urban/rural areas, richer/poorer neighbourhoods, linguistic regions). Regrettably, almost all the German-speaking cantons declined to take part in the survey, with the exception of Aargau. Our sample is, therefore, not representative as regards the linguistic regions. The cantons where schools agreed to take part in the survey are Geneva, the French-speaking part of Bern, Vaud, Ticino and Aargau. The pupils and their parents completed a standardized questionnaire on various dimensions relating to professional aspirations and on their adherence to sexism.

Sample

Pupils

The young people who took part in the survey were pupils of 20 schools spread over the five selected cantons. They were aged 13 to 15 when they completed the questionnaire (in 2011) and were enrolled in the lower secondary school (i.e. grades 9, 10 and 11). They were thus at a time in their lives when the choice of their future professional training had to be made. The pupils completed the questionnaire on computers in the classroom (in all the French- and German-speaking cantons), or on paper in the classroom (as required by the canton of Ticino). Their distribution by canton of residence and sex is shown in Table 1.1.

Parents

The parents were invited to take part on the basis of their children's participation. A single (paper) copy of the questionnaire was sent to them and could be answered by either parent. In no cases were two questionnaires delivered to the same household. In the end, 1,675 parents returned the completed questionnaire, a response rate of 53 per cent. Of the parents questioned who stated their sex, 69.4 per cent were women (Table 1.2).

TABLE 1.1 Sample of pupils questioned, by gender and canton of residence

	Aargau	Bern	Geneva	Ticino	Vaud	Total
Girls	26	212	477	404	414	1,553
Boys	28	203	463	427	441	1,562
Not stated	0	16	7	48	13	84
Total	54	431	947	879	868	3,179

TABLE 1.2 Sample of parents responding, by gender and canton of residence

	Aargau	Bern	Geneva	Ticino	Vaud	Total
Women	3	150	394	328	243	1,118
Men	0	46	163	202	82	493
Not stated	10	9	13	29	3	64
Total	13	205	570	559	328	1,675

Dependent variable: atypicality of professional aspiration

The pupils were asked in particular to answer the following question: "What occupation do you hope to have when you are 30?" The responses were coded according to the International Standard Classification of Occupations (ISCO). This is a classification devised by the International Labour Organization (ILO) in 1958, revised in 1968 and again in 1988 (International Labour Organization, 1991). We then asscribed to each ISCO code of the occupation wished for by the pupils the percentage of men in the same occupation on the basis of the data of the Federal Population Census 2000 (see Gianettoni et al., 2010 for an identical procedure). A score of 0 means that the profession is performed by 0 per cent of men in Switzerland, and a score of 1 means that the profession is performed by 100 per cent of men in Switzerland (and, for example, a score of .62 means that the profession is performed by 62 per cent of men). The higher this score is for boys the higher they aspire to typical occupations. Conversely, the higher the score is for girls, the less they aspire to typical occupations. Finally, we recoded this variable for boys (score *-1 + 1), in order to obtain a new variable where 0 is associated with a maximal typicality of the aspiration and 1 with a maximal atypicality of the aspiration.

Independent variables

Measures of sexism

We measured the degree of legitimacy of gendered roles and the hierarchy of the sexes using an adapted version of the sexism scale developed by Swim et al. (1995). The 13 items on this scale were adapted[1] for young people after a pretest. Cronbach's alpha was calculated for each sexism score (old-fashioned and modern), separately for the pupils and the parents. As regards modern sexism, Cronbach's alpha for the parents is good (.74) but lower for the pupils (.57). Reliability is weaker for the old-fashioned sexism scores: .55 for the pupils and .51 for the parents. Even eliminating some items from the scale, the Cronbach's alpha did not improve. Moreover, a factor analysis on pupils' and parents' data confirms that the best solution consists of two dimensions: one including all the modern sexism items and the other all the old-fashioned sexism items. For this reason, we decided to use the composed scores but systematically checked that the results based on these scores were consistent with those obtained using the individual items.

Social class

Although sexism structures all social classes, members of lower social classes were found to adhere stronger to explicit sexist items when they feel precarious (Gianettoni & Simon-Vermot, 2010). Because of this possible co-variation between adherence to explicit sexist ideologies and social class, our regression analysis was controlled for indicators of social class. Each pupil was associated with the highest ISEI of both parents. The ISEI (International Socio-Economic Index) is an indicator of the position on a socio-economic scale devised by Ganzeboom, De Graaf and Treinman (Ganzeboom et al., 1992). This is a scale from 0 (very low) to 100 (very high) constructed on the basis of the weighted sum of the average number of years of education and the average income of occupation groups (ISCO code). Each point on the ISEI scale is thus the reflection of the cultural and economic resources of the individuals in a particular occupation. Though often confused with a prestige scale, it differs from the latter in that it does not involve subjective evaluations by members of society.

Results

Descriptive statistics

Pupils' professional aspirations

First of all, we present some descriptive results about pupils' professional aspirations. In Table 1.3 are reported the 10 occupations most often mentioned by boys and girls. On the basis of the information about the number of women and men in any ISCO occupation in Switzerland (according to Federal Population Census 2000), we consider an occupation as masculine when 70 per cent or more of those who perform it are men, as feminine when 70 per cent or more of those who perform it are women and mixed in other cases. This threshold of 70 per cent was also used by previous studies (e.g. Charles & Buchmann, 1994; Jacobs, 1989; Vervecken, Hannover, & Wolter, 2013).

Boys aspire particularly to masculine occupations (IT specialist, architect, professional sportsman, lawyer, police officer, engineer, company director) or gender-mixed occupations (medical doctor, secondary school teacher, chef/pastry chef), while girls are attracted by feminine (nursery school teacher, nurse, primary school teacher, beautician, psychologist), mixed (medical doctor, decorator, secondary school teacher, surgeon) but also atypical occupations (lawyer).

TABLE 1.3   The ten most desired occupations by girls and boys

Girls	%	Boys	%
Medical doctor	9.5	IT specialist	6.8
Decorator, stylist	7.3	Architect	5.7
Teacher (secondary school)	6.1	Medical doctor	4.1
Early childhood educator	5.1	Professional sportsman	3.9
Veterinary	4.6	Lawyer	3.9
Lawyer	4.3	Police officer	3.8
Nurse	3.7	Teacher (secondary school)	3.3
Teacher (primary school)	2.9	Engineer	3.1
Beautician, manicure, make-up specialist	2.9	Cook, pastry cook	3.0
Psychologist	2.4	Company director	2.9
TOTAL	48.8		40.5

When aggregating all the answers, results show that 19.1 per cent of girls aspire to an atypical occupation (i.e. one performed by more than 70 per cent men) while only 6.7 per cent of boys aspire to an occupation performed by more than 70 per cent women. The results show that 32.4 per cent of girls aspire to a typical (feminine) occupation and 64 per cent of boys aspire to a typical (masculine) occupation. Finally 48.5 per cent of girls and 29.3 per cent of boys aspire to a mixed occupation. This gender asymmetry in atypical aspirations has already been observed in other countries (Francis, 2002) and in Switzerland with a representative sample of young people (Gianettoni et al., 2010).

Pupils and parents sexism

The means of sexism variables and their correlations are reported in Tables 1.4 and 1.5.

We can see that globally girls adhere less to modern sexism (F (1, 1526) = 10.21, $p < .01$) and to old-fashioned sexism (F (1, 1526) = 156.18, $p < .001$) compared to boys. The same result is found for their parents: mothers adhere less to modern sexism (F (1, 1526) = 97.57, $p < .001$) and to old-fashioned sexism (F (1, 1526) = 47.52, $p < .01$) compared to fathers. Also, parents adhere less to modern sexism (F (1,1526) = 16.77, $p < .001$) and to old-fashioned sexism (F (1, 1526) = 16.87, $p < .001$) compared to pupils.

Table 1.5 shows that pupils' modern and old-fashioned sexism are correlated with parents' modern and old-fashioned sexism. These two forms of sexism are strongly correlated for parents, but not for pupils.

TABLE 1.4 Means (and standard deviations) of sexism variables by pupils' and parents' sex

Sex	Pupils' old-fashioned sexism	Pupils' modern sexism	Parents' old-fashioned sexism	Parents' modern sexism
Women	2.19 (0.88)	4.42 (0.96)	1.86 (0.85)	3.74 (1.06)
Men	2.87 (1.21)	4.58 (0.96)	2.21 (1.04)	4.33 (1.04)
Total	2.51 (1.10)	4.50 (0.96)	1.97 (0.93)	3.92 (1.09)

TABLE 1.5 Correlation between sexism variables

	1	2	3	4
1. Pupils' old fashioned sexism	–	.03	.20★★★	–.09★★
2. Pupils' modern sexism		–	.05	.15★★★
3. Parents' old fashioned sexism			–	.25★★★
4. Parents' modern sexism				–

TABLE 1.6 Determinants of the atypicality (from 0= max typical to 1= max atypical) of the occupation wished for by pupils

Variable	Model 1			Model 2		
	B	SE	t	B	SE	T
Pupils' sex (boys)	–0.29	0.04	–8.09★★★	–0.33	0.04	–7.84★★★
Highest ISEI of both parents	0.01	0.00	2.22★	0.00	0.00	2.04★
Pupils' modern sexism	–0.01	0.01	–0.75	–0.00	0.01	–0.18
Pupils' old-fashioned sexism	–0.05	0.02	–2.09★	–0.03	0.02	–1.41
Interaction pupils' sex and pupil's old-fashioned sexism	0.03	0.13	1.93★	0.18	0.01	1.29
Parents' modern sexism				–0.02	0.01	–2.97★★
Parents' old-fashioned sexism				–0.06	0.02	–2.46★
Interaction pupils' sex and parents' old-fashioned sexism				0.029	0.015	2.00★

Effects of sexism and social class on the atypicality of pupils' aspirations

To test our hypotheses and analyse the effects of sexism and social class on the atypicality of young people's professional aspirations, we subjected these variables and the significant interaction effects to a linear regression analysis (see Table 1.6).

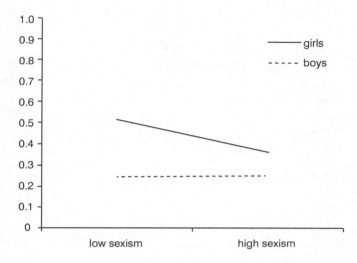

FIGURE 1.1 Interaction between pupils' sex and pupils' old-fashioned sexism on the atypicality of the desired occupation (from 0= min atypical to 1= max atypical)

In the first model, we integrated the sex, the social class indicator and the pupils' sexism; in the second model we added the parents' sexism. Before commenting on the tables, we should point out that, even if the pupils' sexism is positively correlated with the parents' sexism (r = .20, p < .001 for old-fashioned sexism and r = .15, p < .001 for modern sexism, see Table 1.5), we checked that no problem of colinearity arises regarding the variables of sexism.

The results of the first model show that pupils' sex has the stronger influence on the atypicality of professional aspirations: girls aspire more to atypical professions than boys. The parental social class also has an influence on the atypicality of the professional aspiration: the higher the position of the parent's occupation on the socio-economic scale, the more the pupils aspire to atypical occupations.

Concerning the effects of pupils' adherence to sexism on the typicality of their aspirations, significant effects are only observed for old-fashioned sexism. It appears that the fewer pupils adhere to old-fashioned sexism, the more they aspire to atypical occupations. The interaction effect between pupils' sex and pupils' old-fashioned sexism is also significant. Figure 1.1 shows that the more girls adhere to old-fashioned sexism, the less they aspire to gender-atypical occupations (β= –0.08, p < .05). For the boys, by contrast, no link between the two variables appears (β = 0.01, *n.s.*). As consistent with our hypothesis, the rejection of sexist ideologies, at least by girls, allows them to have atypical aspirations, independently of their social class.

The second model additionally integrates parents' variables: in this model, the most significant predictors of the atypicality of aspirations remain the pupils' sex. The impact of social class also remains significant. In contrast, the impact

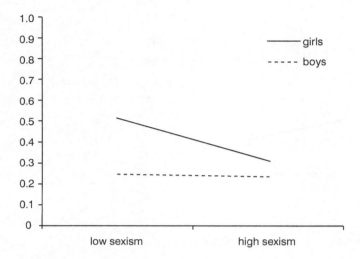

FIGURE 1.2   Interaction between pupils' sex and parents' old-fashioned sexism on the atypicality of the desired occupation (from 0= min atypical to 1= max atypical).

of pupils' old-fashioned sexism disappears. The parents' modern and old-fashioned sexisms have a significant influence on the typicality of the professional aspirations of their children: as expected the more the parents adhere to modern and old-fashioned sexisms the less their children aspire to atypical professions. The conformity of aspirations to gender norms is thus more marked in more sexist familial contexts.

A significant interaction effect also appears between pupils' sex and parents' old-fashioned sexism. Figure 1.2 illustrates that the parents' degree of old-fashioned sexism does not at all influence the degree of typicality of the occupations the boys aspire to ($\beta = -0.01$, *n.s*), while for the girls, the link is clearer: the more their parents adhere to old-fashioned sexism, the more they aspire to typical occupations. ($\beta = -0.11, p < .001$).

Discussion

Holding old-fashioned sexist beliefs is seen to be a significant predictor of the typicality of girls' professional aspirations at the end of their compulsory schooling, but has no influence on boys' career choices. We were able to observe that the more the girls adhere to an old-fashioned sexist vision of society, the more they aspire to gender-typical occupations. By contrast, we found no significant effect of adherence to sexism on the part of the boys on the gendering of their aspirations. This absence of significant effect of sexism among the boys may show that those who wish to work in a "feminine" occupation do not distance themselves from sexist attitudes. The career trajectories of men who enter highly feminized occupations are far different from those of women who move into the "male bastions". Men in occupations predominantly occupied by women tend to have upward careers, leading them to cluster in the upper reaches of the internal occupational hierarchy (Charrier, 2004; Sanchez-Mazas & Casini, 2005). This is almost never the case for women in male-dominated occupations. Therefore, an atypical professional aspiration for boys may express a willing of professional ascent rather than a distancing from the gender system. This interpretation is coherent with some previous results showing that an atypical professional position is associated for young men with a stronger importance accorded to paid work at the expense of family life (Gianettoni et al., 2010).

The absence of significant effects of sexism among the boys may also express the difficulty in finding variables which significantly explain the atypicality of boys' professional aspirations simply because of its scarcity. In our study, like in other research (Francis, 2002; Gianettoni et al., 2010), gender-atypical aspirations are far less frequent among boys compared to those of girls.

The parents' degree of adherence to sexism plays a more important role than pupils' degree of sexism in the pupils' aspirations, including (for modern sexism) those of boys: growing up in a family where modern sexism is more salient, pupils favour more gender-typical professional aspirations. Moreover, the degree of parents' old-fashioned sexism has a significant impact on girl's aspirations: the more the parents adhere to old-fashioned sexism, the more girls aspire to typical occupations. This result shows that primary socialization into gendered roles is an important factor in adolescents' choice of occupation and is, therefore, determinant for their future; it also justifies the need for increasing parental awareness of the role of gender stereotypes on their children' career choices.

Nonetheless, parents' old-fashioned sexism has no effect on boys' professional aspirations. The sub mentioned explanations for the absence of any link between boys' sexism and their aspirations may be also valid for the latter result. However, a bias in our study must be additionally mentioned. Of the parents questioned who stated their sex, 69.4 per cent were women. Some studies showed that same-sex relationships are more influential (Degenne & Forsé, 1994). That could contribute to explain the absence of link between parental sexism (here essentially mothers' sexism) and their sons' professional aspirations.

It is interesting to note that for girls the significant predictor of aspirations is their parents' degree of old-fashioned and modern sexism, whereas for boys it is only their parents' modern sexism. It is fairly easy to understand why the family's departure from the traditional sexist stereotypes (assigning women to the domestic sphere and men to the occupational sphere, etc.) should be an important condition for girls' atypical aspirations. It was less expected that only parental modern sexism would be a significant predictor of boys' aspirations. It may, however, be hypothesized that this result reflects the fact that boys dare to choose atypicality perceived as devaluing in society in general, only when their families are strongly anti-sexist, rejecting beliefs such as "there is no longer a need for feminism" which are part of modern sexism.

Finally, we would like to point out that in a general way our results show a stronger link between sexism and professional aspirations for girls than for boys. This suggests that a distancing from the gender system, through a rejection of sexism is more important for those who occupy a dominated position in the gender system. Also, atypicality has not the same significance for girls and boys. For the latter, as said above, choosing gender-atypical occupations can be a "winning strategy". It is also important to note that the effect of sexism manifests itself independently of social class and is, therefore, not a simple reflection of class membership. While it appears that belonging to a higher social class favours transgression of gender norms (see also Duru-Bellat and Jarousse, 1996), the family's degree of sexism nonetheless influences the probability of atypical aspirations in all social strata.

Practical implementations

To conclude this chapter, we would like to highlight two practical implementations of our results. First of all, since the gendering of professional aspirations is embedded in general sexist ideologies, any political measure developed in order to increase atypical professional orientations should take into account the complexity of gender hierarchies manifesting in social practices and institutions. Political input aiming only to change individual practices (for example, reinforcement of the attractiveness of technical formations for girls) without a political pressure at an institutional level (for example promotion of laws reducing gender discriminations in "masculine" work places) will not be efficient to transform the gender system and the place assigned to men and women in the society.

Second, our results showed the significant role of the gendered primary socialization on professional aspirations. This process must be taken into account when developing political actions in order to reduce gender inequalities. Given the difficulties to act directly in the family sphere, a work of deconstruction of gender stereotypes in child-care institutions (school, nurseries) is necessary to counter sexism that often structures the family systems and, therefore, to ensure an egalitarian input for all children.

Acknowledgements

This research was founded by the Swiss National Science Foundation under the National Research Program NRP 60 "Gender Equality".

We would like to thank the other members of the project "Professional aspirations and orientations of girls and boys towards the end of compulsory school: what determinants for more equality?": Carolina Carvalho Arruda, Jacques-Antoine Gauthier, Dinah Gross, Dominique Joye, Elisabeth Issaieva Moubarak-Nahra and Karin Müller. We also would like to thank Klea Faniko and three anonymous reviewers for their very useful comments and suggestions on a previous version of this chapter.

Note

1 e.g. 'sexual discrimination', used in the original version of the sexism scale, was not understood by young people and was replaced by 'inequalities between men and women'.

References

Barak, A., Feldman, S., & Noy, A. (1991). Traditionality of children's interests as related to their parents' gender stereotype and traditionality of occupations. *Sex Roles, 24,* 511–524. doi:10.1007/BF00289336

Baudelot, C., & Establet, R. (2001). La scolarité des filles à l'échelle mondiale [Girls' schooling at a global level]. In T. Blöss (Ed.), *La dialectique des rapports hommes-femmes* (pp. 103–124). Paris: PUF.

Charles, M., & Buchmann, M. (1994). Assessing micro-level explanations of occupational sex segregation: Human capital development and labor market opportunities in Switzerland. *Schweizerische Zeitschrift für Soziologie, 20,* 595–620.

Charrier, P. (2004). Comment envisage-t-on d'être sage-femme quand on est un homme? L'intégration professionnelle des étudiants hommes sage-femmes [How one considers becoming a midwife when you are a man? Professional integration of men in midwife training]. *Travail, Genre et Société, 12,* 105–124.

Cochran, D. B., Wang, E. W., Stevenson, S. J., Johnson, L. E., & Crews, C. (2011). Adolescent occupational aspirations: Test of Gottfredson's theory of circumscription and compromise. *The Career Development Quarterly, 59,* 412–427. doi:10.1002/j.2161-0045.2011.tb00968.x

Degenne, A., & Forsé, M. (1994). *Les réseaux sociaux* [Social networks]. Paris: Armand Colin.

Delphy, C. (2001). *L'ennemi principal. Tome 2: Penser le genre* [The greatest enemy. Vol 2: Thinking gender]. Paris: Syllepse.

Duru-Bellat, M. (2004). *L'école des filles: Quelle formation pour quels rôles sociaux?* [Girls' school: Which formation for which social roles?]. Paris: L'Harmattan.

Duru-Bellat, M. & Marie, Jarousse J-P. (1996). Le masculin et le féminin dans les modèles éducatifs parentaux [Masculinity and femininity in educational parental models]. Économie et statistique, 293, 77–93.

Eccles, J. S., Jacobs, J. E., & Harold, R. D. (2010). Gender role stereotypes, expectancy effects, and parents' socialization of gender differences. *Journal of Social Issues, 46,* 183–201. doi:10.1111/j.1540-4560.1990.tb01929.x

England, P., Allison, P., & Wu, Y. (2007). Does bad pay cause occupations to feminize? Does feminization reduce pay, and how can we tell with longitudinal data? *Social Science Research, 36,* 1237–1256. doi:10.1016/j.ssresearch.2006.08.003

Farmer, H. (1997). *Diversity and women's career development*. London: Sage.

Francis, B. (1996). Doctor/nurse, teacher/caretaker: Children's gendered choice of adult occupation in interviews and rôle plays. *British Journal of Education and Work, 9,* 47–58. doi:10.1080/0269000960090304

Francis, B. (2002). Is the future really female? The impact and implications of gender for 14–16 years old career choices. *Journal of Education and Work, 15,* 75–88. doi:10.1080/13639080120106730

Ganzeboom, H., De Graaf, P., & Treiman, D. J. (1992). A Standard International Socio-Economic Index of Occupational Status. *Social Science Research, 21,* 1–56.

Gauthier, J-A., & Gianettoni, L. (2013) Socialisation séquentielle et identité de genre liées à la transition de la formation professionnelle à l'emploi [Sequencial socialisation and gender identity linked to transition from vocational school to employment]. *Revue Suisse de Sociologie, 39,* 33–55.

Gianettoni, L. & Simon-Vermot, P. (2010). Quand la menace d'exclusion professionnelle renforce le genre: Représentations et identités de genre auprès de jeunes sans emploi. [When professional exclusion reinforces gender: Gender identity and gender representations among unemployed youth]. *Nouvelles Questions Féministes 29(3),*76–90.

Gianettoni, L., Simon-Vermot, P., & Gauthier, J-A. (2010). Orientations professionnelles atypiques: Transgression des normes de genre et effets identitaires [Atypical professional orientations: Gender norms transgression and identity impact]. *Revue Française de Pédagogie, 173,* 41–50.

Gottfredson, L. (1981). Circumscription and compromise: A developmental theory of occupational aspirations. *Journal of Counseling and Development, 82,* 49–57.

Grossenbacher, S. (2006). Vers l'égalité des sexes à l'école [Towards gender equality in school]. *Que font les cantons pour instaurer l'équité entre hommes et femmes dans le système éducatif ?* [What do cantons do to promote gender equality in educational spheres Aarau : CSRE.

Guichard-Claudic, Y., Kergoat, D., & Vilbrod, A. (2008). *L'inversion du genre. Quand les métiers masculins se conjuguent au féminin… et réciproquement.* [Gender inversion. When masculine jobs are occupied by women and conversely]. Rennes: Presses Universitaires de Rennes.

Guilley, E., Carvalho, C., Gauthier, J-A., Gianettoni, L., Gross, D., Joye, D., Moubarak, E., & Müller, K. (2014). *Maçonne ou avocate: Rupture ou reproduction sociale ? Une enquête sur les aspirations professionnelles des jeunes en Suisse aujourd'hui* . [Bricklayer or lawyer: Social rupture or social reproduction? A survey on current professional aspirations of Swiss young people]. Final scientific report NRP 60 "Gender Equality" (Project number: 4060- 40_129289). Genève, Lausanne: SRED, LINES.

Jacobs, J. A. (1989). *Revolving Doors: Sex segregation and women's careers.* Stanford, CA: Stanford University Press.

Lemarchant, C. (2008). Orientations atypiques de lycéens et lycéennes au sein de filières techniques et professionnelles [Students' atypical orientations in technical and vocational trainings]. In Y. Guichard-Claudic, D. Kergoat, & A. Vilbrod (Eds.) *L'inversion du genre: Quand les métiers masculins se conjuguent au féminin et réciproquement* (pp. 57–69). Rennes: Presses Universitaires de Rennes.

Lightbody, P. & Durndell, A. (1996). Gendered career choice: Is sex-stereotyping the cause or the consequence ? *Educational Studies, 22,* 133–146. doi:10.1080/0305569960220201

Olsen, W. & Walby S. (2004). Modelling gender pay gaps. *EOC Working Paper Series, 17.* Manchester: Equal Opportunities Commission.

Plante, I., de la Sablonnière, R., Aronson, J. M., & Théorêt, M. (2013). Gender stereotype endorsement and achievement-related outcomes: The role of competence beliefs and task values. *Contemporary Educational Psychology, 38,* 225–236. doi:10.1016/j.cedpsych.2013.03.004

Sanchez-Mazas, M. & Casini, A. (2005). Egalité formelle et obstacles informels à l'ascension professionnelle: les femmes et l'effet "plafond de verre" [Formal equality and informal obstacles to professional careers: women and "glass ceiling" effect]. *Information sur les Sciences Sociales, 44,* 141–173.

Sikora, J. & Saha, L. J. (2011). *Lost talent? The occupational expectations and attainments of young Australians.* Adelaïde: National Centre for Vocational Education Research.

Swim, J., Aikin, K., Hall, W., & Hunter, B. (1995). Sexism and racism: Old-fashioned and modern prejudice. *Journal of Personality and Social Psychology, 68*, 199–214. doi: 10.1037/0022-3514.68.2.199

TREE (2013). *Documentation du projet TREE 2000–2012*. [TREE project documentation 2000–2012]. Basel: TREE.

Vervecken, D., Hannover, B., & Wolter, I. (2013). Changing (S)expectations: How gender fair job descriptions impact children's perceptions and interest regarding traditionally male occupations. *Journal of Vocational Behavior, 82*, 208–220. doi:10.1016/j. jvb.2013.01.008

Vondracek, F. W., Lerner, R. M., & Schulenberg, J. E. (1986). *Career development: A life-span developmental approach*. Hillsdale, NJ: Erlbaum.

Vouillot, F. (2007). L'orientation aux prises avec le genre [Orientation in a gender perspective]. *Travail, genre et societés [Work, gender and societies], 18*, 87–108.

Whiston, S. C. & Keller, B. K. (2004). The influences of the family of origin on career development: A review and analysis. *The Counseling Psychologist, 32*, 493–568. doi: 10.1177/0011000004265660

2

HOW GENDER STEREOTYPES OF ACADEMIC ABILITIES CONTRIBUTE TO THE MAINTENANCE OF GENDER HIERARCHY IN HIGHER EDUCATION

Catherine Verniers, Virginie Bonnot, Céline Darnon, Benoît Dompnier, and Delphine Martinot

Despite continuous improvement in women's education over the last decades, a gender hierarchy favouring men in higher education still persists in the majority of OECD countries (Fiske & Unesco, 2012). Female disadvantage is twofold. First, women are still underrepresented in the fields typically considered as the most profitable ones, whether this profitability is measured in terms of salary, power, or prestige (European Commission, 2009)—namely the science, technology, engineering, and mathematics fields (i.e. STEM fields). Second, although female students outperform their male counterparts from elementary to secondary school and represent the majority of undergraduate students, there is paradoxically a loss of women at each step of the academic ladder—referred to as the leaky pipeline—leading to their underrepresentation at the doctoral level and among researchers (Pell, 1996).

Extensive literature has documented several explanations for the gender gap in higher education, ranging from biological to sociocultural factors (for reviews, see Ceci, Ginther, Kahn, & Williams, 2014; Ceci, Williams, & Barnett, 2009; Halpern et al., 2007; Hyde, 2014). Among these factors, research in social psychology puts special emphasis on gender stereotypes. The concept of gender stereotype refers to the set of psychological characteristics considered typical of females or of males and particularly prescribed or proscribed within a given society (Prentice & Carranza, 2002). Women and men are expected to differ in terms of personality characteristics, with women typically considered as more communal and less agentic than men (e.g. Heilman, 2001; Williams et al., 1979), as well as their ability in academic domains, with women expected to have a higher verbal capacity but lower math ability than men (e.g. Guimond & Roussel, 2001). According to two major theoretical perspectives in social psychology— namely, the stereotype threat hypothesis (Steele & Aronson, 1995) and the internalisation hypothesis (Eccles-Parsons et al., 1983)—gender stereotypes impair women's performance in counter stereotypical domains and constrain their academic choices. The aim of the present chapter is to illustrate a potential additional role of gender stereotypes on academic paths by adopting a system justification perspective. Specifically, it is argued that gender stereotypes—in addition to their effect on an individual's performance and personal career decisions—are being used to justify the existing gender hierarchy in higher education.

Traditional socio-psychological explanations for stereotype-congruent academic performance and academic behaviours

Traditionally, the stereotype internalisation hypothesis argues that low- and high-status group members construe their self-concept of abilities on the bases of what competences society expects them to have (e.g. Allport, 1954; Eccles-Parsons et al., 1983). Research on socialisation processes related to the gender achievement gap has focused on how the stereotypic views of others implicitly affect both women's and men's self-perceptions of abilities and attitudes toward mathematics, literature, and language arts (e.g. Eccles, Jacobs, & Harold, 1990; Nosek, Banaji, & Greenwald, 2002). In a recent study designed to investigate implicit gender-STEM stereotypes (i.e. defined as the association of the group concept "men" with the attribute concept "STEM"), Smeding (2012) found that females enrolled in engineering studies held weaker implicit gender-math stereotypes than females in humanities and that this implicit stereotype was not related to math performance for the former, but was negatively related to math performance for the latter. The author suggested that female engineering students could have benefited from an early counter-stereotypic family socialisation environment likely to foster their math achievement and willingness to enter engineering school. This interpretation finds support in research focusing on younger students and highlighting that girls and boys raised in families characterised by traditional gender roles are more likely to make gendered academic choices than adolescents raised in families marked by counter-stereotypical gender roles (Carvalho Arruda, Guilley, & Gianettoni, 2013). Moreover, once internalised, and besides its long-term impact on self-perceived competence and attitudes, stereotype internalisation might also alter performance through temporary interferences in working memory due to self-doubts activated when confronted with challenging tasks in the stereotyped domain (Bonnot & Croizet, 2007a).

However, even when they reach higher levels of academic attainment in counter-stereotyped domains and have not internalised gender stereotypes, women might still be at risk of displaying stereotype-congruent behaviours (lower performance, choice of stereotypical careers, etc.) in situations conducive to stereotype threat (Steele, 1997). Indeed, research based on the stereotype threat hypothesis (Spencer, Steele, & Quinn, 1999) initially indicated that girls' and women's performance decreases when evaluative situations activate their bad reputation in math. For instance, Neuville and Croizet (2007) among primary school girls and Huguet and Régner (2007) among middle school girls demonstrated that girls performed worse than equally qualified boys on a math test when the negative stereotype associated with their math abilities was made salient. Moreover, in a recent review, Appel and Kronberger (2012) found evidence that stereotyped individuals are at risk of experiencing negative effects of stereotype threat not only during test taking but also at the preparation and learning stages (for additional meta-analyses on stereotype threat, see also Nguyen & Ryan, 2008; Picho, Rodriguez, & Finnie, 2013). Ultimately, to protect themselves from the repeated negative effects of stereotype threat, women and girls can present chronic disengagement from math-related domains and prefer stereotypically feminine academic fields (Appel & Kronberger, 2012). Thus, regardless of whether the gender stereotypes are internalised or lead female students to transitory and chronic disengagement from math-related domains, they might affect career decisions in several ways, creating and sustaining gender inequalities in higher education.

In sum, both internalisation and stereotype threat hypotheses suggest that the gender stereotype related to math ability prevents females from fully expressing their competence in math, thereby reducing their willingness to enter related careers. In addition to these hypotheses, grounded at the inter-individual and situational or "positional" level of analysis (respectively, internalisation and stereotype threat hypotheses), taking into account an ideological level of analysis (Doise, 1982) when examining the need to rationalise unequal social arrangements between the sexes will increase our understanding of women's choices and the maintenance of gender inequalities.

System justification theory and gender stereotypes as rationalisation tools

Gender hierarchy in higher education would be justified and maintained, at least in part, by gender stereotypes related to students' abilities and school-related personality traits. Indeed, important theorists in social psychology, such as Allport (1954) and Tajfel (1982), have argued that stereotypes stem from a necessity to rationalise social roles division. Jost and Banaji (1994) have incorporated this idea in a broader conception of the need for rationalisation. Indeed, according to system justification theory, system justification can be defined as a "psychological process by which an individual perceives, understands and explains an existing situation or arrangement and whose result is this situation or arrangement maintenance" (Jost & Banaji, 1994, p. 10). It is understandable that high-status group members are motivated to justify and preserve a system that benefits them. Therefore, the main proposition of system justification theory is to predict that even members of a low-status group might not always recognise the arbitrary feature of social status based on group belonging. Consistent findings have demonstrated system justification among the disadvantaged group members in artificial and natural groups, including ethnic minorities and women, in both the United States and Europe (e.g. Jost & Kay, 2005; Jost, Pelham, Sheldon, & Sullivan, 2003; Ståhl, Eek, & Kazemi, 2010). Moreover, some studies have established the presence of a system justification tendency among children and adolescents. For instance, Henry and Saul (2006) demonstrated that the most impoverished Bolivian children and adolescents endorsed system-justifying beliefs, suggesting an early motivation to justify the status quo among the disadvantaged group members. Elcheroth and Spini (2007) replicated this finding in Western Europe by showing that French secondary students from low-status groups justified the existing social arrangement more than their high-status counterparts.

This need to legitimise inequalities can have consequences for a number of psychological processes, including the use of stereotypes, judgment, and memory. According to this theory, stereotypes constitute tools that allow for an easy explanation of groups' differential status. Some are more competent than others in some domains, so they deserve to have higher positions in the social hierarchy. Thus, gender stereotypes are likely to function like essentialist instruments, allowing for the justification and the reinforcement of inequalities (Glick & Fiske, 2001; Jackman, 1996). Therefore, according to the system justification approach, it could be assumed that the system justification motive contributes to the emergence of stereotypes which in turn contribute to the maintenance of the existing social hierarchies. Successive studies have provided consistent illustrations of the role of gender stereotypes in the justification of the status quo (e.g. Calogero & Jost, 2011; Ståhl et al., 2010), especially the role of complementary gender stereotypes (e.g. Jost & Kay, 2005). Gender stereotypes are defined as complementary insofar as their content ascribes to each group a set of strengths and weaknesses. For instance, Laurin, Kay, and Shepherd (2011) demonstrated that, in order to justify gender inequalities in terms of salaries earned immediately after graduating, women self-stereotyped as more communal (relationship-oriented and warm) and less agentic (competent and assertive) than those in a control condition. Moreover, self-stereotyping as communal rather than agentic increased their satisfaction with the general social system. Three factors can explain why the complementary gender stereotypes can contribute to supporting the status quo. First, they provide the illusion that the division of labour is inevitable and even desirable as each gender group is deemed to be well-suited to endorse a specific social role (Eagly & Steffen, 1984; Hoffman & Hurst, 1990). Second, they reinforce the belief that the system is balanced as no single group owns the monopoly of advantages (Jost & Kay, 2005; Kay & Jost, 2003). Third, they disarm women's protests through the ascription of a set of favourable traits, rewarding women who follow the prescribed gender roles rather than those who challenge the status quo (Eagly & Mladinic, 1994; Glick & Fiske, 2001). In sum, a growing body of evidence suggests that gender stereotypes can justify and maintain the distribution of gender roles in society. We argue that this justifying and maintenance function occurs very particularly in the academic context in which gender stereotypes related to students' ability in specific academic domains can appear as especially relevant rationalisation tools of gender inequalities.

Justifying properties of gender stereotypes ascribed to students

Gender stereotypes related to students' ability in mathematics and science versus verbal domains

The most studied gender stereotype in the field of education is undoubtedly the stereotype focused on mathematic/scientific and verbal abilities. Research has consistently indicated that teachers, parents, and students are aware of, and often endorse, a gender stereotype favourable to men in terms of math and science abilities and favourable to women in terms of language and reading abilities (e.g. Chatard, Guimond, & Selimbegovic, 2007; Gunderson, Ramirez, Levine, & Beilock, 2012). In this respect, the gender stereotype of students' abilities in specific academic domains can be considered a complementary stereotype as defined by Jost and Kay (2005), with the property of justifying and maintaining the gender system. We argue that these functions stem largely from several implications that this gender stereotype has for female students' education path. Specifically, it is now well established that the stereotype assuming male students' superiority in math can harm female students' confidence in their math ability (Bandura, Barbaranelli, Vittorio Caprara, & Pastorelli, 2001; Bonnot & Croizet, 2007b), impair their performance (Smith & Hung, 2008), and constrain their career aspirations (Chazal, Guimond, & Darnon, 2012; Cheryan, 2012).

In an attempt to update our knowledge of gender stereotypes related to academic abilities, a recent study examined math and reading ability stereotype awareness among French fifth graders (Martinot, Bagès, & Désert, 2012). To this aim, participants had to answer a series of direct and indirect questions related to the academic abilities of either male or female targets, such as "How well do people think girls do in math?" This formulation allows for assessing children's awareness of the gender stereotype. Importantly, the ages of the stereotyped targets varied, thereby enabling the authors to assess the gender stereotype ascribed to both adults and children. The findings indicated that these young participants were aware of a gender stereotype favourable to girls and women in reading. Regarding mathematics, the participants were aware of a gender stereotype favourable to males only when the target was an adult. When the target was a child, the pupils believed that people thought that girls succeed as well as boys in math. Thus, the gender stereotype in math, contrary to the stereotype about reading ability, fluctuated as a function of the target's age (see also Plante, Théorêt, & Favreau, 2009). One could argue that this shift in the gender stereotype regarding math abilities reflects the increase in girls' performance over the last decades. However, beyond this kernel-of-truth-based interpretation, the rationalization hypothesis suggests that this gender stereotype might have emerged and now persists in an effort to justify existing gender gaps in students' career paths (Hoffman & Hurst, 1990). More precisely, describing girls and boys as equally skilled in math, but women as less competent than men, suggests that female students can challenge male students on simple, academic tasks, but not in advanced levels of math. Therefore, such a stereotype allows for justifying girls' success during secondary school while simultaneously rationalising men's domination in STEM at university.

A more direct test of the justifying function of gender stereotypes in math and verbal abilities was recently provided by Bonnot and Jost (2014), who asked male and female university students to estimate their competence and recall their past achievement scores in math and verbal domains. This was done either before or after system justification scales were administered, thereby allowing for a manipulation of system justification salience. These scales did not mention gender stereotypes—neither those related to general traits nor those specific to intellectual abilities. Completing the system justification scales before assessing their personal competence and recalling past achievement scores provided participants with an opportunity to think about the legitimacy of the social system to begin with (high system justification salience condition). In the low system justification salience condition, male and female students did not differ in their assessments. However, when system justification concerns were high in salience, male and female participants made more stereotype-consistent assessments. Specifically, men reported higher math competence and recalled higher past math achievement scores than women whereas women reported higher verbal competence than men. These effects held even after adjusting for participants' system justification scores, thereby demonstrating the power of system justification motives that led to stereotype-consistent self-perceptions, regardless of participants' personal attitudes towards system legitimacy. This study also illustrated the role that system justification concerns can have on biasing autobiographical memories for past achievement. Again, these biased memories and self-perceptions, when justification of the system is needed, might explain why—despite equal math achievement—female students enter math-related fields less often than their male counterparts.

The evidence suggests that gender stereotypes related to math and verbal abilities could persist in an attempt to justify female and male students' academic paths (Martinot et al., 2012)—an assumption reinforced by the fact that female students rely on this stereotype when system justification is made salient (Bonnot & Jost, 2014). However, we suspect that the assumed women's inferiority in math ability (and their assumed complementary superiority in verbal domains) is not sufficient for justifying all gender inequalities in higher education.

Gender stereotypes related to students' school-related personality traits and academic potential

We suggest that the justification of female students' underrepresentation in the high prestige fields of higher education necessarily implies the devaluation of girls' general school performance. Thus, in addition to the gender stereotype related to specific academic domains, a broader gender stereotype in terms of successful students' school-related personality traits and potential for future academic success is likely to contribute to this devaluation. The fact that girls' academic performance is less valued than that of boys' has already been pointed out in the discourse surrounding boys' underachievement. Thus, girls' academic success would actually reflect meaningless and inauthentic learning achieved through heavy work, which would signal their lack of inherent smartness (Hodgetts, 2008; Jackson & Dempster, 2009). In addition, in a recent study designed to assess adolescents' awareness of a gender stereotype in terms of students' school-related personality traits, Verniers, Dompnier and Martinot (2015) highlighted that secondary students were aware of quite an ambivalent gender stereotype towards female students. Specifically, French students from grade 7 to 12 were aware that a girl who succeeds in school is perceived as more compliant and hardworking than a boy who succeeds, whereas a boy who succeeds in school is perceived as being more assertive and having a greater potential to improve his intellect. In other words, French adolescents are aware that equally successful students are perceived differently as a function of their gender. Whereas girls are seen as careful, quiet, and polite, boys are seen as leaders, dominant, and decisive. One could consider that, all in all, each gender group has its own strengths. However, the characteristics ascribed to female students seem to be linked less to the potential for future success at a high level than those ascribed to male students. Moreover, awareness of a gender stereotype describing girls as more compliant than boys could contribute to devaluing girls' achievement by reducing their superiority to "a trick of the light, a matter of their compliance, obedience, or seduction of teachers by the neat appearance of their work" (Cohen, 1998, p. 21). According to the gender stereotype related to general academic achievement, girls are also seen as more hardworking than boys, yet at the same time the more effort a girl provides, the less she is seen as having the potential for future achievement. On the contrary, a boy is perceived as working less hard than a girl, but as having the potential to make fruitful efforts by which he could improve his intelligence (Verniers & Martinot, 2015b). Once again, this gender stereotype provides an ambivalent portrait of the female students that tends to minimise their qualities and, thus, to reinforce the belief that the gender system is balanced as no single group possesses all qualities (Jost & Kay, 2005; Kay & Jost, 2003).

The gender stereotype of general academic achievement contributes not only to depreciating girls' performance and their potential for future success, but probably also to rationalising the gender gap in higher education. Indeed, the school-related personality traits ascribed to successful female and male students are precisely those expected in female- and male-dominated fields of higher education, respectively. In a recent study, undergraduate French students pursuing various majors rated the extent to which compliance, assertiveness, effort, and intelligence were predictive of success in female-dominated fields (humanities, literature, and paramedical) and male-dominated fields (sciences and technology, mathematics, and engineering) of higher education (Verniers & Martinot, 2015a). The results indicated that compliance was deemed to predict success in feminine fields of higher education more than in masculine ones. On the contrary, assertiveness, effort, and intelligence were related to success in the masculine fields of study more than in the feminine ones. Again relying on system justification theory, the fact that the characteristics ascribed to successful female and male secondary students match the attributes expected in the female- and male-dominated higher education fields, respectively, provides the illusion that the gender gap in higher education is inevitable and even desirable as each gender group is deemed to be well-suited to succeed in specific fields (Hoffman & Hurst, 1990; Jost & Banaji, 1994). Even if more direct evidence that these specific stereotypes arise in an attempt to justify social order, these results indicate that it might indeed fulfil two major justifying functions: fostering the illusion of a balanced system in which female and male students have different strengths and weaknesses and rationalising students' academic paths by tying them to students' inherent attributes.

Practical implementations

When teachers, counselors, educators, parents, have to judge and evaluate students, or when they help them decide about their future academic orientations, most of the time, they mainly focus their advices and estimations on the way students self-describe, on their personal preferences, as well as on their past obtained performances in various areas. Thus, these pieces of information are basically considered as objective pieces of information about *who* the students really *are*. However, the research reported in the present chapter underlines that far from being objective representations of who students are, performances, self-descriptions and preferences are strongly affected by gender stereotypes, and that important motivations to justify the system may contribute to produce and maintain these very unequal perceptions among girls and boys. For instance, exposure to information describing the gender gap in higher education and their detrimental effects on women's career opportunities in an attempt to encourage counter-stereotypical choices may, ironically, increase students' motivation to legitimate this unequal arrangement. Thus, students may endorse gender stereotypes of academic abilities and define themselves in a stereotypical way in an attempt to justify the current gender gap in higher education. In this sense, we think teachers, educators, parents, counselors should be particularly vigilant not to consider students' performances and self-descriptions as being the pure reflection of their personal abilities and preferences, especially in a context where system justification concerns are highly salient. Such an error would not only lead to misinterpretations. This would also contribute *in fine* to reproduce and maintain the gender hierarchy.

Conclusion and perspectives

The present chapter proposed that system justification theory/motives help understand the maintenance of gender inequalities in higher education and more precisely the apparent paradox between girls' school overachievement and their underrepresentation in prestigious study majors and careers. We argued that an explanation of this paradox can be found in processes by which social arrangements are legitimised, even at the expense of personal and group interest, as is proposed by system justification theory (Jost & Banaji, 1994; Jost, Banaji, & Nosek, 2004; Jost & Hunyady, 2005). Our main argument was that gender stereotypes related to students' abilities in specific academic domains and gender stereotypes ascribing different school achievement-related personality traits to female and male students could contribute to the perpetuation of the gender gap in higher education. Thus, we were able to show that females' math reputation varies depending on how old the target is, in a way that matches the current reality—namely, women are still stereotyped as less competent than men in math whereas girls are perceived to be as equally competent as boys. Moreover, in a context that makes concerns related to system justification salient, women and men self-assessed in line with gender stereotypes of academic abilities. In addition, girls' overachievement is devalued through a gender stereotype of general academic achievement. Indeed, secondary school students are aware that a successful girl in school is perceived as more compliant and less assertive than a successful boy, who is perceived as more likely to make productive efforts to improve his level of intelligence. Finally, the school-related traits perceived to drive success in female- and male-dominated domains of higher education also closely match this stereotype.

However, because of the novelty of this approach, strong and consistent evidence is lacking. In an attempt to show that a system justification motive drives academic and career choices made by female and male students, future research should demonstrate that contexts requiring system justification influence these choices. It should also examine whether relying on these stereotypes makes people more satisfied with the system. Future studies should also take into account ideologies surrounding the academic system. Indeed, according to McCoy and Major (2007), priming justifying ideologies, such as meritocracy, increases self-stereotyping among disadvantaged group members. Therefore, it seems necessary to explore more broadly the role of other ideologies that might be especially important in an academic system, such as school meritocracy (Duru-Bellat & Tenret, 2009) and the norm of internality in the school context (Pansu, Dubois, & Dompnier, 2008) in the justification and maintenance of females' underrepresentation in the most prestigious fields of education.

References

Allport, G. W. (1954). *The Nature of Prejudice*. Cambridge, MA: Addison-Wesley.

Appel, M., & Kronberger, N. (2012). Stereotypes and the achievement gap: Stereotype threat prior to test taking. *Educational Psychology Review*, *24*, 609–635. doi:10.1007/s10648-012-9200-4

Bandura, A., Barbaranelli, C., Vittorio Caprara, G., & Pastorelli, C. (2001). Self-efficacy beliefs as shapers of children's aspirations and career trajectories. *Child Development*, *72*, 187–206. doi:10.1111/1467-8624.00273

Bonnot, V., & Croizet, J.-C. (2007a). Stereotype internalization and women's math performance: The role of interference in working memory. *Journal of Experimental Social Psychology*, *43*, 857–866. doi:10.1016/j.jesp.2006.10.006

Bonnot, V., & Croizet, J.-C. (2007b). Stereotype internalization, math perceptions, and occupational choices of women with counter-stereotypical university majors. *Swiss Journal of Psychology*, *66*, 169–178. doi:10.1024/1421-0185.66.3.169

Bonnot, V., & Jost, J. T. (2014). Divergent effects of system justification salience on the academic self-assessments of men and women. *Group Processes & Intergroup Relations*, *17*, 453–464. doi:10.1177/1368430213512008

Calogero, R. M., & Jost, J. T. (2011). Self-subjugation among women: Exposure to sexist ideology, self-objectification, and the protective function of the need to avoid closure. *Journal of Personality and Social Psychology*, *100*, 211–228. doi:10.1037/a0021864

Carvalho Arruda, C., Guilley, E., & Gianettoni, L. (2013, August 12). Quand filles et garçons aspirent à des professions atypiques [When girls and boys aspire to atypical occupations]. *Revue HR Today*. Retrieved from http://www.nfp60.ch/SiteCollectionDocuments/Projekte/nfp60_%20joye_publikation_hr_today.pdf

Ceci, S. J., Ginther, D. K., Kahn, S., & Williams, W. M. (2014). Women in academic science: A changing landscape. *Psychological Science in the Public Interest*, *15*, 75–141. doi:10.1177/1529100614541236

Ceci, S. J., Williams, W. M., & Barnett, S. M. (2009). Women's underrepresentation in science: Sociocultural and biological considerations. *Psychological Bulletin*, *135*, 218–261. doi:10.1037/a0014412

Chatard, A., Guimond, S., & Selimbegovic, L. (2007). ' How good are you in math?' The effect of gender stereotypes on students' recollection of their school marks. *Journal of Experimental Social Psychology*, *43*, 1017–1024.

Chazal, S., Guimond, S., & Darnon, C. (2012). Personal self and collective self: When academic choices depend on the context of social comparison. *Social Psychology of Education*, *15*, 449–463. doi:10.1007/s11218-012-9199-x

Cheryan, S. (2012). Understanding the paradox in math-related fields: Why do some gender gaps remain while others do not? *Sex Roles*, *66*, 184–190. doi:10.1007/s11199-011-0060-z

Cohen, M. (1998). 'A habit of healthy idleness': Boys' underachievement in historical perspective. In D. Epstein, J. Elwood, V. Hey, & J. Maw (Eds.), *Failing Boys? Issues in Gender and Achievement* (19–34). Buckingham, England: Open University Press.

Doise, W. (1982). *L'explication en psychologie sociale* [Levels of explanation in social psychology]. Paris, France: Presses Universitaires de France.

Duru-Bellat, M., & Tenret, É. (2009). L'emprise de la méritocratie scolaire: quelle légitimité? [What legitimacy for scholastic meritocracy and its way in France?] *Revue française de sociologie*, *50*, 229–258.

Eagly, A. H., & Mladinic, A. (1994). Are people prejudiced against women? Some answers from research on attitudes, gender stereotypes, and judgments of competence. *European Review of Social Psychology*, *5*, 1–35. doi:10.1080/14792779543000002

Eagly, A. H., & Steffen, V. J. (1984). Gender stereotypes stem from the distribution of women and men into social roles. *Journal of Personality and Social Psychology, 46*, 735–754. doi:10.1037/0022-3514.46.4.735

Eccles, J. S., Jacobs, J. E., & Harold, R. D. (1990). Gender role stereotypes, expectancy effects, and parents' socialization of gender differences. *Journal of Social Issues, 46*, 183–201. doi:10.1111/j.1540-4560.1990.tb01929.x

Eccles-Parsons, J., Adler, T., Futterman, R., Goff, S. B., Kaczala, C. M., Meece, J. L., & Midgley, C. (1983). Expectancies, values, and academic behaviors. In J. T. Spence (Ed.), *Achievement and achievement motivation* (pp.75–146). San Francisco, CA: Freeman.

Elcheroth, G., & Spini, D. (2007). Classes sociales et jugements normatifs de jeunes français: la justification du système par les défavorisés revisitée [Social classes and norm judgments by French youths: The justification of the system through underprivileged people revisited]. *Les cahiers internationaux de psychologie sociale, 75–76*, 117–131.

European Commission. (2009). *Gender segregation in the labour market: root causes, implications and policy responses in the EU*. Luxemburg: European Commission, Directorate-General for Employment, Social Affairs and Equal Opportunities, Unit G. *Retrieved from http://ec.europa.eu/social/BlobServlet?docId=4028&langId=en*

Fiske, E. B., & Unesco. (2012). *Atlas mondial de l'égalité des genres dans l'éducation* [World atlas of gender equality in education]. Paris: Unesco. Retrieved from http://www7. bibl.ulaval.ca/doelec/lc/L/Atlas_mondial_egalite_Fiske.pdf

Glick, P., & Fiske, S. T. (2001). An ambivalent alliance: Hostile and benevolent sexism as complementary justifications for gender inequality. *American Psychologist, 56*, 109–118. doi:10.1037/0003-066X.56.2.109

Guimond, S., & Roussel, L. (2001). Bragging about one's school grades: Gender stereotyping and students' perception of their abilities in science, mathematics, and language. *Social Psychology of Education, 4*, 275–293. doi:10.1023/A:1011332704215

Gunderson, E. A., Ramirez, G., Levine, S. C., & Beilock, S. L. (2012). The role of parents and teachers in the development of gender-related math attitudes. *Sex Roles, 66*, 153–166. doi:10.1007/s11199-011-9996-2

Halpern, D. F., Benbow, C. P., Geary, D. C., Gur, R. C., Hyde, J. S., & Gernsbache, M. A. (2007). The science of sex differences in science and mathematics. *Psychological Science in the Public Interest, 8*, 1–51. doi:10.1111/j.1529-1006.2007.00032.x

Heilman, M. E. (2001). Description and prescription: How gender stereotypes prevent women's ascent up the organizational ladder. *Journal of Social Issues, 57*, 657–674. doi:10.1111/0022-4537.00234

Henry, P. J., & Saul, A. (2006). The development of system justification in the developing world. *Social Justice Research, 19*, 365–378.

Hodgetts, K. (2008). Underperformance or "getting it right"? Constructions of gender and achievement in the Australian inquiry into boys' education. *British Journal of Sociology of Education, 29*, 465–477.

Hoffman, C., & Hurst, N. (1990). Gender stereotypes: Perception or rationalization? *Journal of Personality and Social Psychology, 58*, 197–208. doi:10.1037/0022-3514.58.2.197

Huguet, P., & Régner, I. (2007). Stereotype threat among schoolgirls in quasi-ordinary classroom circumstances. *Journal of Educational Psychology, 99*, 545–560. doi:10.1037/0022-0663.99.3.545

Hyde, J. S. (2014). Gender similarities and differences. *Annual Review of Psychology, 65*, 373–398. doi:10.1146/annurev-psych-010213-115057

Jackman, M. R. (1996). *The Velvet Glove: paternalism and conflict in gender, class, and race relations*. Berkeley, CA: University of California Press.

Jackson, C., & Dempster, S. (2009). "I sat back on my computer … with a bottle of whisky next to me": Constructing "cool" masculinity through "effortless" achievement in secondary and higher education. *Journal of Gender Studies*, *18*, 341–356.

Jost, J. T., & Banaji, M. R. (1994). The role of stereotyping in system-justification and the production of false consciousness. *British Journal of Social Psychology*, *33*, 1–27. doi:10.1111/j.2044-8309.1994.tb01008.x

Jost, J. T., & Hunyady, O. (2005). Antecedents and consequences of system-justifying ideologies. *Current Directions in Psychological Science*, *14*, 260–265.

Jost, J. T., & Kay, A. C. (2005). Exposure to benevolent sexism and complementary gender stereotypes: Consequences for specific and diffuse forms of system justification. *Journal of Personality and Social Psychology*, *88*, 498–509.

Jost, J. T., Banaji, M. R., & Nosek, B. A. (2004). A Decade of System Justification Theory: Accumulated Evidence of Conscious and Unconscious Bolstering of the Status Quo. *Political Psychology*, *25*, 881–920.

Jost, J. T., Pelham, B. W., Sheldon, O., & Sullivan, B. N. (2003). Social inequality and the reduction of ideological dissonance on behalf of the system: Evidence of enhanced system justification among the disadvantaged. *European Journal of Social Psychology*, *33*, 13–36. doi:10.1002/ejsp.127

Kay, A. C., & Jost, J. T. (2003). Complementary justice: Effects of "Poor but Happy" and "Poor but Honest " stereotype exemplars on system justification and implicit activation of the justice motive. *Journal of Personality and Social Psychology*, *85*, 823–837.

Laurin, K., Kay, A. C., & Shepherd, S. (2011). Self-stereotyping as a route to system justification. *Social Cognition*, *29*, 360–375. doi:10.1521/soco.2011.29.3.360

McCoy, S. K., & Major, B. (2007). Priming meritocracy and the psychological justification of inequality. *Journal of Experimental Social Psychology*, *43*, 341–351. doi:10.1016/j.jesp.2006.04.009

Martinot, D., Bagès, C., & Désert, M. (2012). French children's awareness of gender stereotypes about mathematics and reading: When girls improve their reputation in math. *Sex Roles*, *66*, 210–219. doi:10.1007/s11199-011-0032-3

Neuville, E., & Croizet, J.-C. (2007). Can salience of gender identity impair math performance among 7–8 year old girls? The moderating role of task difficulty. *European Journal of Psychology of Education*, *22*, 307–316. doi:10.1007/BF03173428

Nguyen, H.-H. D., & Ryan, A. M. (2008). Does stereotype threat affect test performance of minorities and women? A meta-analysis of experimental evidence. *Journal of Applied Psychology*, *93*, 1314–1334. doi:10.1037/a0012702

Nosek, B. A., Banaji, M. R., & Greenwald, A. G. (2002). Math = male, me = female, therefore math ≠me. *Journal of Personality and Social Psychology*, *83*, 44–59.

Pansu, P., Dubois, N., & Dompnier, B. (2008). Internality-norm theory in educational contexts. *European Journal of Psychology of Education*, *23*, 385–397. doi:10.1007/BF03172748

Pell, A. N. (1996). Fixing the leaky pipeline: Women scientists in academia. *Journal of Animal Science*, *74*, 2843–2848.

Picho, K., Rodriguez, A., & Finnie, L. (2013). Exploring the moderating role of context on the mathematics performance of females under stereotype threat: A meta-analysis. *The Journal of Social Psychology*, *153*, 299–333. doi:10.1080/00224545.2012.737380

Plante, I., Théorêt, M., & Favreau, O. E. (2009). Student gender stereotypes: Contrasting the perceived maleness and femaleness of mathematics and language. *Educational Psychology*, *29*, 385–405. doi:10.1080/01443410902971500

Prentice, D. A., & Carranza, E. (2002). What women should be, shouldn't be, are allowed to be, and don't have to be: The contents of prescriptive gender stereotypes. *Psychology of Women Quarterly*, *26*, 269–281. doi: 10.1111/1471-6402.t01-1-00066

Smeding, A. (2012). Women in Science, Technology, Engineering, and Mathematics (STEM): An investigation of their implicit gender stereotypes and stereotypes' connectedness to math performance. *Sex Roles*, *67*, 617–629. doi:10.1007/s11199-012-0209-4

Smith, C. S., & Hung, L.-C. (2008). Stereotype threat: Effects on education. *Social Psychology of Education*, *11*, 243–257. doi:10.1007/s11218-008-9053-3

Spencer, S. J., Steele, C. M., & Quinn, D. M. (1999). Stereotype threat and women's math performance. *Journal of Experimental Social Psychology*, *35*, 4–28. doi:10.1006/jesp.1998.1373

Ståhl, T., Eek, D., & Kazemi, A. (2010). Rape victim blaming as system justification: The role of gender and activation of complementary stereotypes. *Social Justice Research*, *23*, 239–258. doi:10.1007/s11211-010-0117-0

Steele, C. M. (1997). A threat in the air. How stereotypes shape intellectual identity and performance. *The American Psychologist*, *52*, 613–629. doi:10.1037/0003-066X.52.6.613

Steele, C. M., & Aronson, J. (1995). Stereotype threat and the intellectual test performance of African Americans. *Journal of Personality and Social Psychology*, *69*, 797–811. doi:10.1037/0022-3514.69.5.797

Tajfel, H. (1982). Social psychology of intergroup relations. *Annual Review of Psychology*, *33*, 1–39. doi:10.1146/annurev.ps.33.020182.000245

Verniers, C., & Martinot, D. (2015a). Characteristics expected in fields of higher education and gender stereotypical traits related to academic success: a mirror effect. *Social Psychology of Education*. Advance online publication. doi:10.1007/s11218-015-9312-z.

Verniers, C., & Martinot, D. (2015b). Perception of students' intelligence malleability and potential for future success: Unfavourable beliefs towards girl. *British Journal of Educational Psychology*. Advance online publication. doi: 10.1111/bjep.12073

Verniers, C., Dompnier, B., & Martinot, D. (2015). The feminisation of school hypothesis called into question among junior and high school students. Manuscript submitted for publication.

Williams, J. E., Daws, J. T., Best, D. L., Tilquin, C., Wesley, F., & Bjerke, T. (1979). Sex-trait stereotypes in France, Germany, and Norway. *Journal of Cross-Cultural Psychology*, *10*, 133–156. doi:10.1177/0022022179102002

3

DEVELOPMENT OF PHYSICAL ACTIVITY LEVELS OF GIRLS AND BOYS IN EARLY SCHOOL YEARS

A psychosocial perspective

Boris Cheval, Aïna Chalabaev, and Julien Chanal

Physical activity (PA) is defined by the American College of Sports Medicine as any movement of the body produced by the skeletal muscles that requires energy expenditure. It includes a collection of behaviors encompassing sport, conditioning exercise and life-style PA. Moderate-to-vigorous PA (MVPA) has proven to be effective in the primary and secondary prevention of many chronic diseases (see Warburton, Charlesworth, Ivey, Nettlefold, & Bredin, 2010, for a review). Despite these benefits, the population is mostly sedentary (e.g. Haskell et al., 2007; Sjöström, Oja, Hagströmer, Smith, & Bauman, 2006), and some social groups are even more inactive than others. This is particularly the case for girls, female adolescents, and women (e.g. Dumith, Gigante, Domingues, & Kohl, 2011; Hines, 2004; Knisel, Opitz, Wossmann, Keteihuf, 2009; Van Tuyckom, Scheerder, & Bracke, 2010). Indeed, females are less active (e.g. Capersen, Pereira, Curran, 2000; Trost, Pate, Sallis, Freedson, Taylor, Dowda, & Sirard, 2002), participate less in motor activities (Hines, 2004), and quit PA more than males (e.g. Dumith et al., 2011). Given that sports participation in childhood significantly predicts participation during adulthood (Perkins, Jacobs, Barber, & Eccles, 2004; Telema, Yang, Viikari, Valimaki, Wanne, & Raitakari, 2005), early differences observed between boys and girls could lead to sex inequalities in health in adulthood. It is thus crucial to identify factors likely to explain such differences in youth.

As children spend about half of their waking hours in school (Fox, Cooper & McKenna, 2004), this context appears as a key determinant in promoting PA (Meyer, Roth, Zahner, Gerber, Puder, Hebestreit, & Kriemler, 2013; Pate, Davis, Robinson, Stone, McKenzie, & Young, 2006; Pate & O'Neill, 2008). For example, a recent school-based program with Swiss elementary school children revealed an increase of 18 percent in MVPA during the school day, when physical education (PE) lessons are proposed (Kriemler et al., 2010).

However, although PE lessons may enhance students' MVPA on average, one may wonder whether boys and girls benefit in the same way from the PA opportunities within PE classes. This question was not examined in Kriemler et al.'s (2010) study and necessitates further investigation. To fill this gap, the current study combined a psychological approach with a social perspective to shed light on how the gender stereotypes associated to physical activities explain sex differences in terms of behavioral commitment during PE lessons.

According to social psychologists, natural biological factors are not sufficient to explain sex differences in general (e.g. Wood & Eagly, 2012), and in PA in particular (e.g. Knisel et al., 2009). They propose that these differences are the result of a complex interplay between biological, social, and psychological processes, notably through the influence of gender roles (i.e. shared beliefs about attributes that are typical and desirable for each sex; e.g. Wood & Eagly, 2012). Sport is generally perceived as a masculine domain (e.g. Clément-Guillotin, Chalabaev, & Fontayne, 2012), as it emphasizes masculine characteristics such as strength and competitiveness (e.g. Hardin & Greer, 2009). Previous research revealed that children know at an early age (i.e. kindergarten children) the gender roles existing in the PA domain (e.g. Riemer & Visio, 2003). Accordingly, because PE lessons are essentially based on sports, gender roles could be a key element to understand why, in early school years, girls may generally practice less than boys. It is an important question as it could thereafter explain sex differences in daily-life MVPA observed during adulthood.

A possible way to investigate this question is to examine it at the level of specific sports. Although school, through PE, exposes children to sport as a masculine domain at a general level, it is noteworthy that at a more specific level, sports are gender-typed as more or less appropriate for females, males, or both. Research has indeed found that some sports are consistently perceived as feminine (e.g. dancing or gymnastics), whereas others are perceived as neutral (e.g. tennis or swimming) or masculine (e.g. rugby or fighting sport) (e.g. Hardin & Greer, 2009; Riemer & Visio, 2003; Schmalz & Kerstetter, 2006). Accordingly, we assume that girls' and boys' PA behaviors during PE classes may vary depending on the sport taught during the lesson, because gender role beliefs are specific to each sport. Specifically, we can expect that girls would have a lower level of practice when compared to boys, especially when the sport taught is typed as masculine rather than feminine or neutral.

Furthermore, gender roles are believed to lead to their behavioral confirmation through different social psychological mechanisms (for a review in the PA domain, see Chalabaev, Sarrazin, Fontayne, Boiché, & Clément-Guillotin, 2013). Notably, they may affect individuals through their internalization into the self during the socialization process, resulting in sex differences in self-perceptions, motivations, and sport participation in favor of boys (e.g. Boiché, Plaza, Chalabaev, Guillet, & Sarrazin, 2014; Fredricks & Eccles, 2005). One may wonder whether the effects of gender roles increase with age as a result of the accumulation of social and personal pressures to conform to them (e.g.

Wood & Eagly, 2012). Specifically, as they grow up, children may progressively integrate the gender roles associated with physical activities, and sex differences in MVPA could, therefore, be more pronounced as children age.

A recent study provides tentative support to this hypothesis, by showing that endorsement of pro-masculine stereotypes increased as students grew older (Boiché, Chalabaev, & Sarrazin, 2014). However, sex differences in MVPA were not assessed. The literature on gender prejudice development also corroborates this hypothesis, by revealing that some sex differences may increase during adolescence as a function of increased interest in the other sex group (e.g. Rudman & Glick, 2008). For example, Lemus, Moya, and Glick (2010) argued that whereas sexism appears to decrease with age, it seems to increase with romantic relationship experience. Overall, while these different studies corroborate a gender role accumulation effect hypothesis, they are specific to adolescent individuals. Moreover, other research supports the concurrent hypothesis that sex differences in MVPA could be marked as soon as early school years. Indeed, it has been observed that knowledge of activities' gender-typing (e.g. Alfieri, Ruble, & Higgins, 1996; Serbin, Poulin-Dubois, Colborne, Sen, & Eichstedt, 2001), and of sports' gender-typing in particular (Riemer & Visio, 2003), may occur at an early age. Therefore, whether sex differences increase during elementary school years remains an empirical question.

The present study

Based on this literature review, the objective of the current study was to examine whether sex differences in objective MVPA depend on gender-typing of activities taught during PE lessons and children's age, among elementary school children. Specifically, we examined if sex differences in MVPA exist at an early age, and whether they become more pronounced as children grow up. Three cohorts of children (grade 5 to grade 7) were included in the current study. Their time spent in objective MVPA during programed PE lessons were measured twice using an accelerometer, with an interval of one year between the measures. This design allowed us to examine these sex differences depending on children's grade and time measurement. We hypothesized, first, that boys would have a higher level of objective PA during PE classes than girls, but only (or more strongly) when activities performed are typed as masculine (H1). Second, the hypothesis on the evolution of sex differences with age was more exploratory, as past research is inconsistent with this regard (e.g. Boiché et al., 2014; Riemer & Visio, 2003). Specifically, we examined whether sex differences in MVPA depending on sports' gender-typing are more important in children in higher grades (H2) and on the second time measurement (H2 bis).

Method

Participants and procedures.

Participants were Swiss elementary school students (N=1.099, 51.2 percent of boys) from 17 elementary schools from the canton of Geneva, in Switzerland. Data were collected twice during the 2012 and 2013 winter period. First wave of data collection concerned 309 students from 5th grade, 274 from 6th grade and 378 from 7th grade. Second wave concerned 186 students from 5th grade, 161 from 6th grade and 199 from 7th grade. Lessons were taught by PE teachers (N=13) in mixed-sex classes (the mean sample size of PE classes was 20–25 students). Voluntary students were equipped with accelerometers before the PE class by the research assistants. Recorded lessons were randomly chosen on teachers' availability and schedule. No instructions were given about the lessons and activities taught.

Sports' gender-typing

The categorization of the activities taught in PE lessons as perceived as more appropriate for males, females, or both, was based on categorizations established in previous work (e.g. Hardin & Greer, 2009; Riemer & Visio, 2003). As most studies revealed similar categorizations (for a review see Chalabaev et al., 2013), we did not measure how children gender-typed the activities in the current study. Specifically, two experts in the field independently coded each activity based on past relevant research on sport's gender-typing. After they completed their coding, they discussed about potential discrepancies. No discrepancies emerged. The 142 lessons used for this study were composed for 37.8 percent by sports typed as masculine (e.g. football, rugby), 39.3 percent as neutral (e.g. volley-ball, badminton), and only for 22.5 percent by activities typed as feminine (e.g. floor gymnastics, gym apparatus). In this study we combined neutral and feminine activities together. Neutral and feminine activities were grouped together for two main reasons. First, at a conceptual level, it allows to compare PA that are stereotyped as not appropriate for girls (i.e. masculine) versus PA stereotyped as appropriate for girls (i.e. feminine and neutral). Second, at a practical level, in our sample, feminine activities were limited to gymnastics activities, that is, gym apparatus and gym floor (see Table 3.1 for more details). It would, therefore, have been difficult to draw meaningful inferences about non-masculine activities without grouping feminine and neutral activities together.

Measures

Objective physical activity.

Each student was asked to wear a three-axis accelerometer (Actigraph GT3X+; Pensacola, USA) throughout the duration of one PE session, as a measure of

TABLE 3.1 The type of physical activities taught in physical education lessons

Women-typed PA		Neutral PA		Men-typed PA	
Rigging	14.10%	Tchukball	9.20%	Handball	9.80%
Gym floor	8.40%	Collective game	6.30%	Wrestling	7.70%
		Rings	5.60%	Basket-ball	5.60%
		Volley	3.50%	Rugby	4.90%
		Badminton	3.50%	Team sports	4.20%
		Jump	3.50%	Hockey	3.50%
		Courses	2.10%	Football	2.10%
		Kingball	1.40%		
		Throws	1.40%		
		Other	3.20%		
	22.50%		39.70%		37.80%

The percentage corresponds to the percentage of time in total that the specific activity was taught in physical education lessons.

elementary students' PA intensity level. An elastic band with snapping buckles was threaded through the unit and cinched around a child's waist with the device placed in line with the right hip. Based on Trost, Loprinzi, Moore, and Pfeiffer's (2011) review, the activity count cut-offs identified by Evenson and colleagues for 15-s epochs were applied to vertical axis data and corresponded to sedentary (i.e. ≤1.5 MET, ≤ 25 counts), light (i.e. > 1.5 MET , > 26 and < 3 MET, < 573 counts), moderate (i.e. ≥3 MET, ≥574 and < 6MET, < 1002 counts), and vigorous intensity (i.e. ≥ 6 MET, ≥ 1003 counts per 15-s epochs) (Evenson, Catellier, Gill, Ondrak and McMurray, 2008). The mean percent of epochs spent in MVPA was used as the dependent variable.

Data analysis

First, descriptive statistics were performed to present our data depending on our main variables. As the data were collected during real PE lessons during two different school years, few students took part twice. Thus, multilevel modeling was used because it permitted us to correctly estimate parameters of repeated measurement design with unbalanced data. Five models were built. In these models, measurement time was the level one and children the level two. Model 1 only investigated the effect of sex on objective MVPA, whereas Model 2 permitted us to test if this relationship was moderated by children's age. Age was operationalized by a categorical variable named cohort. The two parameters relative to the cohort effect in the tables results represent the difference between the reference cohort (cohort that does not appear in the parameter estimates) and the cohort considered in the fixed effects. Model 3 permitted us to examine the interaction effect between sex and sport's gender-typing on objective MVPA. Model 4 and 5 were conducted to examine if developmental effects exist in the sex by sport's gender-typing interaction. In other word, these models permitted us to test if the internalization of the gender-typed activities a) appeared as young as eight years old and b) if this effect is more important as children grow up. In the first model, we created an interaction term between sex and sport's gender-typing with the cohort variable. Therefore, the two interaction terms determine if the interaction between sex and sport's gender-typing differ between cohort 1 (8 years) and the other cohort consider in the interaction term (see Table 3.2). In Model 5, we created an interaction term with the variable time. This interaction term effect determines if the sex by gender-typing activity is different in our sample the second year of measurement. In all models, categorical variables were dummy coded.

The individual percentage of MVPA during the PE session was used as dependent variable. Multilevel modeling permits us to deal with the hierarchical structure of the data. Specifically, the variability associated with PE classes as well as PE teachers were integrated as random factors in the model.

Results

Descriptive analyses

Table 3.2 provides information about the characteristics of the participants and of the PE lessons.

Model 1: Overall sex differences in objective MVPA during PE classes

Multilevel regression analyses were conducted to examine if sex predicted objective MVPA (see Table 3.3). As can be seen in Figure 3.1, results revealed that girls had a significantly lower level of objective MVPA than boys ($b = -4.39$, $p < .001$).

Model 2: Variation of sex differences in objective MVPA during PE classes according to the cohort (i.e. age)

Multilevel regression analyses were conducted to examine the interactive effect between sex and cohort on objective MVPA. Results revealed that the relationship between sex and objective MVPA in cohort 1 did not significantly differ from that in cohort 2 ($b = -0.16$, $p < .92$), but was marginally different from that in cohort 3 ($b = -1.88$, $p = .065$) (see Table 3.3). As can be seen in Figure 3.2, boys had a higher percentage of MVPA than girls throughout the cohorts; however this difference was marginally more pronounced in cohort 3 compared with cohort 1 [Mean difference = 3.56 percent (cohort 1) vs. 3.74 percent (cohort 2) and 5.44 percent (cohort 3)].

TABLE 3.2 Participants' characteristics and physical activity during physical education lessons

	Total sample	Sex		Grade		
		Girls	Boys	Fifth	Sixth	Seventh
Time 1						
n	961	475	486	309	274	378
n Boys (%)	486 (50.5)	–	–	154 (49.8)	138 (50.4)	194 (51.3)
n Fifth-grade children (%)	309 (32.1)	155 (32.6)	154 (31.6)	–	–	–
n Sixth-grade children (%)	274 (28.4)	136 (28.6)	138 (28.4)	–	–	–
n Seventh-grade children (%)	381 (39.5)	184 (38.7)	194 (39.9)	–	–	–
% of masculine activities	36.5	38.3	35.6	41.7	43.0	27.5
% of PE spent in MVPA	30.44	28.51	32.40	31.84	31.50	28.30
Age in months	118.35 (11.16)	118.21 (11.30)	118.49 (11.02)	105.78 (6.20)	116.47 (5.71)	128.46 (5.98)
Time 2						
n	546	283	263	186	161	199
n Boys (%)	263 (51.8)	–	–	86 (46.2)	75 (46.5)	102 (51.2)
n Fifth-grade children (%)	186 (34.0)	100 (35.5)	86 (32.6)	–	–	–
n Sixth-grade children (%)	161 (29.4)	86 (30.4)	75 (28.5)	–	–	–
n Seventh-grade children (%)	199 (36.4)	97 (34.2)	102 (38.8)	–	–	–
% of masculine activities	44.2	44.2	44.3	49.4	59.2	27.3
% of PE spent in MVPA	31.96	29.80	34.28	33.72	32.00	30.50
Age in months	128.85 (11.61)	128.18 (11.89)	129.57 (11.28)	114.70 (5.76)	124.69 (4.95)	138.86 (5.24)

Values are means (standard deviations), unless stated differently; PE = physical education; MVPA = moderate-to-vigorous physical activity.

TABLE 3.3 Multilevel regression model to examine variation of sex differences in objective MVPA[a] during PE classes depending on gender-typing of the activities taught, student's grade, and times measurement

Predictors	Model 1		Model 2		Model 3		Model 4		Model 5	
	b	SE	b	SE	b	SE	b	SE	b	SE
Fixed Effects										
Intercept	33.24	1.35***	34.28	1.55***	33.69	1.47***	34.64	1.79***	36.65	2.63***
Sex[b]	-4.39	0.42***	-3.56	0.76***	-3.42	0.51***	-2.50	0.97**	-2.33	1.02*
Cohort 2			-0.14	1.28			0.57	1.60		
Cohort 3			-2.81	1.24*			-3.34	1.64*		
Cohort 2 × Sex			-0.17	1.09			-0.60	1.34		
Cohort 3 × Sex			-1.88	1.01			-1.59	1.25		
Gender-typed sport[c]					-0.91	1.40	-0.72	2.06	-0.43	2.35
Gender-typed sport × Sex					-2.66	0.78***	-2.46	1.40	-4.33	1.46**
Cohort 2 × Gender-typed sport							-2.37	2.53		
Cohort 3 × Gender-typed sport							-1.59	2.45		
Cohort 2 × Sex × Gender-typed sport							-0.64	2.03		
Cohort 3 × Sex × Gender-typed sport							-1.62	1.89		
Time									-0.13	0.11
Time × Sex									-0.05	0.04
Time × Gender-typed sport									-0.03	0.10
Time × Sex × Gender-typed sport									0.08	0.07

Random Effects

Intercept	16.53	2.69	16.59	2.68	16.41	2.68	16.49	2.60	17.85	2.89
PE classes	40.88	5.72	39.71	5.61	40.53	5.66	39.65	5.63	39.45	5.75
PE teachers	18.02	9.02	18.03	8.96	18.38	9.13	17.52	8.77	13.01	7.25
Error	40.25	2.63	39.88	2.63	39.86	2.62	39.21	2.60	40.27	2.75
–2 Log likelihood	11208.497		11022.633		11194.115		11002.090		10359.177	

Notes

[a] Percentage of MVPA during specific PE lessons

[b] Boys = 0, Girls = 1

[c] Non-masculine sport = 0, Masculine sport = 1

PA = Physical Activity; MVPA = moderate to vigorous physical activity

PE= Physical Education

p<.10, * p<.05, ** p<.01, ***p<.001

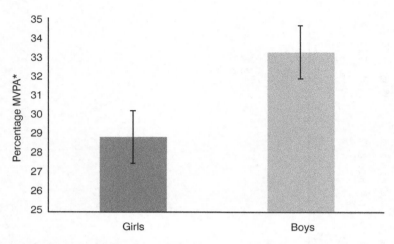

FIGURE 3.1 Sex differences in objective MVPA during PE lessons

Notes
MVPA = moderate to vigorous physical activity
PE = physical education

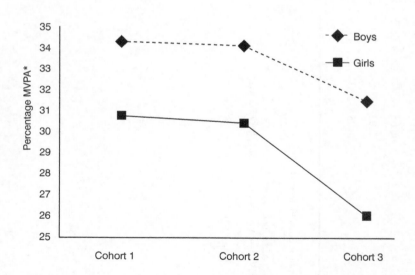

FIGURE 3.2 Interaction between sex and cohort on objective MVPA during PE lessons

Notes
MVPA = moderate to vigorous physical activity
PE = physical education

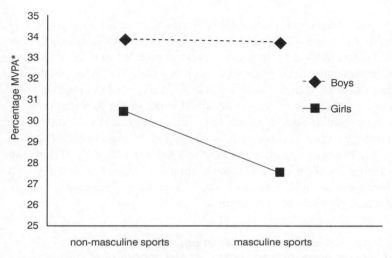

FIGURE 3.3   Interaction between sex and sport's gender-typed on objective MVPA during PE lessons

Notes
MVPA = moderate to vigorous physical activity
PE = physical education

Model 3: Variation of sex differences in objective MVPA during PE classes according to the sport's gender-typing

We predicted that boys would have a higher level of objective MVPA during PE classes than girls, but more strongly when activities performed are typed as masculine. Multilevel regression analyses were conducted to examine the interactive effect of sex and sport's gender-typing on objective MVPA. Aligned with H1, results revealed that the relationships between sex and objective MVPA was moderated by sport's gender-typing ($b = -2.66$, $p < .001$) (see Table 3.3). As can be seen in Figure 3.3, the difference in mean level of objective MVPA between boys and girls was more pronounced in masculine (-6.08 percent) than in feminine and neutral (–3.42 percent) sports.

Model 4: Variation of sex differences in objective MVPA during PE classes according to the sport's gender-typing and student's grades

We explored whether sex differences in MVPA depending on the gender-typing of activities taught would be more important in higher school year children (H2). Multilevel regression analyses were conducted to examine the interactive effect of sex and sport's gender-typing on objective MVPA depending on children's school year. Results revealed that the interactive effect between sex and sport's gender-typing on objective MVPA in cohort 1 did not significantly differ from that in cohort 2 ($b = 0.64$, $p < .75$) or from that in cohort 3 ($b = -1.62$, $p < .39$) (see Table 3.3). In addition, results revealed that the interactive effect between sex and sport's gender-typing on objective MVPA in cohort 2 did not significantly differ from that in cohort 3 ($b = -2.26$, $p < .24$). However, even if the interactive effects were not statistically distinct in the different cohorts, results are in line with the developmental hypothesis. Specifically, the interactive effect was not significant in cohort 1 ($b = -2.47$, $p < .08$) and in cohort 2 ($b = -1.82$, $p < .22$), but became significant in cohort 3 ($b = -4.09$, $p < .001$). As can be seen in Figure 3.4, the mean difference in objective MVPA between boys and girls was more important in masculine activities, and this difference was more pronounced in higher school year children.

Model 5: Variation of sex differences in objective MVPA during PE classes according to sport's gender-typing and measurement time

We next explored whether sex differences in MVPA, depending on the gender-typing of sports taught, would be more important on the second measurement time (H2 bis). Results revealed that the interactive effect between sex and physical activity's gender-typing on objective MVPA did not significantly differ depending on the measurement time ($b = 0.08$, $p < .221$) (see Table 3.3). As can be seen in Figure 3.5, the mean difference in objective MVPA between boys and girls was more important in masculine activities. However, the characteristics of the interaction between sex and sport's gender-typing did not significantly depend on measurement times.

Discussion

Main findings

Promoting regular PA is part of the public health priorities given its extensive health benefits (Warburton, et al. 2010), but low participation rates still remain (Haskell et al., 2007), especially among females (e.g. Knisel et al., 2009; Van Tuyckom et al., 2010). These gaps between females and males could lead to sex inequalities in health; it is thus crucial to better understand them. The current study drew on a social psychological approach to test the assumption that sex differences in MVPA during PE lessons among elementary school children can be partly explained by the gender-typing of the activities taught and the children's age. Two major findings were observed. First, boys had an overall higher percentage of objective MVPA during PE classes, but this sex difference was more pronounced for masculine activities, than for neutral or feminine ones. Second, this gender-typing effect was more pronounced in higher school year children.

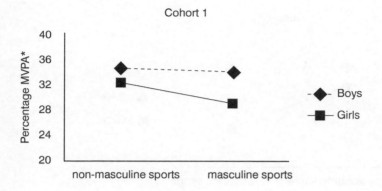

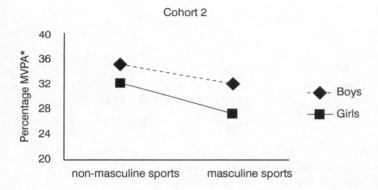

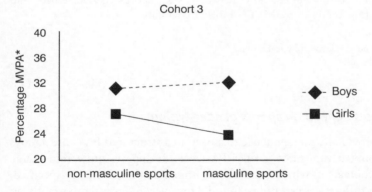

FIGURE 3.4 Three-way interaction between sex, sport's gender-typed and cohort membership on objective MVPA during PE lessons

Notes
MVPA = moderate to vigorous physical activity
PE = physical education

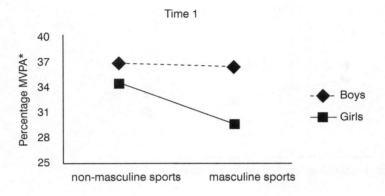

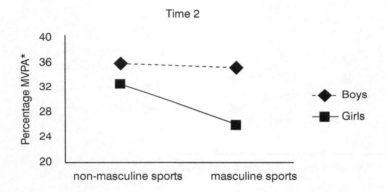

FIGURE 3.5 Three-way interaction between sex, sport's gender-typed and measurement time on objective MVPA during PE lessons

Notes
MVPA = moderate to vigorous physical activity
PE = physical education

Sex differences depend on sport's gender-typing.

Our results provide further evidence that even in a structured PA context, boys and girls do not demonstrate similar PA levels. It appears quite remarkable that even in contexts in which behaviors to implement are explicitly specified, significant sex differences can still be found. However, and most importantly, an interactive effect between sex and activity's gender-typing was corroborated. As expected, boys had a higher level of objective MVPA during PE classes than girls, but this sex difference was stronger when activities performed were typed as masculine, rather than feminine or neutral. These results are in accordance with past research showing that since sport is viewed as a male domain (e.g. Clément-Guillotin et al., 2012), differences in disfavor of girls and women are observed in sport participation (e.g. Fredricks & Eccles, 2005). The current study provides a more detailed picture of these differences, by showing that if we look at a more specific level, they are less pronounced in physical activities that are seen as more neutral or feminine (e.g. Hardin, & Greer, 2009; Schmalz & Kertestetter, 2006; Riemer & Visio, 2003). In line with a social psychological explanation of sex differences in PA, it suggests that the gender roles associated with the PE activities students participate in may influence their activity levels. The next step consists in better understanding the mechanisms through which this influence may occur. Several psychosocial mechanisms have been identified in the literature (e.g. Chalabaev et al., 2013). First, sex differences in PA engagement may be due to societal pressures to conform to gender roles, notably through significant others' disapproval of counter-stereotypic behaviors and approval of stereotypic ones (e.g. Wood & Eagly, 2012). Second, sex differences in PA may be explained by internalization of gender stereotypes into self-perceptions, leading girls to have lower perceived ability in this domain than boys, and in turn, lower PA levels (e.g. Fredricks & Eccles, 2005). Third, sex differences in PA could be due to stereotype threat effects (Steele, 1997): facing negative ingroup stereotypes when participating in masculine activities in PE classes may generate negative thoughts, worries, and avoidance responses (Chalabaev, Dematte, Sarrazin, & Fontayne, 2014). In turn, this psychological discomfort could lead girls to disengage from this domain. Our data do not allow us to identify which of these psychological mechanisms explain the results. It would be interesting to examine this question in future research in order to facilitate the development of efficient interventions.

Sex differences depend on sport's gender-typing and children's age

Even if the gender-typing effect did not significantly differ depending on students' school year, the results are aligned with the developmental perspective. Specifically, the interactive effect between sex and sport's gender-typing was only significant in cohort 3. Interestingly, this sex difference was more strongly driven by a decrease in girls' PA level than by an increase in boy's PA level, during lessons based on masculine sports (see Figure 3.2). This finding is in accordance with previous studies revealing that if boys are typically more active than girls, this difference becomes more pronounced as age increases through childhood and adolescence (e.g. Riddoch, et al., 2004; Strauss, Rodzilsky, Burack, & Colin, 2001). However, we believe our study goes beyond this by suggesting that this sex difference should be more or less pronounced depending on the gender-typing of the activities taught. Interestingly, these findings could help to understand previous inconsistencies regarding sex differences in PA within a PE elementary context. Indeed, within this context, whereas some studies revealed no significant difference between boys and girls (e.g. Tudor-Locke, Lee, Morgan, Beighle, & Pangrazi, 2006; Nettlefold, McKay, Warburton, McGuire,

Bredin & Naylor, 2011), others revealed that boys spent more time in MVPA than girls (e.g. Meyer et al., 2013; see Fairclough & Stratton, 2006, for a review). Therefore, the current results suggest that these inconsistencies in previous research could be a by-product of the identification of development of gender-typing according to the methodologies and the age of the participants.

Practical implementations

These findings have implications for applied contexts as well as for future research. In fact, given PE's influence on children's overall PA (Fairclough & Stratton, 2006), and that children's overall PA predicts fitness activities during adulthood (Perkins et al., 2004; Telema et al., 2005), ensuring that all children benefit equally from these PA opportunities is a professional duty for the teacher. The current results stressing the sex differences in behavioral engagement during PE classes in disfavor of girls, should invite them to adjust their practice. Different solutions may be considered: first, teachers could program fewer activities that are perceived as masculine; second, reducing the perception of the masculine character of some activities taught (e.g. rugby, or fighting sports) could help to reduce the significant sex differences in behavioral commitment during PE lessons; third, a recent meta-analysis indicates that interventions programs that catered for girls only are more efficient in increasing physical activity than programs targeting both boys and girls (Biddle, Braithwaite, & Pearson, 2014). Implementation of such strategies could be facilitated by education programs that target teachers, in order to (a) raise their awareness of the problem of sex inequalities within PE lessons, (b) help them to understand how they can prevent this problem, and to (c) provide teachers with strategies to foster girls PA behaviors. For example, learning how to present a masculine sport (e.g. fighting sport), how to interact with girls, as well as the kind of vocabulary to use so that this sport does not appear as a domain reserved for males seems an important perspective.

Limitations

Several limitations to this study exist. First, while we assumed that the sex differences observed were due to the internalization of gender roles, we did not assess either children's endorsement of the gender-typing of activities, or how they internalized these gender roles into the self (i.e. by measuring their perceived value of physical activities and their sport competence). This limitation notwithstanding, we consider these results as a basis for future research and hope that other researchers will join us to investigate different possible mechanisms and moderators of these effects. Second, the three age cohorts ranged from eight to twelve years. Accordingly, it was not possible to examine whether the gender-typing effect increases during adolescence. Longer monitoring periods would be valuable in future research.

Conclusion

In conclusion, this study demonstrated that, as in everyday life, PE is marked by sex differences in terms of behavioral commitment in disfavor of girls. It appears that even among young children (i.e. eight years old) these sex differences are more pronounced when physical activities taught are considered as masculine, rather than neutral. These findings reinforce the utility of a psychological approach, rather than biological, to explain these sex differences. Finally, a clear implication of the present findings is that PE teachers should be particularly attentive to the way in which they present the activities to teach, and especially when these activities are considered as masculine. We hope that these results will sensitize the educational community in order to ensure that boys and girls have the same quality of education. Such awareness appears to hold a great promise to avoid the courses taught at school leading to sex inequalities in health during adulthood.

References

Alfieri, T., Ruble, D. N., & Higgins, E. T. (1996). Gender stereotypes during adolescence: Developmental changes and the transition to junior high school. *Developmental Psychology, 32*, 1129–1137. doi:10.1037/0012-1649.32.6.1129

Biddle, S. J. H., Braithwaite, R., & Pearson, N. (2014). The effectiveness of interventions to increase physical activity among young girls: A meta-analysis. *Preventive Medicine, 62*, 119–131. doi:10.1016/j.ypmed.2014.02.009

Boiché, J., Chalabaev, A., & Sarrazin, P. (2014). Development of sex stereotypes relative to sport competence and value during adolescence. *Psychology of Sport and Exercise, 15*, 212–215. doi:10.1016/j.psychsport.2013.11.003

Boiché, J., Plaza, M., Chalabaev, A., Guillet, E., & Sarrazin, P. (2014). Social antecedents and consequences of sport gender stereotypes during adolescence. *Psychology of Women Quarterly, 38*, 259–274. doi:10.1177/0361684313505844

Capersen, C. J., Pereira, M. A., & Curran, K. M. (2000). Changes in physical activity patterns in the United States, by sex and cross-sectional age. *Medicine and Science in Sports and Exercise, 32*, 1601–1609. doi:10.1097/00005768-200009000-00013

Chalabaev, A., Dematte, E., Sarrazin, P., & Fontayne, P. (2014). Creating regulatory fit under stereotype threat: Effects on performance and self-determination among junior high school students. *International Review of Social Psychology, 27*, 119–132.

Chalabaev, A., Sarrazin, P., Fontayne, P., Boiché, J., & Clément-Guillotin, C. (2013). The influence of sex stereotypes and gender roles on sport participation and performance: Review and future directions. *Psychology of Sport and Exercise, 14*, 136–144. doi:10.1016/j.psychsport.2012.10.005

Clément-Guillotin, C., Chalabaev, A., & Fontayne, P. (2012). Is sport still a masculine domain? A psychological glance. *International Journal of Sport Psychology, 43*, 67–78.

Dumith, S. C., Gigante, D. P., Domingues, M. R., & Kohl, H. W. (2011). Physical activity change during adolescence: A systematic review and a pooled analysis. *International Journal of Epidemiology, 40*, 685–698. doi:10.1093/ije/dyq272

Evenson, K. R., Catellier, D. J., Gill, K., Ondrak, K. S., & McMurray, R. G. (2008). Calibration of two objective measures of physical activity for children. *Journal of Sports Sciences, 26*, 1557–1565. doi:10.1080/02640410802334196

Fairclough, S. J., & Stratton, G. (2006). A review of physical activity levels during elementary school physical education. *Journal of Teaching in Physical Education, 25*, 239–257.

Fox, K. R., Cooper, A. C., & McKenna, J. (2004). The school and the promotion of children's health-enhancing physical activity: Perspectives from the UK. *Journal of teaching Physical Education, 23*, 336–355.

Fredricks, J. A., & Eccles, J. S. (2005). Family socialization, gender, and sport motivation and involvement. *Journal of Sport and Exercise Psychology, 27*, 3–31.

Hardin, M., & Greer, J. D. (2009). The influence of gender-role socialization, media use and sports participation on perceptions of gender-appropriate sports. *Journal of Sport Behavior, 32*, 207–226.

Haskell, W. L., Lee, I. M., Pate, R. R., Powell, K. E., Blair, S. N., Franklin, B. A., ... Bauman A. (2007). Physical activity and public health: Updated recommendation for adults from the American College of Sports Medicine and the American Heart Association. *Medicine and Science in Sports and Exercise, 39*, 1423–1434. doi:10.1161/CIRCULATIONAHA.107.185649

Hines, M. (2004). Androgen, estrogen, and gender: Contributions of the early hormone environment to gender-related behavior. In A. H. Eagly, A. E. Beall, & R. J. Sternberg (Eds.), *The Psychology of Gender* (2nd ed., pp. 9–37). New York: Guilford Press.

Knisel, E., Opitz, S., Wossmann, M., & Keteihuf, K. (2009). Sport motivation and physical activity of students in three European schools. *International Journal of Physical Education, 46*, 40–53.

Kriemler, S., Zahner, L., Schindler, C., Meyer, U., Hartmann, T., Hebestreit, H., ... Puder J.J. (2010). Effect of school based physical activity programme (KISS) on fitness and adiposity in primary schoolchildren: Cluster randomised controlled trial. *British Medical Journal, 340*, c785. doi:10.1136/bmj.c785

Lemus, S., Moya, M., & Glick, P. (2010). When contact correlates with prejudice: Adolescents' romantic relationship experience predicts greater benevolent sexism in boys and hostile sexism in girls. *Sex Roles, 63*, 214–225. doi:10.1007/s11199-010-9786-2

Meyer, U., Roth, R., Zahner, L., Gerber, M., Puder, J. J., Hebestreit, H., & Kriemler, S. (2013). Contribution of physical education to overall physical activity. *Scandinavian Journal of Medicine and Science in Sports, 23*, 600–606. doi:10.1111/j.1600-0838.2011.01425.x

Nettlefold, L., McKay, H. A., Warburton, D. E., McGuire, K. A., Bredin, S. S., & Naylor P. J. (2011). The challenge of low physical activity during the school day: at recess, lunch and in physical education. *British Journal of Sports Medicine, 45*, 813–819. doi:10.1136/bjsm.2009.068072

Pate, R. R., & O'Neill, J. R. (2008). Summary of the American Heart Association scientific statement: Promoting physical activity in children and youth: a leadership role for schools. *Journal of Cardiovascular Nursing, 23*, 44–49. doi:10.1097/01.JCN.0000305056.96247.bb

Pate, R. R., Davis, M. G., Robinson, T. N., Stone, E. J., McKenzie, T. L., & Young, J. C. (2006). Promoting physical activity in children and youth: a leadership role for schools: A scientific statement from the American Heart Association Council on Nutrition, Physical Activity, and Metabolism (Physical Activity Committee) in collaboration with the Councils on Cardiovascular Disease in the Young and Cardiovascular Nursing. *Circulation, 114*, 1214–1224. doi:10.1161/CIRCULATIONAHA.106.177052

Perkins, D., Jacobs, J., Barber, B., & Eccles, J. (2004). Childhood and adolescent sports participation as predictors of participation in sports and physical fitness activities during young adulthood. *Youth and Society, 35*, 495–520. doi:10.1177/0044118X03261619

Riddoch, C. J., Andersen, L. B., Wedderkopp, N., Harro, M., Klasson-Heggebo, L., Sardinha, L. B., Cooper, A. R., & Ekelund, U. (2004). Physical activity levels and patterns of 9-and 15-yr-old European children. *Medicine and Science in Sports and Exercice, 36*, 86–92. doi:10.1249/01.MSS.0000106174.43932.92

Riemer, B. A., & Visio, M. E. (2003). Gender typing of sports: An investigation of Metheny's classification. *Research Quarterly for Exercise and Sport, 74*, 193–205. doi:10.1 080/02701367.2003.10609081

Rudman, L.A., & Glick, P. (2008). *The Social Psychology of Gender: How power and intimacy shape gender relations* (pp.204–230). New York: Guilford Press.

Schmalz, D., & Kerstetter, D. (2006). Girlie girls and manly men: Children's stigma consciousness of gender in sports and physical activities. *Journal of Leisure Research, 38*, 536–557.

Serbin, L. A., Poulin-Dubois, D., Colburne, K. A., Sen, M. G., & Eichstedt, J. A. (2001). Gender stereotyping in infancy: Visual preferences for and knowledge of gender-stereotyped toys in the second year. *International Journal of Behavioral Development, 25*, 7–15. doi:10.1080/01650250042000078

Sjöström, M., Oja, P., Hagströmer, M., Smith, B. J., & Bauman, A. (2006). Health enhancing physical activity across European Union countries: The Eurobarometer study. *Journal of Public Health, 14*, 291–300. doi:10.1007/s10389-006-0031-y

Steele, C. M. (1997). A threat in the air: how stereotypes shape intellectual identity and performance. *American Psychologist, 52*, 613. doi: 10.1037/0003-066X.52.6.613

Strauss, R. S., Rodzilsky, D., Burack, G., & Colin, M., (2001). Psychosocial correlates of physical activity in healthy children free. *Archiche of Pediatrics Adolescent Medicine, 155*, 897–902. doi:10.1001/archpedi.155.8.897

Telema, R., Yang, X., Viikari, J., Valimaki, I., Wanne, O., & Raitakari, O. (2005). Physical activity from childhood to adulthood: A 21-year tracking study. *American Journal of Preventive Medicine, 28*, 267–273. doi:10.1016/j.amepre.2004.12.003

Trost, S. G., Pate, R. R., Sallis, J. F., Freedson, P. S., Taylor, W. C., Dowda, M., Sirard, J. (2002). Age and gender differences in objectively measured physical activity in youth. *Medicine and Science in Sports and Exercise, 34*, 350–355. doi:0195-9131/02/3402-0350/$3.00/0

Tudor-Locke, C., Lee, S. M., Morgan, C. F., Beighle, A., Pangrazi, R. P. (2006). Children's pedometer-determined physical activity during the segmented school day. *Medicine and Science in Sports and Exercise, 38*, 1732–1738. doi:10.1249/01.mss.0000230212.55119.98

Van Tuyckom, C., Scheerder, J., & Bracke, P. (2010). Gender and age inequalities in regular sports participation: A cross-national study of 25 European countries. *Journal of Sports Sciences, 28*, 1077–1084. doi:10.1080/02640414.2010.492229

Warburton, D., Charlesworth, S., Ivey, A., Nettlefold, L., & Bredin, S. (2010). A systematic review of the evidence for Canada's physical activity guidelines for adults. *International Journal of Behavioral Nutrition and Physical Activity, 7*, 39. doi:10.1186/1479-5868-7-39

Wood, W., & Eagly, A. H. (2012). Biosocial construction of sex differences and similarities in behavior. In M. P. Zanna & J. M. Olson (Eds.), *Advances in Experimental Social Psychology* (Vol. 46, pp. 55–112). San Diego: Academic Press.

4

GENDER IN PATIENT–PHYSICIAN INTERACTIONS

Valérie Carrard and Marianne Schmid Mast

Introduction

Physicians have high status and high power in many respects. For one thing, physicians are considered as having high status and prestige because the job is socially highly valued and physicians are typically well paid. They thus have an economically superior standing compared to the majority of their patients. The medical knowledge the patients seek when consulting a physician also adds to the physician's high power or status. And, the medical visit implies most of the time that the patient is ill and/or in pain and in a vulnerable, thus subordinate, position. Moreover, being a physician is still associated with being male (Lenton, Blair, & Hastie, 2001) and being humane or caring was more associated with being a female than a male physician (Fennema, Meyer, & Owen, 1990). This highlights that power and gender and their interplay are important to consider when investigating how physicians and patients interact. This is the goal of the present chapter.

Women are underrepresented in high status positions and this includes women physicians. The non-profit research group Catalyst Research (Catalyst Research, 2013a) reports that in business in the US, women represent only 4.2 per cent of CEOs, 8.1 per cent of the top earners, 16.6 per cent of board seats, and 14.3 per cent of executive officers. Yet, what is seldom known is that the picture is even worse in healthcare and social assistance where women represent fewer than 0.1 per cent of CEOs, 13.7 per cent of board directors, and 15.8 per cent of executive officers (Catalyst Research, 2013b). Women represent 32 per cent of physicians worldwide (between 2001 and 2004; World Health Organization, 2013). More and more women enter medical school (Jolliff, Leadley, Coakley, & Sloane, 2012), but they are less likely than male doctors to be found in a leading position (Catalyst Research, 2013b).

As is the case for women in high-status jobs in general, female physicians also face similar challenges. Female leaders are typically evaluated less favourably than their male counterparts and this evaluation is particularly negative when women leaders adopt a masculine leadership style (Eagly & Karau, 2002). In the present chapter, we will examine to what extent female physicians are affected by the same evaluations as female leaders in general. We will also discuss how female and male physicians differ in their interaction style toward their patients, how patients behave differently towards their female and male physicians and how the sex composition of the physician–patient dyad affects consultation outcomes. Moreover, we will analyse how gender stereotypes can affect the medical interaction and its outcomes.

The patient–physician interaction

Since physicians are the depositary of the medical knowledge the patients are seeking, patients and physicians usually have an asymmetric relationship where physicians have control over the interaction, they set the agenda, they have the medical knowledge and competence, and they can provide access to treatment options. Physicians differ in the extent to which they share this power with their patients and patients themselves differ in how empowered they are. Roter and Hall (2006) propose a classification scheme describing four prototypical medical interaction styles according to the division of power between the patient and the physician.

1   Paternalism is an interaction style in which the physician takes control of the situation. The patient is passive thus not involved in the setting of the agenda and the decision-making process and receives little information during the interaction.
2   Consumerism is a setting in which the patient takes control over the agenda and the medical interaction. The physician is still the one providing information, but all the decisions are taken by the patient.
3   Default is an interaction style characterized by both patient and physician being low in power. Neither of them takes control over the agenda or the decision-making. The goals and role of each interaction partner remains vague.

TABLE 4.1 Medical interaction styles according to the distribution of control (Roter & Hall, 2006, p.26)

Patient Control	Physician control	
	Low	High
Low	Default	Paternalism
High	Consumerism	Mutuality

4   Mutuality is a style defined by the sharing of power between the patient and the physician, characterized by egalitarianism and partnership. Patient and physician exchange information. They will build together an agenda, and negotiate the issue of the situation in order to have a shared decision-making process.

The traditional and still most common medical interaction style is the paternalistic one (Roter & Hall, 2006), although the physician–patient interaction has moved to a more egalitarian relationship in the past decades. Nowadays, the recommended medical interaction style is patient-centredness (Institute of Medicine, 2001) described as care that "respects the individuality, values, ethnicity, social endowments, and information needs of each patient. The primary design idea is to put each patient in control of his or her own care" (Berwick, 2002, p.84–85).

Patient-centredness has been shown to be beneficial for the patients as well as for the physicians. Patient-centred physicians have patients who are more satisfied (Bensing et al., 2001), who trust the physician more (Aruguete & Roberts, 2000), adhere better to the physician's treatment recommendations (Robinson, 2006), and are less likely to sue their physicians for malpractice (Ambady, LaPlante et al., 2002).

Sex in the patient–physician interaction

In the following, we summarize findings from the literature on how female doctors interact with their patients as compared to male doctors. We also present research exploring how physicians treat male and female patients and how the sex composition of the physician–patient dyad affects both physicians and patients. All along, we also report findings on how sex influences patients' satisfaction. We focus our review on empirical studies conducted in the fields of internal medicine and general practice. These are the fields in which most of these studies are conducted and the focus on a broader field enables us to draw more generalizable conclusions concerning patient–physician interactions.

Physician sex

Physician sex affects how the physician behaves and interacts with his or her patients and patients react differently to the sex of the physician.

Physician sex and physician behaviour.

A meta-analysis by Roter, Hall, and Aoki (2002) showed that although female and male physcians show some similarities in their interactions with patients like the quality of the medical information provided, the amount of negative talk, or how much social conversation such as greetings they exchange with their patients, physicians' behaviour shows considerable differences depending on physician sex. Female physicians have longer visits (on average 2 min longer) and ask more closed questions. They explore more the implication of the illness, diagnosis, and treatment for the daily life context of their patients, and ask more psychosocial questions (i.e. questions related to illness impact on patients' psychological and emotional state). Female doctors also display warmer behaviours toward their patient with more positive talk such as agreements, encouragements, and reassurance, as well as more positive non-verbal communication like smiling, nodding, or a friendly tone of voice. As compared to male physicians, female physicians build partnerships with their patients more actively during the consultations and interrupt their patients less than do male physicians (Rhoades, McFarland, Finch, & Johnson, 2001).

All in all, those results show that female physician behaviour corresponds more to the pattern of patient-centredness (Roter & Hall, 2004; Roter et al., 2002) characterized by more caring and more sharing. Moreover, the female physicians' behaviour reflects typical female behaviour observed in non-clinical populations: More emotion expression (both verbally and non-verbally), more self-disclosure, and more egalitarianism in social relations (Brody & Hall, 2008; Dindia & Allen, 1992; Fischer, 2000).

Physician sex and patient behaviour.

In non-clinical settings, it has been shown that people treat men and women differently in conversations. People gaze more and smile more at women, approach women more closely, and self-disclose more to women (Dindia & Allen, 1992; Hinsz & Tomhave, 1991). In the medical setting, patients behave differently when facing a female physician as compared to when facing a male physician (Hall & Roter, 2002). Patients consulting with a female physician express more positive communication, such as agreement, than when consulting with a male physician. Patients talk more, provide more medical information and more psychosocial information when with a female physician. This can be due to the active partnership building shown by female physicians. Patients of female physicians also show more empowered behaviour such as more interruptions and they behave in a more dominant way. In sum, when facing a female physician, patient behaviour tends to be more positive, participative, and empowered (Hall & Roter, 1998, 2002).

Physician sex and patient satisfaction.

As described above, compared to male physicians, female physicians display more patient-centredness. This physician interaction style has shown to be related to more positive interaction outcomes (Ambady, Koo, Rosenthal, &

Winograd, 2002; Ambady, LaPlante, et al., 2002; Aruguete & Roberts, 2000; Bensing et al., 2001). Given that female physicians use the interaction style that is related to better patient outcomes (e.g. satisfaction) we would expect the female physicians to have more satisfied patients. Astonishingly, it is not the case. A meta-analysis by Hall, Blanch-Hartigan, and Roter (2011) reports that the difference in patient satisfaction between female and male physicians is significant, but so small ($r < 0.04$) that we cannot state female physicians are more positively evaluated as compared to male physicians. This paradox can be explained by the fact that gender stereotypes affect how patients perceive and evaluate female and male physicians. We discuss the effects of stereotypes in the physician–patient interaction later in this chapter.

Patient sex

Patient sex also influences the communication between physicians and patients. Female patients differ from male patients in that they have different medical problems, different bodies, their preferences for the type of physician interaction style are different, and their behaviour in the medical encounter differs as does the behaviour of the physicians in function of the sex of the patient (Kiesler & Auerbach, 2006; Verbrugge, 1989).

Patient sex and patient behaviour.

Female patients use more positive statements. They engage in more emotionally concerned talk and express their feelings more than male patients who talk more about facts when with their physician (Stewart, 1983). Female patients display more disagreement and speak in a less bored and less calm voice (Hall & Roter, 1995). Female patients also ask more questions and show more interest (Hall & Roter, 1998; Wallen, Waitzkin, & Stoeckle, 1979). All in all, patient behaviour depends more on physician sex than on patient sex (Roter, Lipkin Jr., & Korsgaard, 1991).

Patient sex and physician behaviour.

Physician behaviour is influenced by their patient's sex. Physicians ask female patients more questions about what they think and how they feel than male patients (Hall & Roter, 1998; Stewart, 1983; Wallen et al., 1979). Female patients also receive more emotionally concerned statements from their physicians (Hall & Roter, 1995, 1998) and are addressed with more empathy (Hall, Irish, Roter, Ehrlich, & Miller, 1994a; Hooper, Comstock, Goodwin, & Goodwin, 1982). Physicians provide more information to female than to male patients (Hall & Roter, 1998) and speak in a calmer, less dominant way to female patients than to male patients (Hall et al., 1994a). However, it has also been shown that physicians express more disagreements, speak in a more bored voice (Hall & Roter, 1995), and interrupt female patients more than they do male patients (Rhoades et al., 2001). In sum, physicians tend to respond to female patients with more emotional and egalitarian behaviours than toward male patients. At the same time, physicians also express more dominance in their behaviours toward female patients than toward male patients.

Patient sex and patient satisfaction.

Physicians use a more patient-centred interaction style toward female patients than toward male patients. We thus would expect female patients to be more satisfied. However, similar as in the case of the physician, there is no significant influence of patient sex on satisfaction with the medical consultation (Hall & Dornan, 1990; Jenkinson, Coulter, Bruster, Richards, & Chandola, 2002; Mead, Bower, & Hann, 2002).

Sex dyads

Relatively little research has looked at the sex composition of the dyad and how it affects the interaction behaviour between physician and patient and consultation outcomes.

Male physician with male patient.

Koss and Rosenthal's (1997) study of interactional synchrony (coordination of behaviours between two people) showed that male–male dyads were the ones with the least coordination between patient and physician. The male–male dyad is also the one with the lower patients' rating of the physicians' tendency to include them in the decision-making process (Kaplan, Gandek, Greenfield, Rogers, & Ware, 1995). Male physician–male patient dyads are characterized by the greatest amount of physician speaking time as compared to patient speaking time (Hall et al., 1994a), and by the highest level of physician dominance (Roter et al., 1991). To summarize, it seems that the male physician–male patient dyad is characterized by power differences between the physician and the patient with the male physician showing more dominant behaviour and the male patient being more submissive.

Male physician with female patient.

The male physician–female patient dyad is the least well documented. The only relevant finding in the research is that this dyad has been shown to be the one with the least amount of patient-centredness from the physician (Law & Britten, 1995).

Female physician with female patient.

The female–female dyad is characterized by more mutuality (Hall, Irish, Roter, Ehrlich, & Miller, 1994b), more patient-centredness (Law & Britten, 1995), and more interactional synchrony (coordination of behaviours between the persons; Koss & Rosenthal, 1997). In this dyad, consultation times are longer (Franks & Bertakis, 2003) and the amounts of speaking time between the physician and the patient are more equal (Hall et al., 1994a). This is also the dyad in which the physician shows more positive statements, emotional exchange, nodding, and interest cues like back-channelling (Hall et al., 1994a; Irish & Hall, 1995; van den Brink-Muinen, van Dulmen, Messerli-Rohrbach, & Bensing, 2002).

Female physician with male patient.

The female physician–male patient dyad is the one where the physician uses the least amount of technical language, smiles the most, but also used the most dominant tone of voice in the beginning of the consultation, the friendliest tone of voice in the end and the most interested and anxious tone of voice all along the consultation (Hall et al., 1994a). In this dyad, the male patient used the most dominant and bored tone of voice, but also made more partnership statements (Hall et al., 1994a). We can see that the interaction between female physician and male patient is characterized by discordant behaviours. This can reflects uneasiness felt by both partners in a situation where a woman, by handling a higher power position in front of a man in a lower power position, challenges the stereotypes associated with sex. We will see more about gender stereotypes and their impact on the patient–physician interaction in our next subchapter.

Sex composition of the dyad and patient satisfaction.

There is only scarce research exploring sex composition of the dyad and its effects on medical interaction outcomes. Nevertheless, their findings showed that sex dyads influence patient satisfaction. Female patients trusted female physicians more than male physicians and overall rated more positively the consultation when consulting with a female physician (Derose, Hays, McCaffrey, & Baker, 2001). In the female–female dyad, a greater patient satisfaction is linked with more occurrences of the female physician's typical behaviours: positivity, egalitarianism, and psychosocial orientation (Hall et al., 1994b). When focusing on the link between interruptions and patient satisfaction, we can interestingly note that for the female–female dyad more interruptions is positively related to patient satisfaction, but they are negatively related for the consultation involving a man (patient or physician; Hall et al., 1994b). It seems thus that sex composition influences the way interruptions are experienced by patients. Sex combination also influences the way expressed physician uncertainty is perceived. A study showed that expression of uncertainty leads to dissatisfaction only when the physician is a women and the patient a man (Cousin, Schmid Mast, & Jaunin-Stalder, 2013). All in all, the sex dyads that are less likely to lead to patient's satisfaction are the ones with opposed sex. In absolute terms, the lowest satisfaction rate is the male patients' consulting with a younger female physician and female–female dyads are the ones which are more often related to patient satisfaction (Hall et al., 1994b).

Gender stereotypes

Stereotypes describe how a person belonging to a specific group typically is or behaves (Burgess & Borgida, 1999; Heilman, 2001). Among other things, women are expected to be communal, indecisive, weak, gentle, and emotional and men are expected to be agentic, decisive, strong, bold, and rational (Burgess & Borgida, 1999). Stereotypes are also prescriptive and define how a person belonging to a specific group should behave (Burgess & Borgida, 1999; Heilman, 2001). Gender prescriptive stereotypes overlap with the descriptive ones. Women should thus show the behaviours that stereotypically characterize them (e.g. communal or gentle) and should not behave in a manly way (e.g. agentic or bold; Heilman, 2001).

The *lack of fit* model (Heilman, 1983, 1995) states that when the expectations about the attributes of a job are in line with the attributes stereotypically associated with the person in this job, the evaluation of this person will be positive. However, when there is a lack of correspondence between the attributes associated with the job and those associated with the job holder, the evaluation of the person will be negative. The expectations linked to being a physician include both, the feminine caring and communal aspect, but it also contains much of the male-typical attributes such as technical and medical competence, and status (Roter & Hall, 2006). Women are stereotypically seen as low status and this is where the lack of fit for women physicians comes in: being a physician necessitates conveying power and status but that is not how women are typically seen. This incongruence between gender expectations and job attributes can explain why female physicians do not have patients that are much more satisfied than patients of male physicians. Patient-centredness showed more by female physicians should lead to much better satisfaction with female physicians, but the lack of fit between what women should be like and what physicians should be like attenuates this expected link.

The lack of fit models also comes into play when looking at the way female and male physicians interact with their patients. When the female physician behaves in a male-typical way (e.g. showing less patient-centred communication), this incongruence is associated with a more negative evaluation and when the female physician behaves in a female-typical way, this is linked to more positive evaluations of her by the patients. To illustrate, people indicated greater satisfaction with a female physician when she behaved according to what is expected from her in terms of gender stereotypes (e.g. more gazing at the patient, more forward lean, softer voice) whereas satisfaction ratings for male physicians depended less on their gender-congruent behaviour (Schmid Mast, Hall, & Roter, 2008). Also, female patients were particularly satisfied with female physicians who showed a caring, thus gender role congruent interaction style, whereas in male–male interactions, the physician communication style did not affect patient satisfaction (Schmid Mast et al., 2008). The lack of fit model can also explain why female physicians do not get credit for using a more patient-centred interaction style but male physicians do (Hall, Roter, Blanch-Hartigan, Schmid Mast, & Pitegoff, 2014). It seems as if when women doctors are expected to use a more patient-centred interaction style and when they do, they simply confirm what was expected from them. If they do not, this is when they obtain less favourable evaluations. For men, when they show the non-expected patient-centred communication style, they are perceived as going out of their way to accomodate their patients by using an unexpected positive communication and then this gets noticed by patients in a positive way. The lack of fit between the level of expected patient-centred behaviour and the level of actually shown patient-centred behaviour seems to be the driving factor for how patients evaluate their physicians. The lack of fit draws the attention to scrutinizing the physician's behaviour.

Conclusion and outlook

Sex of the physician and sex of the patient as well as the sex composition of the physician–patient dyad affects how both physicians and patients behave during the medical interaction and it affects the quality of the interaction and its outcomes. Not only are there differences in how female and male doctors behave and communicate with their patients, there are also differences in how female and male doctors are perceived and evaluated by their patients. Both of these aspects affect consultation outcomes.

Outlook

Many areas remain under-researched. For instance, there is a gap in the literature concerning gender differences according to different fields of medical specialization. This chapter is based on internal medicine and general practice because most of the gender studies in medical communication have been conducted in these fields. Nevertheless, the different medical specializations imply differences concerning the goal of the consultation – for example bad news delivery for oncology, or purely information provision for surgery. It would thus be interesting to see whether, and how, male and female physicians are evaluated differently when the consultation goals and the implications differ. Interestingly, gender segregation has labelled certain medical specializations as being more female (like pediatric) or male (like surgery; Boulis, Jacobs, & Veloski, 2001) and medical students tend to choose their specialization accordingly (van Tongeren-

Alers et al., 2011). Future researches might want to focus more on the gender specificities of the different medical specializations.

There is more research needed to investigate how the sex composition of the dyad affects the way a consultation unfolds and what the consultation outcomes are. Research so far suggests that the female physician–male patient dyad might be particularly problematic. With the feminization of medicine (Levinson & Lurie, 2004) – meaning an increased percentage of women becoming doctors over the years – this sex constellation will become more frequent in the future and thus deserves more scrutiny in order to know how to counteract potential negative effects.

Also, the role of the gender stereotypes is not completely clear. Some research shows that women doctors profit from adopting a feminine interaction style, others show that female doctors should avoid a masculine interaction style, and others show that women doctors are not rewarded for using a patient-centred interaction style. Future research might want to address which conditions or which aspects of the female physician communication style exactly affect the medical consultation outcomes.

Practical implementations

How female physicians can counteract potentially negative evaluations or profit more from using the state-of-the-art communication style is not an easy task. Although some studies show that adherence to the more female-typical communication style can be beneficial for female physicians (Schmid Mast et al., 2008), we would not like to suggest that behaving in a more female way is the way to go, especially because empirical evidence also shows that when female physicians do this by, for instance, showing more patient-centredness, they do not necessarily get credit for it (Hall et al., 2014). So one piece of advice for female doctors is to avoid male-typical behaviour, because this has a relatively consistent negative influence on how they are evaluated (Eagly & Karau, 2002). We also think that the physician stereotype will develop toward including more female-typical aspects and we then would expect less difference in the evaluation of female and male physicians. By bringing the female physician role model to greater prominence, people's stereotypes about physicians might change and include more feminine attributes (e.g. warmth, caring, empathy).

Individual differences in patients are another important factor. Not all patients harbour gender stereotypes to the same extent. For example, the more hostile sexist a male patient was, the less satisfied he indicated he would be after a consultation with a female physician because he perceived the female physician as less patient-centred in her communication style (Klöckner Cronauer & Schmid Mast, 2014). This reaction can be explained by a rejection of womanly behaviours (like patient-centredness) or by a rejection of women in relatively high-status positions by hostile sexist men.

So physician training might want to include knowledge about gender stereotypes physicians can encounter in their daily practice and training in interpersonal sensitivity to pick up on whether their patients are particularly affected by gender stereotypes. With more awareness of gender stereotypes, physicians would better understand their patients needs, preferences, and reaction and could react to them accordingly.

Conclusion

The physician–patient relationship is a particularly interesting relationship in which to study gender and power effects because unlike in many other leadership positions, the expectations concerning a physician are not completely masculine; there are many aspects of gender stereotypical female behaviour included in the expectations people harbour towards a physician: empathy, caring, etc. In that sense, it is a relationship that has the potential to result in fewer gender differences than other hierarchical relationships.

References

Ambady, N., Koo, J., Rosenthal, R., & Winograd, C. H. (2002). Physical therapists' nonverbal communication predicts geriatric patients' health outcomes. *Psychology and Aging, 17*, 443–452. doi: 10.1037/0882-7974.17.3.443

Ambady, N., LaPlante, D., Nguyen, T., Rosenthal, R., Chaumeton, N., & Levinson, W. (2002). Surgeons' tone of voice: A clue to malpractice history. *Surgery, 132*, 5–9. doi: 10.1067/msy.2002.124733

Aruguete, M. S., & Roberts, C. A. (2000). Gender, affiliation, and control in physician–patient encounters. *Sex Roles, 42*, 107–118. doi: 10.1023/A:1007036412480

Bensing, J., van Dulmen, S., Kallerup, H., Visser, A., Borrell, F., Finset, A., & Zimmermann, C. (2001). The European Association for Communication in Healthcare. *Patient Education and Counseling, 43*, 1–4. doi: 10.1016/S0738-3991(01)00125-2

Berwick, D. M. (2002). A user's manual for the IOM's 'Quality Chasm' Report. *Health Affairs, 21*, 80–90. doi: 10.1377/hlthaff.21.3.80

Boulis, A., Jacobs, J., & Veloski, J. J. (2001). Gender segregation by specialty during medical school. *Academic Medicine, 76*, 65–67. doi: 10.1097/00001888-200110001-0022

Brody, L. R., & Hall, J. A. (2008). Gender and emotion in context. In M. Lewis, J. M. Haviland-Jones, & L. Feldman Barret (Eds.), *Handbook of emotions* (pp. 395–408). New York: The Guilford Press.

Burgess, D., & Borgida, E. (1999). Who women are, who women should be: Descriptive and prescriptive gender stereotyping in sex discrimination. *Psychology, Public Policy, and Law, 5*, 665–692. doi: 10.1037/1076-8971.5.3.665

Catalyst Research. (2013a, July 1). *Pyramid: Women in S&P 500 Companies*. Retrieved from http://www.catalyst.org/knowledge/us-women-business

Catalyst Research. (2013b, May 21). *Pyramid: Women in U.S. Healthcare*. Retrieved from http://www.catalyst.org/knowledge/women-us-healthcare

Cousin, G., Schmid Mast, M., & Jaunin-Stalder, N. (2013). When physician expressed uncertainty leads to patient dissatisfaction: A gender study. *Medical Education, 47*, 923–931. doi: 10.1111/medu.12237

Derose, K. P., Hays, R. D., McCaffrey, D. F., & Baker, D. W. (2001). Does physician gender affect satisfaction of men and women visiting the emergency department? *Journal of General Internal Medicine, 16,* 218–226. doi: 10.1046/j.1525-1497.2001.016004218.x

Dindia, K., & Allen, M. (1992). Sex differences in self-disclosure: A meta-analysis. *Psychological Bulletin, 112,* 106–124. doi: 10.1037/0033-2909.112.1.106

Eagly, A. H., & Karau, S. J. (2002). Role congruity theory of prejudice toward female leaders. *Psychological Review, 109,* 573–598. doi: 10.1037//0033-295x.109.3.573

Fennema, K., Meyer, D., & Owen, N. (1990). Sex of physician: Patients' preferences and stereotypes. *The Journal of Family Practice, 30,* 441–446.

Fischer, A. H. (2000). *Gender and Emotion: Social psychological perspectives.* Cambridge: Cambridge University Press.

Franks, P., & Bertakis, K. D. (2003). Physician gender, patient gender, and primary care. *Journal of Women's Health, 12,* 73–80. doi: 10.1089/154099903321154167.

Hall, J. A., & Dornan, M. C. (1990). Patient sociodemographic characteristics as predictors of satisfaction with medical care: A meta-analysis. *Social Science & Medicine, 30,* 811–818. doi: 10.1016/0277-9536(90)90205-7

Hall, J. A., & Roter, D. L. (1995). Patient gender and communication with physicians: Results of a community-based study. *Women's Health, 1,* 77–95.

Hall, J. A., & Roter, D. L. (1998). Medical communication and gender: A summary of research. *The Journal of Gender-Specific Medicine, 1,* 39–42. doi: 10.1001/jama.288.6.756.

Hall, J. A., & Roter, D. L. (2002). Do patients talk differently to male and female physicians? A meta-analytic review. *Patient Education and Counseling, 48,* 217–224. doi: 10.1016/S0738-3991(02)00174-X

Hall, J. A., Blanch-Hartigan, D., & Roter, D. L. (2011). Patients' satisfaction with male versus female physicians: A meta-analysis. *Medical Care, 49,* 611–617. doi: 10.1097/MLR.0b013e318213c03f

Hall, J. A., Irish, J. T., Roter, D. L., Ehrlich, C. M., & Miller, L. H. (1994a). Gender in medical encounters: An analysis of physician and patient communication in a primary care setting. *Health Psychology, 13,* 384–392. doi: 10.1037/0278-6133.13.5.384

Hall, J. A., Irish, J. T., Roter, D. L., Ehrlich, C. M., & Miller, L. H. (1994b). Satisfaction, gender, and communication in medical visits. *Medical Care, 32,* 1216–1231. doi: 10.1097/00005650-199412000-00005

Hall, J. A., Roter, D. L., Blanch-Hartigan, D., Schmid Mast, M., & Pitegoff, C. A. (2014). How patient-centered do female physicians need to be? Analogue patients' satisfaction with male and female physicians' identical behaviours. *Health Communication* (ahead-of-print). doi: 10.1080/10410236.2014.900892

Heilman, M. E. (1983). Sex bias in work settings: The lack of fit model. In B. Staw & L. Cummings (Eds.), *Research in Organizational Behaviour* (pp. 269–298). Greenwich, CT: JAI Press.

Heilman, M. E. (1995). Sex stereotypes and their effects in the workplace: What we know and what we don't know. *Journal of Social Behaviour and Personality, 10,* 3–26. doi: 10.1016/j.riob.2012.11.003

Heilman, M. E. (2001). Description and prescription: How gender stereotypes prevent women's ascent up the organizational ladder. *Journal of social issues, 57,* 657–674. doi: 10.1111/0022-4537.00234

Hinsz, V. B., & Tomhave, J. A. (1991). Smile and (half) the world smiles with you, frown and you frown alone. *Personality and Social Psychology Bulletin, 17,* 586–592. doi: 10.1177/0146167291175014

Hooper, E. M., Comstock, L. M., Goodwin, J. M., & Goodwin, J. S. (1982). Patient characteristics that influence physician behaviour. *Medical Care, 20*, 630–638. doi: 10.1097/00005650-198206000-00009

Institute of Medicine. (2001). *Improving the 21st Century Healthcare System. Crossing the quality chasm: A new healthcare system for the 21st century*. Washington, DC: National Academy Press.

Irish, J. T., & Hall, J. A. (1995). Interruptive patterns in medical visits: The effects of role, status and gender. *Social Science & Medicine, 41*, 873–881. doi: 10.1016/0277-9536(94)00399-E

Jenkinson, C., Coulter, A., Bruster, S., Richards, N., & Chandola, T. (2002). Patients' experiences and satisfaction with health care: Results of a questionnaire study of specific aspects of care. *Quality and Safety in Health Care, 11*, 335–339. doi: 10.1136/qhc.11.4.335

Jolliff, L., Leadley, J., Coakley, E., & Sloane, R. A. (2012). *Women in U.S. Academic Medicine and Science: Statistics and benchmarking report 2011–2012*. Washington, DC: Association of American Medical College.

Kaplan, S. H., Gandek, B., Greenfield, S., Rogers, W., & Ware, J. E. (1995). Patient and visit characteristics related to physicians' participatory decision-making style: Results from the Medical Outcomes Study. *Medical Care, 33*, 1176–1187. doi: 10.1097/00005650-199512000-00002

Kiesler, D. J., & Auerbach, S. M. (2006). Optimal matches of patient preferences for information, decision-making and interpersonal behaviour: Evidence, models and interventions. *Patient Education and Counseling, 61*, 319–341. doi: 10.1016/j.pec.2005.08.002

Klöckner Cronauer, C., & Schmid Mast, M. (2014). Hostile sexist male patients and female doctors – A challenging encounter. *The Patient: Patient-Centered Outcomes Research, 7*, 37–45. doi: 10.1007/s40271-013-0025-0

Koss, T., & Rosenthal, R. (1997). Interactional synchrony, positivity, and patient satisfaction in the physician-patient relationship. *Medical Care, 35*, 1158–1163. doi: 10.1097/00005650-199711000-00007

Law, S. A., & Britten, N. (1995). Factors that influence the patient centredness of a consultation. *The British Journal of General Practice, 45*, 520–524. doi: 10.1097/00005650-199711000-00007

Lenton, A. P., Blair, I. V., & Hastie, R. (2001). Illusions of Gender: Stereotypes evoke false memories. *Journal of Experimental Social Psychology, 37*, 3–14. doi: 10.1006/jesp.2000.1426

Levinson, W., & Lurie, N. (2004). When most doctors are women: What lies ahead? *Annals of Internal Medicine, 141*, 471–474. doi: 10.7326/0003-4819-141-6-200409210-00013

Mead, N., Bower, P., & Hann, M. (2002). The impact of general practitioners' patient-centredness on patients' post-consultation satisfaction and enablement. *Social Science & Medicine, 55*, 283–299. doi: 10.1016/S0277-9536(01)00171-X

Rhoades, D. R., McFarland, K. F., Finch, W. H., & Johnson, A. O. (2001). Speaking and interruptions during primary care office visits. *Family Medicine, 33*, 528–532.

Robinson, J. D. (2006). Nonverbal communication and physician–patient interaction: Review and new directions. In V. Manusov & M. L. Patterson (Eds.), *The Sage handbook of nonverbal communication* (pp. 437–459). Thousand Oaks, CA: Sage.

Roter, D. L., & Hall, J. A. (2004). Physician gender and patient-centered communication: A critical review of empirical research. *Annual Review of Public Health, 25*, 497–519. doi: 10.1146/annurev.publhealth.25.101802.123134

Roter, D. L., & Hall, J. A. (2006). *Doctors Talking with Patients/Patients Talking with Doctors: Improving communication in medical visits* (2nd ed.). Westport, CT: Praeger.

Roter, D. L., Hall, J. A., & Aoki, Y. (2002). Physician gender effects in medical communication: A meta-analytic review. *Journal of the American Medical Association, 288*, 756–764. doi: 10.1001/jama.288.6.756

Roter, D. L., Lipkin Jr., M., & Korsgaard, A. (1991). Sex differences in patients' and physicians' communication during primary care medical visits. *Medical Care, 29*, 1083–1093. doi: 10.1097/00005650-199111000-00002

Schmid Mast, M., Hall, J. A., & Roter, D. L. (2008). Caring and dominance affect participants' perceptions and behaviours during a virtual medical visit. *Journal of General Internal Medicine, 23*, 523–527. doi: 10.1007/s11606-008-0512-5

Stewart, M. (1983). Patient characteristics which are related to the doctor-patient interaction. *Family Practice, 1*, 30–36. doi: 10.1093/fampra/1.1.30

van den Brink-Muinen, A., van Dulmen, S., Messerli-Rohrbach, V., & Bensing, J. (2002). Do gender-dyads have different communication patterns? A comparative study in Western-European general practices. *Patient Education and Counseling, 48*, 253–264. doi: 10.1016/S0738-3991(02)00178-7

van Tongeren-Alers, M., van Esch, M., Verdonk, P., Johansson, E., Hamberg, K., & Lagro-Janssen, T. (2011). Are new medical students' specialty preferences gendered? Related motivational factors at a Dutch medical school. *Teaching and Learning in Medicine, 23*, 263–268. doi: 10.1080/10401334.2011.586928

Verbrugge, L. M. (1989). The twain meet: Empirical explanations of sex differences in health and mortality. *Journal of Health and Social Behaviour, 30*, 282–304. doi: 10.2307/2136961

Wallen, J., Waitzkin, H., & Stoeckle, J. (1979). Physician stereotypes about female health and illness: A study of patient's sex and the informative process during medical interviews. *Women & Health, 4*, 135–146. doi: 10.1300/J013v04n02_03

World Health Organization. (2013). Health workforce by gender distribution by country. *Global Health Observatory Data Repository*, July 2. Retrieved from http://apps.who.int/gho/data/node.main.A1449?lang=en

PART II

Women's struggles in the workplace

5

THE EFFECTS OF STEREOTYPES OF WOMEN'S PERFORMANCE IN MALE-DOMINATED HIERARCHIES

Stereotype threat activation and reduction through role models

Ioana Latu and Marianne Schmid Mast

Introduction

Despite recent progress in increasing gender equality, hierarchies remain male-dominated in most political and business domains. For example, across the world, only 21.8 percent of members of parliament are female (The Inter-Parliamentary Union, 2014), and of the 196 nations across the world, only 22 are led by women. Women are also underrepresented in the business domain, a trend that tends to increase as we consider higher levels of the hierarchy. For instance, although women comprise 47.3 percent of the US labor force, the percentage of women occupying top leadership positions, such as Fortune 500 CEOs, remains quite low – 5.2 percent (Catalyst, 2015).

Gender stereotypes also reflect this disadvantage for women in male-dominated domains, as women are generally less likely than men to be associated with leadership (Koenig, Eagly, Mitchell, & Ristikari, 2011). How harmful are those stereotypes for women with leadership aspirations? Are they powerful enough to lead women to perform and feel worse in leadership? And if this is the case, what can we do about it?

In the current chapter we first discuss the consequences of negative stereotypes on women's performance and self-related cognitions in leadership domains. Second, we explore effective strategies to reduce the impact of negative stereotypes for women in leadership. Please see Figure 5.1 for a visual representation of the contents of this chapter.

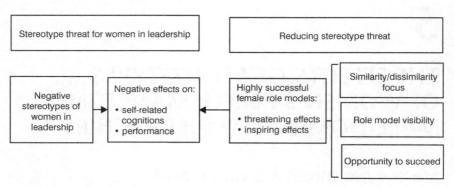

FIGURE 5.1 Chapter overview

Gender stereotypes in male-dominated hierarchies

Stereotypes are cognitive structures that contain our beliefs about certain social groups. Inherent to stereotyping is the belief that all members of the groups share the same characteristics (Judd, Ryan, & Park, 1991). Research has documented several stereotypes of men and women: women are seen as more communal, whereas men as more agentic (Rudman & Glick, 2001), women as more egalitarian, whereas men as more hierarchical (Schmid Mast, 2004), women more fitting with teaching jobs, whereas men with engineering and accounting jobs (White & White, 2006).

Within leadership, political, and business domains, gender stereotypes continue to disadvantage women, as evident from several research paradigms. For example, in Schein's *think manager – think male paradigm* participants rated leaders, women, and men on several traits such as intuitive, dominant, curious, competent, emotionally stable (Schein, 1973; Schein, Mueller, Lituchy, & Liu, 1996). Across 40 studies, leader stereotypical traits correlated more strongly with masculine traits (intraclass correlation = .62) compared to feminine traits (intraclass correlation = .25), according to a meta-analysis published in 2011 (Koenig et al., 2011). In other words, leaders are stereotypically seen as more similar to male compared to female stereotypes. Research from the agency-communion paradigm (Powell & Butterfield, 1984, 1989) yielded similar findings, with good leader stereotypes being perceived as having more agentic (masculine) than communal (feminine) characteristics. Drawing from the role congruity model (Eagly & Karau, 2002) and the lack-of-fit model (Heilman, 1983, 2001), this mismatch between leader stereotypes and feminine stereotypes poses a potential threat for women who aspire to become leaders because it makes feminine qualities undesirable for leadership, possibly leading to negative evaluations of female leaders (Heilman, Block, & Martell, 1995).

Not only is there a mismatch between leader stereotypes and female stereotypes, but once women are considered in the leadership context, research shows that individuals tend to hold negative stereotypes of female managers.

For example, female managers were attributed more negative attributes compared to male managers (Heilman et al., 1995). Although there has been some improvement in individuals' explicit gender stereotypes in the last few decades such that female managers are seen as more assertive, more ambitious, and less submissive than in the past (Duehr & Bono, 2006; Stoker, Van der Velde, & Lammers, 2012), we still see negative stereotypes of female managers at implicit (relatively unconscious) levels. For example, across two studies (Latu et al., 2011) we found that women were more likely than men to be implicitly associated with incompetent managerial traits (e.g. *follower, incompetent, ignorant*), whereas men were more likely than women to be implicitly associated with competent managerial traits (e.g. *leader, competent, knowledgeable*).

The consequences of gender stereotypes for women's performance and self-related cognitions

How do these stereotypes affect women in male-dominated domains? We will review the literature on the effects of gender-leadership stereotypes on women's performance and self-related cognitions, which we define as any thoughts about the self that are assessed through self-report measures and can include self-evaluations, self-stereotypes, leadership aspirations, and entrepreneurial intentions.

A wealth of research has suggested that being aware of negative stereotypes about our ingroup can negatively affect performance in the relevant domain, a phenomenon known as stereotype threat (Steele, 1997; Steele & Aronson, 2000). Stereotype threat is a situational factor and it can be activated in three different ways (Nguyen & Ryan, 2008): blatant (explicitly stating the target group's inferiority, for example that women are not as good at math as men), moderately explicit (stating that a math test, for example, produces gender differences without specifying which group tends to perform better), and implicit (making gender salient, through emphasizing test diagnosticity, exposing women to gender stereotypic commercials, or manipulating the gender composition of the group).

In terms of outcomes, across several studies, women who were primed with negative gender stereotypes showed decreased performance on math tests (Schmader & Johns, 2003; Spencer, Steele, & Quinn, 1999) as well as decreased interest in quantitative domains, such as mathematics, engineering and computer science (Davies, Spencer, Quinn, & Gerhardstein, 2002). Overall, stereotype threat has an important, negative effect on women's performance and self-related cognitions in STEM (science, technology, engineering, and mathematics). The idea is that women's concerns about confirming negative stereotypes about their gender group (e.g. the stereotype that women are not good at math) can interfere with their performance and self-related cognitions, possibly because of unsuccessful attempts to suppress self-relevant stereotypes (Logel, Iserman, Davies, Quinn, & Spencer, 2009) and subsequent decreased working memory capacity (Schmader & Johns, 2003) or increased arousal (Ben-Zeev, Fein, & Inzlicht, 2005).

Although the evidence is sparser, stereotype threat seems also to affect women's self-related cognitions in leadership domains. Women exposed to TV commercials depicting women in gender stereotypical roles (e.g. homecoming queen) were less interested in choosing a leadership role in a subsequent task (Davies, Spencer, & Steele, 2005). Similarly, gender stereotype threat activation decreased women's entrepreneurial intentions (Gupta & Bhawe, 2007) and women's confidence in their likelihood of reaching their career aspirations (von Hippel, Issa, Ma, & Stokes, 2011). It also had more profound implications on women's identities, such that female leaders who experienced stereotype threat were more likely to separate their female identity from their work-related identity (Von Hippel, Issa et al., 2011). Overall, these damaging effects on women's leadership self-related cognitions are dangerous for women in male-dominated domains because they can lead women to withdraw from leadership and business domains that evoke such a stereotype threat.

Negative stereotypes not only affect women's self-related cognitions, but also their actual performance on several leadership tasks. In a hypothetical managerial decision-making task (Bergeron, Block, & Echtenkamp, 2006), participants played the role of a manager whose role was to make decisions for six memos dealing with complex organizational issues, such as granting maternity leave, recruiting, sexual harassment, permitting a job training course, hiring a manager, selecting a research firm. Each of these memos had a correct answer, against which participants' decisions were coded by two independent coders. Women who performed this managerial task under stereotype threat showed a decrease in both the quantity and the quality of their managerial decisions. Similarly, women under stereotype threat activation adopted a more masculine communication style, which in turn led to more negative evaluations and less managerial effectiveness (von Hippel, Wiryakusuma, Bowden, & Shochet, 2011). In a leadership task such as influencing and motivating employees, stereotype threat led to decreased leadership performance for those female participants low in self-efficacy (Hoyt & Blascovich, 2010). Finally, negotiation skills have also been affected by stereotype threat. When negative leadership-gender stereotypes were activated (i.e. when stereotypically feminine traits were linked to poor negotiation outcomes), women performed less well than men (Kray, Thompson, & Galinsky, 2001; Tellhed & Björklund, 2011). Overall, these findings show that not only do women *feel* threatened and discouraged when negative leadership stereotypes are activated, but their performance actually suffers.

Reducing the negative consequences of gender stereotypes

How can we reduce the negative effects of stereotype threat for women in leadership? Several strategies of stereotype threat removal have proved to be efficient, such as changing the successful negotiator stereotype, such that it becomes less masculine. This strategy involves training participants to associate stereotypically feminine traits (emotional expressivity, listening skills, interpersonal sensitivity) with the stereotype of successful negotiators (Kray, Galinsky, & Thompson, 2002). Another successful strategy is that of self-affirmation, in which participants are encouraged to think about values that are important to themselves prior to performing the evaluation task (von Hippel, Wiryakusuma et al., 2011).

In addition to these strategies, research has been successful at identifying individual differences which moderate women's response to stereotype threat. For example, research shows that women with high levels of leadership self-efficacy are more likely to show heightened levels of leadership aspiration, leader self-identification, and performance when exposed to highly successful role models (Hoyt, 2013; Hoyt & Blascovich, 2010). Also, believing that leadership ability is malleable ("leaders are made") rather than fixed ("leaders are born") led to more positive reactions to role models (Burnette, Pollack, & Hoyt, 2010; Hoyt, Burnette, & Innella, 2012). Finally, having a less proactive personality seems to predict positive reactions to role models (Gupta & Bhawe, 2007).

Overall, situational factors such as the explicitness of the stereotype, the group sex-composition, and the power of the person can also modulate the responses to stereotype threat (for a review of the quantitative performance literature see Nguyen & Ryan, 2008). In addition to these situational factors, factors related to interpersonal relations are also important. Particularly, in the remainder of the chapter we focus on role models: exposing women to counterstereotypic exemplars of their own group – highly successful, powerful women, who through their success have disproved the negative stereotype of women in leadership. This is a particularly controversial strategy for reducing the negative effects of stereotypes and thus empowering women in male-dominated hierarchies.

Research on female role models in leadership shows that exposure to such highly successful women can have both negative and positive effects. On the one hand, incredibly successful women can empower women in leadership, by challenging negative stereotypes and making women feel that they can do it too (assimilation effects). On the other hand, they can lead to negative effects, because women exposed to other highly successful women may feel threatened and discouraged, ultimately leading them to believe that they could never achieve that level of success (contrast effects). Using social comparison theory (Festinger, 1954) and more specifically the selective accessibility model (Mussweiler, 2003) as a theoretical framework, we will present research supporting both these claims (including our research) and later attempt to resolve this debate.

According to the social accessibility model applied to social comparisons, when comparing to others, people may take one of two strategies. They can either engage in similarity testing, which implies selectively focusing on similarities with the role model. Alternatively they can engage in dissimilarity testing, which implies selectively focusing on dissimilarities to the role model.

Contrast: threatening effects.

Social comparison with highly successful others can lead either to contrast or assimilation effects (Mussweiler, 2003). Contrast occurs when comparisons with a highly successful person have unintended negative effects – for example, participants primed with Albert Einstein experienced decreased performance on intelligence tests (Dijksterhuis et al., 1998). Overall, highly successful others that are relevant to self (LeBoeuf & Estes, 2004) but whose success seems unattainable (Lockwood & Kunda, 1997) tend to elicit contrast, thus hurting self-evaluations and performance. This hypothesis was indeed supported when exposing women to highly successful female leaders. For example, women exposed to other highly successful women showed lower self-evaluations (Hoyt & Simon, 2011; Parks-Stamm, Heilman, & Hearns, 2008), weaker self-leadership associations (Rudman & Phelan, 2010), and lower leadership aspirations (Hoyt & Simon, 2011). For instance, exposure to high-level female leaders before performing a leadership task led women to self-report lower self-evaluations, greater feelings of inferiority, and lower leadership aspirations compared to exposure to high-level male leaders or controls (Hoyt & Simon, 2011). Similarly, exposing women to a successful female CEO decreased their competence self-ratings (Parks-Stamm, Heilman, & Hearns, 2008). Women's self-stereotypes were also affected: priming with highly successful women (professor at Stanford Business School, organ transplant surgeon, president of the Global Financial Services division) led to weaker self-leadership associations and less interest in those high-power occupations (Rudman & Phelan, 2010). Exposures to women in high-profile leadership positions also led to increased self-stereotyping, deflated career goals, and less likelihood to associate leadership with the self at an explicit level (Asgari, Dasgupta, & Stout, 2012). These negative effects were only reversed when the leader was explicitly presented as being similar to the participant, consistent with Mussweiler's selective accessibility model (Mussweiler, 2003; Mussweiler, Rüter, & Epstude, 2004).

Assimilation: inspiring effects.

Although previous research has found evidence of contrast effects on women's self-related cognitions upon exposures to highly successful female role models, the opposite may also occur, an effect called assimilation. Indeed, under certain conditions, targets primed with a stereotype (Dijksterhuis et al., 1998) or a stereotypic exemplar (Osswald, Greitemeyer, Fischer, & Frey, 2010; Taylor, Lord, McIntyre, & Paulson, 2011) show behavioral assimilation, by behaving in ways consistent with the stereotype (e.g. better test performance after being primed with "professor", Dijksterhuis et al., 1998).

The idea of behavior assimilation was supported when we looked at the effects of highly successful female role models on women's *actual behavior* during a leadership task (Latu, Mast, Lammers, & Bombari, 2013). Male and female participants were asked to give a persuasive political speech in front of an audience in a virtual reality environment. While delivering the speech, participants were subtly primed either with the picture of a female political role model (Hillary Clinton or Angela Merkel), or the picture of a male political role model (Bill Clinton), or with no pictures. In a pretest, we insured that our participants perceived the male and female role models as similar on several dimensions such as liking, competence, and power. As a dependent measure, we assessed the length of our participants' speeches, as speaking time is a measure of empowered behavior, with powerful/dominant people tending to speak longer (Schmid Mast, 2002). We also videotaped participants and showed the videotaped speeches to an external coder who evaluated the quality of our participants' speeches, based on the structure and fluency of the discourse, but also nonverbal behaviors such as body posture and voice quality. After delivering the speech, we also asked participants to self-evaluate their performance using several items (e.g. "I was successful in communicating my message during the oral presentation"), using a five-point Likert scale.

Results showed that when delivering a leadership task while being exposed to a male role model or no role models, we find a gender performance gap, with male participants speaking longer than women. However, exposure to female role models increased the length of women's speeches, thus eliminating the gender performance gap of empowered behavior. In fact, women's speeches were 24 percent longer when exposed to a portrait of Hilary Clinton and 49 percent longer when exposed to a portrait of Angela Merkel, compared to the average of the control conditions. Moreover, the longer women spoke the better they were evaluated by external coders and the more positively they self-evaluated their own performance. There was no significant difference between the two female role model conditions. Overall, these findings show that highly successful female role models empower women's actual behavior in a leadership task, and these inspiring effects are further reflected in women's self-evaluations.

Resolving the controversy.

Overall, it seems that exposing women to counterstereotypical (successful) female leaders can sometimes reduce the negative effects of gender-leadership stereotypes through assimilation, but it can also have adverse effects, through contrast effects. How can these contradictory effects be explained? We will consider three possible explanations for these effects and discuss their implications for applied gender issues in male-dominated domains.

First, consistent with the selective accessibility model (Mussweiler, 2003), the extent to which social comparisons lead to assimilation vs. contrast depends primarily on whether individuals focus on similarities or differences with the target. If women exposed to highly successful female role models selectively focus on how they are similar to the female role model (e.g. sharing the same gender, nationality, career aspirations), then it is likely that they would be inspired by those role models through the process of assimilation. However, if women exposed to the same highly successful female role models selectively focus on how they are different from the female role model (e.g. different educational opportunities, socioeconomic status), then it is likely that they would be threatened by the role model through the process of contrast. Mussweiler and colleagues (2004) manipulated the similarity/difference focus in two ways. First, they manipulated the position of the standard (i.e. the role model) who was seen as either extremely or moderately successful. In this case, an extremely successful role model would be seen as less similar, thus eliciting contrast effects. Second, they manipulated the position of the self in relation to the standard – for example, by receiving positive feedback that would temporarily move one's self-views closer to the standard, thus eliciting assimilation effects.

The selective accessibility model was confirmed in the domain of successful female leaders by Asgari and colleagues' findings which showed that when focusing on similarities with the high-profile female leader (e.g. the female leader had ordinary beginnings or attended the same university as the participants), exposures to such successful female role models had inspiring effects by increasing implicit associations between the self and leadership-related words such as leader, ambitious, powerful, achiever, and influential (Asgari et al., 2012). This model is also supported by work on mentorship (Lockwood & Kunda, 1997) which showed that when exposed to role models whose success seems attainable, female participants' self-views were inspired (self-enhancement), whereas when the role models' success seemed unattainable, female participants self-views were threatened (self-deflation). In future studies, participants should rate the extent to which they feel similar to the role model, in order to investigate directly whether women who see themselves as more similar to the role models also experience an inspiring effect, consistent with the selective accessibility model (Mussweiler, 2003).

From an applied perspective, these findings suggest that in order to successfully reduce the effects of negative stereotypes on women in leadership through exposure to role models, several steps need to be taken to insure a similarity focus. These strategies can include highlighting the dimensions on which highly successful female leaders are similar to other women with leadership aspirations, underscoring the fact that sustained effort, and not exceptional luck, explains female leaders' success, or framing success as being attainable by providing opportunities for contact between highly successful female leaders and women with leadership aspirations.

Although Mussweiler's selective accessibility model can explain many of the seemingly conflicting findings in this domain, it does not explain the inspiring effects that we have found in our research. Given that our role models were extremely successful (Hillary Clinton was the Secretary of State of the USA and Angela Merkel the chancellor of Germany), according to the selective accessibility model, we should have found a contrast effect due to a focus on dissimilarities. Thus, additional factors may be used to explain such contrasting findings.

A second factor which may help explain the conflicting effects of female role models' on women's leadership self-cognitions and behaviors is the element of visibility. In Latu and colleagues (2013), the role model was highly and permanently visible (photo hanging on the wall participants were facing during the leadership task). In most other studies, priming with female role models consisted of presenting either photos coupled with written biographical information about the model (Asgari et al., 2012; Hoyt & Simon, 2011; Rudman & Phelan, 2010), or exclusively written biographical information (Parks-Stamm et al., 2008). Importantly, this information was presented to participants before the assessment of leadership self-cognitions or the leadership task. It may be that, in order to be inspiring, female role models need to be continuously visible. This way, women may mimic the actual powerful nonverbal behaviors of the model (e.g. powerful body postures), which could, in turn, lead to more empowered behaviors and enhanced self-related cognitions. From an applied perspective, this finding would underscore the importance of not only having female role models in leadership, but of having visible female role models. Future studies should also establish if the positive effects of role models' visibility are due to role models' power or the mere presence of another female (in which case, exposures to visible female non-leaders would suffice to elicit inspiring effects).

A third factor that may account for the contradicting effects of female role models on women in leadership is the opportunity to succeed. In our study, women exposed to highly successful female role models were given the opportunity to actually perform a leadership task and prove their self-worth. In other studies (Parks-Stamm et al., 2008; Rudman & Phelan, 2010), women exposed to highly successful female role models were not necessarily given an opportunity to act, but immediately completed measures of self-valuations, self-stereotypes, or leadership aspirations. Thus, it is possible that when given the opportunity to act, succeed and feel good about their performance, women would derive their self-evaluations from their behavior during the task. This process would be consistent with the self-perception theory (Bem, 1972), according to which people infer their internal states (in this case self-evaluations) by observing their own behavior (in this case their performance on the leadership task). On the contrary, when there is no opportunity to act and experience domain-related success, women may merely engage in social comparison with the role model, leading to contrasting effects and thus negative effects on self-related cognitions and behaviors. From an applied perspective, this finding would have profound implications for women in leadership, suggesting the importance of giving women plenty of opportunities to act and prove their self-worth in leadership tasks and situations.

Practical implementations

The current chapter offers several practical implementation suggestions. We suggest that in order for successful female role models to inspire women in leadership and reduce stereotype threat, three conditions should be met. We propose that acknowledging and fostering these conditions in applied settings is key to women inspiring women. First, highly successful female role models should be seen as accessible and similar to women who aspire to be leaders, ideally through some form of contact that increases perceived similarity. Second, we recommend increasing the visibility of female role models in leadership contexts. Thus, increasing gender equality at the top is not only the goal, but it also becomes a source of inspiration for other women. Finally, we suggest that women need to be given, and take themselves, the opportunity to act and prove their self-worth in leadership settings.

Conclusions

Negative stereotypes of women in leadership are alive and well. Moreover, they are likely to affect the performance and self-related cognitions of women with leadership aspirations. Fortunately, several strategies have been efficient in protecting women from the negative effects of stereotypes, including exposure to counterstereotypical women – women who have succeeded in leadership, thus disproving the stereotype. These findings show that increasing the number of women in top leadership positions is not only a goal of gender equality, but it can also become the engine that drives gender equality in male-dominated domains. However, given that exposure to highly successful female leaders can have unintended negative effects, it is important to understand the conditions under which women with leadership aspirations are best served and inspired by such incredibly successful women.

References

Asgari, S., Dasgupta, N., & Stout, J. G. (2012). When do counterstereotypic ingroup members inspire versus deflate? The effect of successful professional women on young women's leadership self-concept. *Personality and Social Psychology Bulletin, 38,* 370–383. doi: 10.1177/0146167211431968

Bem, D. J. (1972). Self-perception theory. In L. Berkowitz (Ed.), *Advances in Experimental Social Psychology* (Vol. 6, pp. 1–62). New York: Academic Press.

Ben-Zeev, T., Fein, S., & Inzlicht, M. (2005). Arousal and stereotype threat. *Journal of Experimental Social Psychology, 41,* 174–181. doi: 10.1016/j.jesp.2003.11.007

Bergeron, D. M., Block, C. J., & Echtenkamp, B. A. (2006). Disabling the able: Stereotype threat and women's work performance. *Human Performance, 19,* 133–158. doi: 10.1207/s15327043hup1902_3

Burnette, J. L., Pollack, J. M., & Hoyt, C. L. (2010). Individual differences in implicit theories of leadership ability and self-efficacy: Predicting responses to stereotype threat. *Journal of Leadership Studies, 3,* 46–56. doi: 10.1002/jls.20138

Catalyst. (2015). Women in S&P 500 Companies. Retrieved from http://www.catalyst.org/knowledge/women-sp-500-companies.

Davies, P. G., Spencer, S. J., & Steele, C. M. (2005). Clearing the air: Identity safety moderates the effects of stereotype threat on women's leadership aspirations. *Journal of Personality and Social Psychology, 88,* 276–287. doi: 10.1037/0022-3514.88.2.276

Davies, P. G., Spencer, S. J., Quinn, D. M., & Gerhardstein, R. (2002). Consuming images: How television commercials that elicit stereotype threat can restrain women academically and professionally. *Personality and Social Psychology Bulletin, 28*, 1615–1628. doi: 10.1177/014616702237644

Dijksterhuis, A., Spears, R., Postmes, T., Stapel, D., Koomen, W., van Knippenberg, A., et al. (1998). Seeing one thing and doing another: Contrast effects in automatic behavior. *Journal of Personality and Social Psychology, 75*, 862–871. doi: 10.1037/0022-3514.75.4.862

Duehr, E. E., & Bono, J. E. (2006). Men, women, and managers: Are stereotypes finally changing? *Personnel Psychology, 59*, 815–846. doi: 10.1111/j.1744-6570.2006.00055.x

Eagly, A. H., & Karau, S. J. (2002). Role congruity theory of prejudice toward female leaders. *Psychological Review, 109*, 573–598. doi: 10.1037/0033-295x.109.3.573

Festinger, L. (1954). A theory of social comparison processes. *Human relations*, 7(2), 117–140. doi: 10.1177/001872675400700202

Gupta, V. K., & Bhawe, N. M. (2007). The influence of proactive personality and stereotype threat on women's entrepreneurial intentions. *Journal of Leadership & Organizational Studies, 13*, 73–85. doi: 10.1177/10717919070130040901

Heilman, M. E. (1983). Sex bias in work settings: The Lack of Fit model. *Research in Organizational Behavior, 5*, 269–298.

Heilman, M. E. (2001). Description and prescription: How gender stereotypes prevent women's ascent up the organizational ladder. *Journal of Social Issues, 57*, 657–674. doi: 10.1111/0022-4537.00234

Heilman, M. E., Block, C. J., & Martell, R. F. (1995). Sex stereotypes: Do they influence perceptions of managers? *Journal of Social Behavior & Personality, 10*, 237–252.

Hoyt, C. L. (2013). Inspirational or self-deflating: The role of self-efficacy in elite role model effectiveness. *Social Psychological and Personality Science, 4*, 290–298. doi: 10.1177/1948550612455066.

Hoyt, C. L., & Blascovich, J. (2010). The role of leadership self-efficacy and stereotype activation on cardiovascular, behavioral and self-report responses in the leadership domain. *The Leadership Quarterly, 21*, 89–103. doi: 10.1016/j.leaqua.2009.10.007

Hoyt, C. L., & Simon, S. (2011). Female leaders: Injurious or inspiring role models for women? *Psychology of Women Quarterly, 35*, 143–157. doi: 10.1177/0361684310385216

Hoyt, C. L., Burnette, J. L., & Innella, A. N. (2012). I can do that: The impact of implicit thoeries on leadership role model effectiveness. *Personality and Social Psychology Bulletin, 38*, 257–268. doi: 10.1177/0146167211427922

Judd, C. M., Ryan, C. S., & Park, B. (1991). Accuracy in the judgment of in-group and out-group variability. *Journal of Personality and Social Psychology, 61*, 366–379. doi:10.1037/0022-3514.61.3.366

Koenig, A. M., Eagly, A. H., Mitchell, A. A., & Ristikari, T. (2011). Are leader stereotypes masculine? A meta-analysis of three research paradigms. *Psychological Bulletin, 137*, 616–642. doi: 10.1037/a0023557

Kray, L. J., Galinsky, A. D., & Thompson, L. (2002). Reversing the gender gap in negotiations: An exploration of stereotype regeneration. *Organizational Behavior and Human Decision Processes, 87*, 386–409. doi: 10.1006/obhd.2001.2979

Kray, L. J., Thompson, L., & Galinsky, A. (2001). Battle of the sexes: Gender stereotype confirmation and reactance in negotiations. *Journal of Personality and Social Psychology, 80*, 942–958. doi: 10.1037/0022-3514.80.6.942

Latu, I. M., Mast, M. S., Lammers, J., & Bombari, D. (2013). Successful female leaders empower women's behavior in leadership tasks. *Journal of Experimental Social Psychology, 49*, 444–448. doi: 10.1016/j.jesp.2013.01.003

Latu, I. M., Stewart, T. L., Myers, A. C., Lisco, C. G., Estes, S. B., & Donahue, D. K. (2011). What we "say" and what we "think" about female managers: Explicit versus implicit associations of women with success. *Psychology of Women Quarterly, 35*, 252–266. doi: 10.1177/0361684310383811

LeBoeuf, R. A., & Estes, Z. (2004). 'Fortunately, I'm no Einstein': Comparison relevance as a determinant of behavioral assimilation and contrast. *Social Cognition, 22*, 607–636. doi: 10.1521/soco.22.6.607.54817

Lockwood, P., & Kunda, Z. (1997). Superstars and me: Predicting the impact of role models on the self. *Journal of Personality and Social Psychology, 73*, 91–103. doi: 10.1037/0022-3514.73.1.91

Logel, C., Iserman, E. C., Davies, P. G., Quinn, D. M., & Spencer, S. J. (2009). The perils of double consciousness: The role of thought suppression in stereotype threat. *Journal of Experimental Social Psychology, 45*, 299–312. doi: 10.1016/j.jesp.2008.07.016

Mussweiler, T. (2003). Comparison processes in social judgment: Mechanisms and consequences. *Psychological Review, 110*, 472–489. doi: 10.1037/0033-295x.110.3.472

Mussweiler, T., Rüter, K., & Epstude, K. (2004). The ups and downs of social comparison: Mechanisms of assimilation and contrast. *Journal of Personality and Social Psychology, 87*, 832–844. doi: 10.1037/0022-3514.87.6.832

Nguyen, H. H. D., & Ryan, A. M. (2008). Does stereotype threat affect test performance of minorities and women? A meta-analysis of experimental evidence. *Journal of Applied Psychology, 93*, 1314–1334. doi: 10.1037/a0012702

Osswald, S., Greitemeyer, T., Fischer, P., & Frey, D. (2010). Moral prototypes and moral behavior: Specific effects on emotional precursors of moral behavior and on moral behavior by the activation of moral prototypes. *European Journal of Social Psychology, 40*, 1078–1094. doi: 10.1002/ejsp.728

Parks-Stamm, E. J., Heilman, M. E., & Hearns, K. A. (2008). Motivated to penalize: Women's strategic rejection of successful women. *Personality and Social Psychology Bulletin, 34*, 237–247. doi: 10.1177/0146167207310027

Powell, G. N., & Butterfield, D. A. (1984). If 'good managers' are masculine, what are 'bad managers'? *Sex Roles, 10*, 477–484. doi: 10.1007/bf00287256

Powell, G. N., & Butterfield, D. A. (1989). The 'good manager': Did androgyny fare better in the 1980s? *Group & Organization Studies, 14*, 216–233. doi: 10.1177/105960118901400209

Rudman, L. A., & Glick, P. (2001). Prescriptive gender stereotypes and backlash toward agentic women. *Journal of Social Issues, 57*, 743–762. doi : 10.1111/0022-4537.00239

Rudman, L. A., & Phelan, J. E. (2010). The effect of priming gender roles on women's implicit gender beliefs and career aspirations. *Social Psychology, 41*, 192–202. doi: 10.1027/1864-9335/a000027

Schein, V. E. (1973). The relationship between sex role stereotypes and requisite management characteristics. *Journal of Applied Psychology, 57*, 95–100. doi: 10.1037/h0037128.

Schein, V. E., Mueller, R., Lituchy, T., & Liu, J. (1996). Think manager—think male: A global phenomenon? *Journal of Organizational Behavior, 17*, 33–41. doi: 10.1002/(sici)1099-1379(199601)17:1<33::aid-job778>3.0.co;2-f

Schmader, T., & Johns, M. (2003). Converging evidence that stereotype threat reduces working memory capacity. *Journal of Personality and Social Psychology, 85*, 440–452. doi: 10.1037/0022-3514.85.3.440

Schmid Mast, M. (2002). Dominance as expresses and inferred through speaking time: A meta-analysis. *Human Communication Research, 28*, 420–450. doi: 10.1093/hcr/28.3.420

Schmid Mast, M. (2004). Men are hierarchical, women are egalitarian: An implicit gender stereotype. *Swiss Journal of Psychology, 63,* 107–111. doi: 10.1024/1421-0185.63.2.107

Spencer, S. J., Steele, C. M., & Quinn, D. M. (1999). Stereotype threat and women's math performance. *Journal of Experimental Social Psychology, 35,* 4–28. doi: 10.1006/jesp.1998.1373

Steele, C. M. (1997). A threat in the air: How stereotypes shape intellectual identity and performance. *American Psychologist, 52,* 613–629. doi: 10.1037/0003-066x.52.6.613

Steele, C. M., & Aronson, J. (2000). Stereotype threat and the intellectual test performance of African Americans. In C. Stangor (Ed.), *Stereotypes and prejudice: Essential readings.* (pp. 369–389). New York: Psychology Press.

Stoker, J. I., Van der Velde, M., & Lammers, J. (2012). Factors relating to managerial stereotypes: The role of gender of the employee and the manager and management gender ratio. *Journal of Business and Psychology, 27,* 31–42. doi: 10.1007/s10869-011-9210-0

Taylor, C. A., Lord, C. G., McIntyre, R. B., & Paulson, R. M. (2011). The Hillary Clinton effect: When the same role model inspires or fails to inspire improved performance under stereotype threat. *Group Processes & Intergroup Relations, 14,* 447–459. doi: 10.1177/1368430210382680

Tellhed, U., & Björklund, F. (2011). Stereotype threat in salary negotiations is mediated by reservation salary. *Scandinavian Journal of Psychology, 52,* 185–195. doi: 10.1111/j.1467-9450.2010.00855.x

The Interparliamentary Union (2014). *Women in parliaments data.* Retrieved from http://www.ipu.org/wmn-e/world.htm

von Hippel, C., Issa, M., Ma, R., & Stokes, A. (2011). Stereotype threat: Antecedents and consequences for working women. *European Journal of Social Psychology, 41,* 151–161. doi: 10.1002/ejsp.749

von Hippel, C., Wiryakusuma, C., Bowden, J., & Shochet, M. (2011). Stereotype threat and female communication styles. *Personality and Social Psychology Bulletin, 37,* 1312–1324. doi: 10.1177/0146167211410439

White, M. J., & White, G. B. (2006). Implicit and explicit occupational gender stereotypes. *Sex Roles, 55,* 259–266. doi:10.1007/s11199-006-9078-z

6

WHEN MERITOCRACY OPPOSES QUOTA POLICY

How education and policy strength impact opinions about affirmative action

Klea Faniko, Fabio Lorenzi-Cioldi, Paolo Ghisletta, Siri Øyslebø Sørensen, Erjona Manushi, Fiorela Shalsi and Marion Chipeaux

Previous studies showed that in comparison with people with a low level of education, those with a high level of education are more supportive to the soft forms of affirmative action policies (AAPs) (Haley & Sidanius, 2006) but less supportive to the strong forms of AAPs (Astin, 1977; Faniko, 2015; Faniko, Lorenzi-Cioldi, & Buschini, 2011; Faniko, Lorenzi-Cioldi, Buschini, & Chatard, 2008; 2012).

In the current research, we focus on support for AAPs and aim to explain why people with high and low level of education differ in their support for different AAPs. We connect to literature considering meritocracy as a mere myth that serves to legitimize social inequalities (e.g. Pratto, Sidanius, Stallworth, & Malle, 1994) to understand why people with a high level of education are less supportive to AAPs than those with a low level.

This research was conducted in Albania, a South-Eastern European post-communist country with a particular history in relation to gender equality policies before and after the fall of the regime. Before 1990, as part of the regime ideology, gender equality was implemented throughout education as well as employment policies in all fields of work. For example, during the communist period, especially from 1970 till 1987, Albania had the highest percentage of women in parliament, ranging from 26.89 to 30 percent with the highest figure of 33.60 in 1974 (Albanian Parliament, 2003). Regardless of these high figures of women's representation in politics, the communist society was still considered patriarchal (Gjermeni, Preçi, Dauti, & Kalaja, 2003).

After the fall of the regime in 1990, women's representation in work participation dropped to extremely low percentages until 2005 (with 4 to 7 percent, with one exception of 15 percent in 1996). During the transitional period, mainstream politics did not allow questions of gender equality and political participation in any of the ex-communist countries (Jalušič & Antić, 2001). This has, however, changed. Indeed, the ex-communist countries went from total rejection to gradual introduction of gender quotas (Antić & Lokar, 2006). More concretely, in Albania the real boost of women representation happened after 2008, with the implementation of the Law 'Gender Equality in Society' which introduced a 30 percent quota for the under-represented gender in all legislative, executive, judicial power bodies as well as in other public-sector institutions (Labor Law No 9970, 2008). Nevertheless, politics is the only field where this law is implemented and monitored publicly so far. Public-sector institutions are not yet clearly benefitting from quotas' implementation.

Affirmative action policies

Although AAPs aim to ensure equal opportunity in employment, education, and politics for all individuals, both the advantaged and the disadvantaged have shown resistance to these policies (Crosby, Sabattini, & Aizawa, 2013; Iyer, 2009). Previous research has established that resistance to AAPs is strongly influenced by factors such as type of affirmative action and individual characteristics (e.g. gender) (Harrison, Kravitz, Mayer, Leslie, & Lev Arey, 2006). More concretely, AAPs differ in degree of strength, forming a continuum ranging from soft to hard forms (Seligman, 1973). At the "soft" end, weak preferential treatments give preference to the minority member if the majority and the minority candidates are equally qualified. At the "hard" end, strong preferential treatments are based exclusively on the applicant's group membership (e.g. quota; for more specific policies, see Harrison et al. 2006). Research shows that attitudes towards AAPs become increasingly negative as more emphasis is given to demographic status rather than to personal qualifications, skills or merit (Kravitz & Klineberg, 2004).

Education, meritocracy, and opinions towards affirmative action policies

Although there is a well-established body of research examining opinions about AAPs, and especially how the strength of AAPs affects such opinions, there is little research on the role of educational level, and the findings are quite inconsistent. For instance, Haley and Sidanius (2006) demonstrated for both women and men, a positive relationship between educational level and support for outreach (a "soft" program which aims at finding qualified people from certain groups), but no relationship for quotas, for minorities members, which in return are considered as strong forms of affirmative action. Kravitz and Klineberg (2000) found higher support for a tiebreak policy that favors African Americans among participants with a high level of education compared with those with a low level of education. Another series of research (Faniko, 2015; Faniko et al. (2008, 2012) showed a significant decrease of support for strong preferential treatment targeted at women among the highly educated. Astin (1977) similarly concluded that the highly educated were less supportive of quotas targeted at African Americans than the less educated individuals. Thus, these evidences clearly suggest that the effect of educational level on support for AAPs depends on the strength of the policy.

To further understand mechanisms linking educational level to degree of support for AAPs, we included the concept of meritocracy in our study. The ideology of meritocracy implies that rewards should be proportional to individual efforts, competence, and hard work (Son Hing, Bobocel, & Zanna, 2002). The educational system contributes to meritocracy endorsement by fostering "the belief that economic success depends essentially on the possession of technical and cognitive skills" (Bowles & Gintis, 1976, p. 102–103).

However, authors, arguing that there is a gap between individual merit and income, have challenged the ideology of meritocracy. Indeed, meritocracy has been criticized as a mere myth that serves to legitimize social inequalities (e.g. Pratto et al., 1994; Son Hing et al., 2011), and concerns about merit may serve to justify reluctance and opposition to AAPs (Aberson & Haag, 2003; Bobocel, Son Hing, Davey, Stanley, & Zanna, 1998). In fact, there is evidence showing that endorsement of meritocracy is associated with opposition towards strong preferential treatments (Aberson, 2007). Strong preferential treatments (e.g. quotas) are seen as primarily based on group membership, favoring target-group members by pushing individual qualifications and competence aside. In contrast, however, endorsement of meritocracy does not generate opposition to soft forms of affirmative action (Bobocel et al., 1998; Aberson & Haag, 2003).

Based on our analysis of the current literature, we claim that effects of educational level should vary as a function of the affirmative action specific policy. Individuals with a high level of education are likely to over endorse the merit principle compared to those with a low level of education (Kunovich & Slomczynski, 2007) and one way to justify their opposition to quotas is to emphasize meritocratic principles (Jost, Banaji, & Nosek, 2004). Taking into consideration the positive relationship between educational level and endorsement of meritocracy on the one hand, and the fact that the quota policy is ambiguous with regard to information about the individual qualifications of the female candidate on the other hand, our first hypothesis predicts that compared to people with a low level, those with a high level of education will show less support for this policy (Hypothesis 1a). When it comes to weak preferential treatment, we can concur with Harrison et al., (2006) that this policy takes both individual merit and group membership into consideration. Hence, weak preferential treatment does clearly less threaten the in-group interests and the advantaged position of individuals with high levels of education. We thus expect that people from the two educational levels should show similar levels of support for weak preferential treatment (Hypothesis 1b).

The relationships between educational level and meritocracy on the one hand, and between meritocracy and support for different forms of affirmative action on the other hand, have been extensively studied. However, the mediational role of meritocracy in the relationship between educational level and support for AAPs has yet to be examined. Hypothesis 2a predicts that the endorsement of meritocracy would mediate the effect of education on support for affirmative action framed as a quota policy, because group membership is emphasized. Conversely, referring to previous findings (e.g. Bobocel et al., 1998) we do not expect a significant relationship between endorsement of meritocracy and support for weak preferential treatment. This soft form of affirmative action takes into account the qualifications of the individual: the target-group member is only considered if his/her qualifications are equivalent to those of the non-target-group member. These policies do not generate opposition on the grounds of merit, and thus we do not expect that endorsement of meritocracy mediates the relationship between educational level and support for weak preferential treatment (Hypothesis 2b).

Study

Participants

Participants were 232 (129 women and 103 men) Albanian full-time workers from various public-sector institutions. In Albania, part-time jobs do not exist in public sector.

Participants' mean age was 40.58 ($SD = 13.75$) years ranging from 20 to 66 years old, and does not correlate with the variables in the model. Low level of education applied to participants without a university degree (N *women* = 47; N *men* = 55) and high level of education applied to participants with a university degree (N *women* = 82; N *men* = 48) (see e.g. Faniko et al., 2008; 2012; Federico & Sidanius, 2002; Sidanius, Pratto, & Bobo, 1996). We should clarify that in Albania the mandatory level of public education is up to 9th grade and there is a high attendance in both high school (through 12th grade) and University (Institute of Statistics, INSTAT, 2014).

Procedure

Participants volunteered to take part in a study on strategies for facilitating access of women to decision-making positions in public-sector institutions. Participants completed a questionnaire consisting of (a) a series of items assessing the preference for the merit principle, (b) a scenario that introduced the situation of women in Albanian public-sector institutions along with a new hiring policy, and (c) a series of items assessing support for the hiring policy.

Measures

Preference for the merit principle

We used the five items from the *Preference for the merit principle (PMP)* scale (Davey, Bobocel, Son Hing, & Zanna, 1999) to measure prescriptive beliefs. Sample items were: *"Promotion decisions ought to take into account the effort workers put into their job"*, *"Members of a work team ought to receive different pay depending on the amount each person contributed"* (1 = strongly disagree, 7 = strongly agree; Cronbach α = .84).

We computed a one-factor confirmatory analysis with the AMOS 18 software (Arbuckle, 2005) to assess the unidimensionality of the PMP scale. Following the recommendations advocated by Kline (1998), several indexes were used to evaluate the goodness of fit of the model. These indexes are the Tucker-Lewis index (TLI), the comparative fit index (CFI), and the root-mean-square error of approximation (RMSEA). We added a residual covariance between two items with high semantic proximity relevance to the model. The final model adjusted well to the data: χ^2 (df=4, n = 232) = 4.49, p = .34, TLI = .99, CFI = .99, RMSEA = .02 (90 per cent confidence interval: [.00; .10]).

Introduction of AAPs

At the outset of the questionnaire, participants read the following bogus description: "According to a recent census carried out in Albanian public-sector institutions, women hold a low number of decision-making positions. Following the publication of this census, several public-sector institutions decided to apply a new hiring policy aimed at increasing the number of educated women in decision-making positions (e.g. director, deputy director, head of unit, and head of office)." One of two AAPs, selected from previous research (e.g. Faniko et al., 2012), was then introduced. In the *weak preferential* treatment condition, participants read: "This policy holds that when a woman and a man are in competition, the woman should be selected if her skills are equivalent to those of the male candidate." In the *quota* condition, participants read: "This policy holds that 30 per cent of decision-making positions are reserved for women. When a woman and a man are in competition for a decision-making position, the woman should be selected in order to attain this quota."

Support for AAPs

Support for the specific AAPs was assessed using five items derived from previous research (see Kravitz & Platania, 1993; Lorenzi-Cioldi, 2002). Sample items were: *"This hiring policy is a good policy,"* and *"I would be willing to work in an organization that applies this hiring policy"* (1 = strongly disagree, 7 = strongly agree, Cronbach α = .70). The items assessing support for AAPs were also analyzed with a one-factor confirmatory model. We again added a residual covariance between two items based on their semantic proximity. The final model adjusted well to the data: χ^2 (df=4, n = 232) = 7.57, p = .11, TLI = .99, CFI = .99, RMSEA = .06 (90 percent confidence interval: [.00; .13]). All of the items assessing preference for the merit principle and support for AAPs had a standardized factor loading of .50 or higher.

A Principal Component Analysis with Varimax-rotation confirmed that items intended to preference for the merit principle and support for AAPs loaded into two separated factors explaining 76.69 per cent of the total variance. The means of these constructs are weakly correlated (r = -.19, p < .005).

Results

Preference for the merit principle

ANOVA on the mean of the preference for the merit principle, with participant educational level and gender as between-subjects predictors, produced an effect for education, $F(1, 228)$ = 15.51, p < .001, $\eta2$ = .06. Consistent with our expectations, participants with a high level of education reported greater endorsement of the merit principle than those with a low level of education (M_{high} = 4.73, SD = 1.47 and M_{low} = 3.39, SD =.90). Women and men expressed similar preferences for the merit principle, (M_{women} = 5.19, SD = 1.19, M_{men} = 4.99, SD = 1.27, $F(1, 228)$ = .16, p = .69, $\eta2$ = .00. Because women (M = 1.64, SD = .48) were more educated than men (M = 1.46, SD = .50), $F(1, 227)$ = 6.83, p = .01, $\eta2$ = .03 we decided to perform an ANCOVA with level of education as the independent variable and gender as the covariate. Consistent with the previous findings, the non-significant effect of gender suggested the same pattern of educational level for both women and men, ruling out the potential confound between gender and education, ($F(1, 228)$ = .28, p = .60, $\eta2$ = .00, effect of gender).

Support for AAPs

To assess the effects of participant gender (female vs. male), participant educational level (low level vs. high level), the type of affirmative action (weak preferential treatment vs. quota), and their interactions, on a total score for support for affirmative action policies, we performed a univariate analysis of variance (ANOVA). Results did not show any gender differences, $F(1, 227)$ = 2.22, p = .13, $\eta2$ = .01 (M_{women} = 4.69, SD = 2.20 M_{men} = 4.24, SD = 2.46). Support for AAPs was lower among participants with a high level of education (M = 4.16, SD = 2.33) than among those with a low level of education (M = 4.91, SD = 2.27), $F(1, 227)$ = 6.00, p < .02, $\eta2$ = .03. There was again greater support for weak preferential treatment (M = 5.96, SD = 1.31) than for the quota policy (M = 3.21, SD = 2.26), $F(1, 227)$ = 112.65, p < .001,

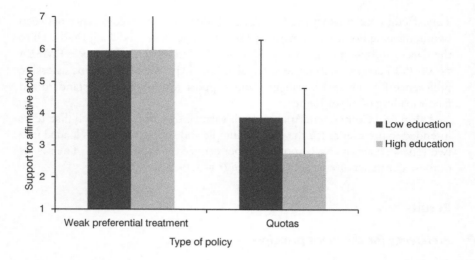

FIGURE 6.1 Means of support for the affirmative action plan as predicted by education and type of policy

$\eta2 = .33$. Finally, the analysis produced the expected Participant Education X Type of affirmative action interaction, the only significant interaction $F(1, 227) = 5.95$, $p < .02$, $\eta2 = .03$. Mean comparisons indicated that participants with a high level of education ($M = 5.97$, $SD = 1.09$) and a low level of education ($M = 5.95$, $SD = 1.53$) did not differ in their support for weak preferential treatment. The quota policy received less support among participants with a high level of education ($M = 2.75$, $SD = 2.05$) than among those with a low level of education ($M = 3.87$, $SD = 2.41$), $p < .001$ (See Figure 6.1). As in the previous analysis, an ANCOVA was conducted with level of education, and type of policy as the independent variables and gender as the covariate. The results showed a non-significant effect of gender as covariate and the same pattern of results for the other independent variable as in the previous analysis, ($F(1, 228) = 2.22$, $p = .14$, $\eta2 = .00$, effect of gender).

Mediating role of meritocracy.

A moderated mediation analysis was performed with structural equation modeling (SEM) to examine the mediating role of preference for the merit principle on the relationship between participant education and support for affirmative action in both the weak preferential treatment condition and the quota condition. We calculated a likelihood ratio test to examine whether the free loadings of both scales were different or equal across the two preferential conditions. The result of the likelihood ratio test showed no significant differences in adjustment between the model with unequal loadings across conditions and the model with constrained loadings of equality across the conditions ($\chi^2 = 8$, $df = 8$, $p = ns$), suggesting that the two scales' items were interpreted similarly across the two conditions. Accordingly, the model with equal loadings across conditions was selected for the following analysis.

To assess the moderated mediation, we tested and compared two statistically nested models. Both models constrained the paths between educational level and preference for the merit principle, and between educational level and support for AAPs to be equal across the two preferential conditions (weak preferential treatment and quota). The path between meritocracy and support for AAPs was freely estimated across the two conditions in a first model, χ^2 (df=90, $n = 232$) = 113.25, $p < .05$, TLI = .98, CFI = .99, RMSEA = .03 (90 percent confidence interval: [.00; .05]), while it was forced to equality across conditions in a second model χ^2 (df=91, $n = 232$) = 138.13, $p < .05$, TLI = .97, CFI = .97, RMSEA = .05 (90 percent confidence interval: [.03; .06]). The model comparison (likelihood ratio test: χ^2 (df=1, $n = 232$) = 24.88, $p < .01$) supported our expectation of a moderated mediation because the former model was superior in fit to the second model. The examination of the paths revealed that the preconditions for the moderated mediations were met. As predicted, the findings suggest that preference for the merit principle mediated the relationship between level of education and support for affirmative action in the quota condition (Hypothesis 2a), but not in the weak preferential treatment condition (Hypothesis 2b). The more educated participants were, the more they supported the merit principle in both policy conditions ($\beta = .29$, $p < .001$). Meritocracy was negatively related to support for affirmative action in the quota condition ($\beta = -.48$, $p < .001$), but not in the weak preferential treatment condition ($\beta = .15$, $p = .14$). In the quota condition, the direct effect of education on support for affirmative action ($\beta = -.25$, $p < .005$) was no longer significant when the effect of preference for the merit principle was controlled for ($\beta = -.04$, $p = .47$). In the weak preferential treatment, both the direct and indirect effects of education on support for affirmative action were not significant ($\beta = .01$, $p = .95$; $b = -.04$, $p = .47$, respectively; see Figure 6.2).

Discussion

Consistent with previous research (e.g. Kravitz & Klineberg, 2000; 2004; Kravitz & Platania, 1993; Lorenzi-Cioldi, 2002), men and women showed less support towards quotas than towards weak preferential treatment. According Son Hing et al. (2002), one interpretation of these findings is that individuals are opposed to AAPs to the extent that the actual policy violates meritocratic principles. With strong forms of AAPs such as a quota, the traditional principle of meritocracy is violated insofar as women may be favored even if they are less qualified than men. Thus, strong forms of AAPs are judged as perverting meritocratic standards and ideals because they give priority to particular social category memberships (Augoustinos, Tuffin, & Every, 2005).

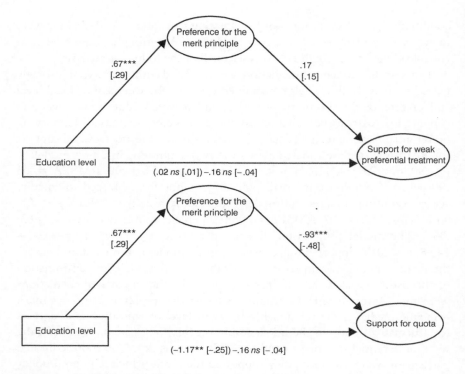

FIGURE 6.2 Mediating role of the preference for the merit principle on the relationship between level of education (low level coded 1; high level coded 2) and support for affirmative action in weak preferential treatment condition and quota condition

Standardized path weights are in square brackets. Unstandardized path weights are out square brackets. The paths weights in parentheses do not control for the effect of the mediator (Note: * p < .05 ; ** p < .01 ; *** p < .001)

In agreement with our predictions, the findings demonstrated that participants with a high level of education, compared to participants with a low level of education, express less support for affirmative action framed as a quota policy. It is worth noting that this pattern of support was similarly in effect among men and among women. Although this null finding concerning participant sex is surprising at a first glance, we claim that the low support for gender quotas found among the highly educated women makes sense in light of the Queen Bee phenomenon. The Queen Bee phenomenon refers to the phenomenon that some women who have been successful in male-dominated organizations tend to behave in ways that derogate rather than help the advancement of other women (see Ellemers, Rink, Derks, & Ryan, 2012; Staines, Tavris, and Jayaratne (1974). Indeed, Queen Bees distance themselves from their group membership and perceive themselves as non-stereotypical members of their gender group (Derks, Ellemers, Van Laar, &

De Groot, 2011; Derks, Van Laar, Ellemers, & De Groot, 2011; Ellemers, Van Den Heuvel, De Gilder, Maass, & Bonvini, 2004). Hence, they oppose AAPs that assist other women's career, especially if these policies are primarily based on group membership. There is evidence that compared to women with a low level of education, highly educated women exhibit more signs of the Queen Bee phenomenon, for instance by rating their personal career commitment as higher than the career commitment of other women or describing themselves as more masculine than the other women (Derks, Ellemers, et al., 2011; Derks, Van Laar, et al., 2011; Ellemers et al., 2004). More importantly, the more highly-educated women emphasize disengagement from their gender group, the less they support AAPs (Faniko, Ellemers, & Derks, 2015; Faniko, Lorenzi-Cioldi, Manushi, Ghisletta, & Chipeaux, 2014).

In order to account for this pattern of support towards AAPs, we developed a model that considered the joint roles of education and meritocracy. Past research (Faniko et al., 2012) demonstrated that effects of education are mediated by the threat to meritocratic beliefs posed by strong preferential treatment. In an extension of Faniko et al.'s (2012) research, the present study assessed the mediational role of merit beliefs on the relation between education and support for strong and weak affirmative action policies. Furthermore, moderated mediation analyses provided evidence for our second hypothesis by showing that the effect of education on support for the quota policy, but not for the weak preferential treatment, was mediated by preference for the merit principle. Thus, the moderated mediation analysis provided evidence for the hypothesized mechanism through which education might influence support for AAPs. It is worth noting that preference for the merit principle can also be considered as an indicator of the self-group distancing. Indeed, ongoing studies provide evidence of strong correlations between the self-group distancing and beliefs in meritocracy (Faniko et al., 2015).

Theoretical implications

Examining the role of education in shaping people's support for AAPs is of both social and theoretical relevance. As Kravitz and Klineberg (2000) mentioned, the relation between education and support for AAPs is poorly and inconsistently documented. Our research sheds light on this relationship.

First, the present findings support the idea that individuals' endorsement of meritocracy might account for the relationship between educational level and support for affirmative action framed as a quota policy. Although the relationships between, on the one hand, endorsement of meritocracy and opposition to AAPs (Aberson, 2007; Bobocel et al., 1998), and, on the other hand, education and meritocracy (Bowles & Gintis, 1976; Kunovich & Slomczynski, 2007), have been documented, the novelty of our findings lies in the fact that (1) meritocracy mediates the relationship between education and support for strong policies of affirmative action, and that (2) it does so among both men and women. The assessment and the documentation of this mediated relationship in this study is a contribution to the literature on factors influencing support for AAPs.

Second, this research was conducted among workers from various public-sector institutions in Albania, an Eastern European country. The majority of the previous studies on support for AAPs relied on student samples from western universities. Employees have actual work experience. It can thus be inferred that this population is directly concerned with hiring policies. Their level of support for AAPs is potentially more relevant and crucial for the implementation of these policies. Furthermore, examining these questions in Albania, outside of the North-American and Western-European context, sheds light on the opinions of a population that is virtually unknown to social psychologists.

Practical implications

This chapter enhances the understanding of how invisible barriers hinder women in accessing decision-making positions. The practical implications of understanding possible resistance to affirmative action policies is at least twofold: first this gives background knowledge for selecting APP measures in a given situation (i.e. in organizations populated with highly educated personnel), and second the knowledge points to the importance of raising an awareness of how different types of APP measures are framed and presented.

As mentioned in the introduction, Albania, where this study was conducted, has adopted legislation promoting gender equality, introducing the uses of gender quotas (30 percent) where women are underrepresented. However action is yet to be taken in terms of enforcing the legislation within the public sector, where the study presented in this chapter was carried out. The analysis showing how meritocracy mediates the relationship between education and support for strong AAPs both amongst men and women can be used to suggest either a gradual introduction of softer AAPs, in order to meet less hostility. Or, if implementing strong AAP (quotas) lessons can be taken in how to present and introduce the policies emphasizing the significance of qualifications and competence of women.

Many countries in Europe, Asia and Africa have implemented, or are implementing, AAPs also outside of political institutions (Fagan et al., 2012). Even though this study was conducted in Albania, the findings raise applicability issues that go beyond the Albanian society, as the ideology of meritocracy is influential in many societies and organizational settings.

Organizations that work on developing and implementing AAPs may benefit from the consideration of psychological processes that influence the degree of support for distinct types of AAPs. Organizations implementing or envisioning implementing AAPs, especially quota policies, should take into consideration the effect of educational level on support for the policy in order to develop working strategies to target potential resistance based on the psychological processes described above. For example, the organizations may enhance support for strong forms of affirmative action by emphasizing that the policy does not contradict meritocracy, but rather makes sure that individual, qualified women are not excluded from being given equal opportunities. This strategy was, for example, applied when gender quotas on corporate boards were introduced in Norway. In order to tackle resistance towards the use of gender quotas, the emphasis was put on the fact that the introduction of gender quotas ensured access to the complete pool of qualified individuals, as more desirable compared to drawing from only half of the qualified population (Bjørkhaug & Sørensen, 2012).

Limitations and future directions

Although the research presented in this chapter provides insights into the complex relationships between education and support for AAPs, it has a number of limitations that should be followed up on in future research.

One limitation to the study at hand is that the data did not examine issues related to self-interest. Some of the past research has revealed the role of self-interest in support for AAPs. However, there is again low consistency in the evidence provided. Some research shows that attitudes towards AAPs are strongly interlaced with issues of self-interest (Harrison et al., 2006), but other research does not show this relationship (e.g. Sears & Funk, 1991). From a self-interest perspective our findings may seem counterintuitive. One might think that in comparison to highly educated people, those with a low level of education would be less supportive of AAPs because these programs do not concern them. Conversely, the extent to which highly educated people feel their personal interest is being served by AAPs is a complex issue and remains a likely proxy of professional status and gender. Highly educated women who already hold positions in decision-making bodies may oppose a quota policy because this program potentially threatens their position, whereas highly educated women who do not hold decision-making positions might support a quota policy because it offers them a way to enter the competition with male peers. We did not address the role of self-interest because this was not a goal of our planned research. Undoubtedly, however, the issue of self-interest deserves more attention in future research. In addition, testing other possible mechanisms such as self-interest in the relationship between level of education and meritocracy will enable a test of alternative models and would provide an enhanced understanding of the effect of educational level on support of APPs.

Finally, a longitudinal design allowing us to tease apart educational effects deriving from participants' social background (e.g. social class), and participants' achieved social mobility (see also Peterson & Lane, 2001) should be considered to complete our cross-sectional approach. Such alternative approaches could also use multilevel methodologies to consider potential moderators such as the progressive deconstruction of traditional beliefs about gender roles and the lively debate on AAPs in our society.

Conclusion

The rapid diffusion of affirmative action policies around the world calls for an increased effort devoted to understanding factors that may help devising good policies for given organizations at the right moment. Based on the vast amount of the psychological literature on attitudes and opinions towards affirmative action, we now know that there are a great number of such factors, and that separate experimental or survey interventions can only capture the role of a very small subset of such factors. The present research makes one step further in the understanding of the mechanisms that produce favorable or unfavorable opinions toward affirmative action policies.

Acknowledgement

This work was supported by a Mobility Grant (SNSF grant IZKOZ1_154264/1) awarded to Klea Faniko.

References

Aberson, C. L. (2007). Diversity, merit, fairness, and discrimination beliefs as predictors of support for affirmative-action policy actions. *Journal of Applied Social Psychology, 37*, 2451–2474. doi:10.1111/j.1559-1816.2007.00266.x

Aberson, C. L., & Haag, S. C. (2003). Beliefs about affirmative action and diversity and their relationship to support for hiring policies. *Analyses of Social Issues and Public Policy, 3*, 121–138. doi:10.1111/j.1530-2415.2003.00018.x

Albanian Parliament. (2003). *Gratë në parlament* [Women in Parliament]. Tirana: Author.

Antić, M. G., & Lokar, S. (2006). The Balkans: From total rejection to gradual acceptance of gender quotas. In D. Dahlerup (Ed.) *Women, Quotas and Politics* (pp. 138–167). London: Routledge.

Arbuckle, J. L. (2005). *Amos 6.0 User's Guide*. Chicago, IL: SPSS.

Astin, A. W. (1977). *Four Critical Years*. San Francisco, CA: Josey-Bass.

Augoustinos, M., Tuffin, K., & Every, D. (2005). New racism, meritocracy and individualism: Constraining affirmative action in education. *Discourse and Society, 16*, 315–340. doi:10.1177/0957926505051168

Bjørkhaug, H., & Sørensen, S. Ø. (2012). Feminism without gender? Arguments for gender quotas on corporate boards in Norway. *Comparative Social Research, 29*, 185–209. doi:10.1108/S0195-6310(2012)0000029010

Bobocel, D. R., Son Hing, L. S., Davey, L. M., Stanley, D. J., & Zanna, M. P. (1998). Justice-based opposition to social policies: Is it genuine? *Journal of Personality and Social Psychology, 75*, 653–669. doi:10.1037/0022-3514.75.3.653

Bowles, S., & Gintis, H. (1976). Schooling in capitalist America revisited. *Sociology of Education, 75*, 1–18.

Crosby, F. J., Sabattini, L., & Aizawa, M. (2013). Affirmative action and gender equality. In: M. K. Ryan & N. R. Branscombe, (Eds.). *The SAGE Handbook of Gender and Psychology* (pp. 484–499). London: Sage Publications.

Davey, L. M., Bobocel, D. R., Son Hing, L. S., & Zanna, M. P. (1999). Preference for the merit principle scale: An individual difference measure of distributive justice preferences. *Social Justice Research, 12*, 223–240. doi:10.1023/A:1022148418210

Derks, B., Ellemers, N., Van Laar, C., & De Groot, K. (2011). Do sexist organizational cultures create the Queen Bee? *British Journal of Social Psychology, 50,* 519–535. doi: 10.1348/014466610X525280

Derks, B., Van Laar, C., Ellemers, N., & De Groot, K. (2011). Gender-bias primes elicit queen-bee responses among senior policewomen. *Psychological Science, 22,* 1243–1249. doi:10.1177/0956797611417258

Ellemers, N., Rink, F. A., Derks, B., & Ryan, M. K. (2012). Women in high places: When and why promoting women into top positions can harm them individually or as a group (and how to prevent this). *Research in Organizational Behavior, 32,* 163–187. doi:10.1016/j.riob.2012.10.003

Ellemers, N., Van Den Heuvel, H., De Gilder, D., Maass, A., & Bonvini, A. (2004). The underrepresentation of women in science: Differential commitment or the queen bee syndrome? *British Journal of Social Psychology, 43,* 1–24. doi:10.1348/0144666042037999

Fagan, C., Menéndez, M. C. G., & Ansón, S. G. (2012). *Women on corporate boards and in top management. European trends and policy.* Hampshire: Palgrave MacMillan.

Faniko, K. (2015). *Genre d'accord, mérite d'abord ? Une analyse des opinions envers les mesures de discrimination positive.* [Gender ok, but merit first ? An analysis of opinions towards Affirmative Action Plans] Bern: Peter Lang.

Faniko, K., Ellemers, N., & Derks, B. (2015). *Creating the Queen Bee: How career experiences of female professionals affect support for affirmative action policies.* Talk at 14th Congress of the Swiss Society of Psychology, Geneva.

Faniko, K., Lorenzi-Cioldi, F., & Buschini, F. (2011). The role of education on opinions toward affirmative action targeted at women in Albania. In J. Kovalčík, M. Muránsky & A. Rochovská (Eds.), *Where do we go from here? Economic trends, social trajectories and policies of identities in post communist capitalism,* (pp. 60–69). Bratislava: Friedrich-Ebert- Stiftung.

Faniko, K., Lorenzi-Cioldi, F., Buschini, F., & Chatard, A. (2008). Affirmative Action Plans that assist women's mobility in Albania: The paradox of education. In S. Fischer & H. Pleines (Eds.), *Crises and Conflicts in Post-socialist Societies. The role of ethnic, political and social identities in Changing Europe* (vol. 4, pp. 209–219). Stuttgart: Ibidem-Publishers.

Faniko, K., Lorenzi-Cioldi, F., Buschini, F., & Chatard, A. (2012). The influence of education on attitudes toward affirmative action: The role of the policy's strength. *Journal of Applied Social Psychology, 42,* 387–413. doi:10.1111/j.1559-1816.2011.00892.x

Faniko, K., Lorenzi-Cioldi, F., Manushi, M., Ghisletta, P., & Chipeaux, M. (2014, July). *When women do not support affirmative action policies. A Queen Bee Syndrome?* Poster presented at the meeting of the European Association of Social Psychology (EASP), Amsterdam, the Netherlands.

Federico, C. M. & Sidanius, J. (2002). Racism, Ideology, and Affirmative Action Revisited: The antecedents and consequences of "Principled Objections" to Affirmative Action. *Journal of Personality and Social Psychology, 82,* 488–502. doi:10.1037//0022-3514.82.4.488

Gjermeni, E., Preçi, Z., Dauti, M., & Kalaja, D. (2003). *Report on gender and agriculture.* Tirana: The Women's Centre.

Haley, H., & Sidanius, J. (2006). The positive and negative framing of affirmative action: A group dominance perspective. *Personality and Social Psychology Bulletin, 32,* 656–668. doi:10.1177/0146167205283442

Harrison, D. A., Kravitz, D. A., Mayer, D. M., Leslie, L. M., & Lev Arey, D. (2006). Understanding attitudes toward affirmative action programs in employment: Summary and meta-analysis of 35 years of research. *Journal of Applied Psychology, 91,* 1013–1036. doi:10.1037/0021-9010.91.5.1013

Institute of Statistics. (2014). *Education in Albania.* Retrieved from http://www.instat.gov. al/en/themes/education.aspx

Iyer, A. (2009). Increasing the Representation and Status of Women in Employment: The Effectiveness of Affirmative Action. In M. Barreto, M. K. Ryan & M. T. Schmitt (Eds.). *The Glass Ceiling in the 21st Century: Understanding barriers to gender equality,* (pp. 257–280) Washington, D.C.: American Psychological Association.

Jalušič, V., & Antić, M. G. (2001). *Women – Politics – Equal Opportunities: Prospects for Gender Equality Politics in Central and Eastern Europe.* Ljubljana: Peace Institute.

Jost, J. T., Banaji, M. R., & Nosek, B. A. (2004). A decade of system justification theory: Accumulated evidence of conscious and unconscious bolstering of the status quo. *Political Psychology, 25,* 881–919. doi:10.1111/j.1467-9221.2004.00402.x

Kline, R. B. (1998). *Principles and Practice of Structural Equation Modeling.* New York: Guilford Press.

Kravitz, D. A., & Klineberg, S. L. (2000). Reactions to two versions of affirmative action among Whites, Blacks, and Hispanics. *Journal of Applied Psychology, 85,* 597–611. doi:10.1037/0021-9010.85.4.597

Kravitz, D. A., & Klineberg, S. L. (2004). Predicting affirmative action attitudes: Interactions of the effects of individual differences with the strength of the affirmative action plan. In N. DiTomaso & C. Post (Eds.), *Research in the Sociology of Work: Diversity in the work force* (pp. 107–130). Amsterdam: Elsevier.

Kravitz, D. A., & Platania, J. (1993). Attitudes and beliefs about affirmative action: Effects of target and of respondent sex and ethnicity. *Journal of Applied Psychology, 78,* 928–938. doi:10.1037/0021-9010.78.6.928

Kunovich, S., & Slomczynski, K. M. (2007). Systems of distribution and a sense of equity: A multilevel analysis of meritocratic attitudes in post-industrial societies. *European Sociological Review, 23,* 649–663. doi:10.1093/esr/jcm026

Labor Law No 9970 (2008). *Gender Equality in Society.* Retrieved from http://www.mpcs. gov.al/dpshb/images/stories/files/ligjet/3.4.1.1._Law_on_gender_equality_in_society. pdf

Lorenzi-Cioldi, F., & Buschini, F. (2008). When the glass ceiling collapses, walls are erected: Positive and negative consequences of psychological essentialism in affirmative action. In S. Badaloni, C. A. Drace, O. Gia, C. Levorato, & F. Vidotto (Eds.), *Under-representation of Women in Science and Technology* (pp. 27–40). Padova: Cleup.

Peterson, B. E., & Lane, M. D. (2001). Implications of authoritarianism for young adulthood: Longitudinal analysis of college experiences and future goals. *Personality and Social Psychology Bulletin, 27,* 678–690. doi:10.1177/0146167201276004

Pratto, F., Sidanius, J., Stallworth, L. M., & Malle, B. F. (1994). Social dominance orientation: A personality variable predicting social and political attitudes. *Journal of Personality and Social Psychology, 67,* 741–763. doi:10.1037/0022-3514.67.4.741

Sears, D. O., & Funk, C. L. (1991). The role of self-interest in social and political attitudes. In M. P. Zanna (Ed.), *Advances in Experimental Social Psychology* (Vol. 24, pp. 1–91). San Diego, CA: Academic Press.

Seligman, D. (1973). How «equal opportunity» turned into employment quotas. *Fortune, 87,* 160–168.

Sidanius, J., Pratto, F., & Bobo, L. (1996). Racism, conservatism, affirmative action, and intellectual sophistication: A matter of principled conservatism or group dominance? *Journal of Personality and Social Psychology, 70,* 476–490. doi:10.1037/0022-3514.70.3.476

Son Hing, L. S., Bobocel, D. R., & Zanna, M. P. (2002). Meritocracy and opposition to affirmative action: Making concessions in the face of discrimination. *Journal of Personality and Social Psychology, 83,* 493–509. doi:10.1037/0022-3514.83.3.493

Son Hing, L. S., Bobocel, D. R., Zanna, M. P., Garcia, D.M., Gee, S., & Orazietti, K. (2011). The merit of meritocracy. *Journal of Personality and Social Psychology, 101,* 433–450. doi:10.1037/a0024618

Staines, G., Tavris, C., & Jayaratne, T. E. (1974). The queen bee syndrome. *Psychology Today,* 7, 55–60.

7

REFINING THE CONDITIONS AND CAUSES OF THE GLASS CLIFF

Hostility, signalling change, or solving the crisis?

Clara Kulich, Vincenzo Iacoviello, and Fabio Lorenzi-Cioldi

Introduction

Considering the distribution of women and men across social hierarchies some progress has been made: Angela Merkel (Chancellor of Germany), Marissa Mayer (CEO of Yahoo), and Karin Bergmann (director of a prestigious theatre in Austria), to name a few, are examples of the impact of the growing permeability of the gender hierarchy. However, women continue to experience barriers in organisational and political spheres (Barreto, Ryan, & Schmitt, 2009). The notion of a *glass ceiling* first appeared in 1986 in *The Wall Street Journal* (Hymowitz & Schellhardt, 1986) to describe these often invisible discriminatory forces that prevent women from attaining top positions in the corporate world. More recently, scholars in the field of gender and leadership have focused on the circumstances under which women may surmount these obstacles, thereby encountering other kinds of gendered barriers. This shift was triggered by a *The Times* article (Judge, 2003) in which a journalist looked at the relationship between company performance and managers' gender in the 100 largest companies of the London Stock Exchange. She observed that the stock-performance of companies with the greatest number of female directors on their boards was poorer than the performance of those with the fewest or no women on the board. Her conclusion was that these women were responsible for the negative corporate outcomes, and thus that it was of little surprise that women were hardly selected for management positions. Intrigued by this interpretation, Ryan and Haslam (2005) undertook a comprehensive analysis of these data taking into account companies' stock-performances before and after director appointments. Their findings provided compelling evidence that adverse circumstances, compared to favourable ones, increase the likelihood of women reaching high-status positions in organisations (Ryan & Haslam, 2005,

2007). Apparently, women in leadership positions face particularly precarious and challenging conditions that increase their risk of failing. Following the glass-ceiling metaphor, Ryan and Haslam called this type of bias the *glass cliff*. The "cliff" highlights the risky nature of these women's leadership positions, and "glass" refers to the invisibility of this differential treatment of women.

We define glass cliff as a woman's increased chances of being selected for positions of power in a time of crisis compared to prosperous times. This does not automatically imply that men are more likely to be chosen in a favourable context compared to women, or that women are more likely to be chosen in precarious contexts compared to men – although we do not exclude these phenomena, they are not considered necessary conditions of a glass cliff. In this chapter, we review the literature on the glass-cliff phenomenon, and we introduce new ideas and findings on the conditions under which glass cliffs occur, and why they occur. In particular, we attempt to identify which type of crisis is most affected by glass-cliff decisions and which mechanisms are at play.

The glass cliff

Following the first empirical examination of the glass cliff (Ryan & Haslam, 2005), a number of experimental and archival studies have illustrated and replicated this phenomenon. Experimental demonstrations typically confront participants with an ailing or a thriving organisation (e.g., international firm), event (e.g., music festival), or political party. Researchers then ask participants to choose between candidates for a leadership position. The candidates differ one from another in sex but not in their competences and CVs. Such scenarios have been presented to high-schoolers and university students, to business leaders and professionals, and to the public at large (e.g., Bruckmüller & Branscombe, 2010; Haslam & Ryan, 2008; Ryan, Haslam, & Kulich, 2010). Moreover, this research has been carried out in such diverse countries as the Netherlands, Spain, Switzerland, the UK, and the US (e.g., Bruckmüller & Branscombe, 2010; Gartzia, Ryan, Balluerka, & Aritzeta, 2012; Haslam & Ryan, 2008; Kulich, Lorenzi-Cioldi, Iacoviello, Faniko, & Ryan, in press; Rink, Ryan, & Stoker, 2013). The findings consistently show that the female candidate is more likely to be selected as the new leader in a struggling than in a thriving organisation (notice that members of other minorities may also experience glass cliffs; see Cook & Glass, 2013; Kulich, Ryan, & Haslam, 2014; Ryan, Haslam, Wilson-Kovacs, Hersby, & Kulich, 2007). Despite the fact that glass cliffs are amply documented, there still remain many questions concerning the exact conditions in which they occur, and their actual causes. Bruckmüller, Ryan, Rink, and Haslam (2014) identified several motivations for glass-cliff decisions. Glass cliffs are a way to discriminate against women, by setting them up for failure. But they may also be a strategic choice aiming to "signal" a change in a company's situation. Bruckmüller et al. also discuss the role of gender stereotypes which create a *think crisis-think female* association.

Accordingly, women are preferred leaders in crisis situations where managing-people skills and the ability to endure a crisis are expected from a leader (Ryan, Haslam, Hersby, & Bongiorno, 2011). Finally, empirical research discounts the idea that women may actively seek such challenging positions (Rink et al., 2013). In this chapter, we will focus on the discrimination and the "signalling change" explanations. Both explanations involve an active role for decision makers. We review the literature on these two explanations, and point at some complexities that call for more research. Moreover, we will present new research that investigates the idea that women may also serve to implement "actual change".

Explaining the glass cliff: hostility

Traditional sexism portrays women as incompetent, especially in masculine contexts such as management (e.g., Eagly, Karau, & Makhijani, 1995; Schein, 2001). Thus, one may hypothesise that sexist attitudes are responsible for glass cliffs because sexist individuals want to make life hard for women who dare to challenge the gender hierarchy (for example by aiming for top positions). When Ryan, Haslam, and Postmes (2007) asked laypeople to explain what they thought the reasons for the glass cliff were, one of the most frequently mentioned causes was indeed hostility against women. Two types of hostility may be at play. First, choosing a woman in precarious circumstances may be motivated by the wish to see her fail. This failure could then be used to justify and legitimise prejudice about women's ineffectiveness in management, and to harm the reputation of women more generally. Second, companies may look for a scapegoat who takes the responsibility for the crisis (e.g., Ryan & Haslam, 2007; Ryan et al., 2007). Thus, hostility against women may actually serve the company by communicating to the outside world that a single person is responsible for the crisis and not the company as a whole. Such an unfortunate role would be likely fulfilled by someone who is not appreciated as an effective leader. Hence, in a hostile-sexist organisation, a woman may be considered the right person for this role. Some indirect evidence for this idea comes from Ryan et al. (2011, Study 3). They showed that in a crisis situation feminine traits are preferred over masculine ones when a manager is hired to take the blame for organisational failure, that is, to act as a scapegoat, or to endure the crisis. Although this preference concerns only feminine traits, one may assume that women are consequently more likely to be preferred as scapegoats.

In summary, independent of the first or the second mechanism stated, a *hostility hypothesis* suggests that sexist (compared to non-sexist) individuals would be more likely to make glass-cliff choices. Empirical research, however, has not warranted this conclusion yet. For instance, Gartzia et al. (2012) presented to employees and managers an unsuccessful-company scenario and new leaders who varied in terms of sex. Inconsistent with the hostility assumption, higher sexism led to a preference for male over female leaders. However, this research did not provide a comparison of poorly and strongly performing company contexts. Hence, in order to examine whether sexist individuals engage in glass-cliff decisions depending on the company context, we did a comparison of a poorly and a strongly performing company. In an experimental study (unpublished data by Kulich, Lorenzi-Cioldi, Iacoviello, Faniko, & Ryan, 2012) professionals in Switzerland first read about either a strongly or a poorly performing company, and then expressed their choice for a candidate (male or female), which was followed by an assessment of participants' hostile sexist attitudes. Paralleling Gartzia et al.'s (2012) findings, results indicated that sexist participants were less likely to choose the female candidate than low-sexist participants. Sexist participants were even less likely to choose a woman in the poor performance condition compared to the strong condition and compared to low-sexist participants.

Although laypeople spontaneously evoke the possibility of hostility as an underlying mechanism (Ryan et al., 2007), empirical evidence suggests that hostile sexism does not predict glass-cliff appointments. Rather, hostile attitudes against women lead to a general preference for men, regardless of company performance. Paradoxically, people with low levels of hostile attitudes tended towards a glass cliff (although these results did not reach significance). However, as Ryan et al. (2011) demonstrated, gender stereotypes still play a role. This occurs at a subtle or implicit level, as women may be considered as more suitable for passive roles of enduring a crisis because of the traits that they are associated with. Moreover, people seem happier to expose women than men to such stressful positions because women are deemed to possess the competences to cope with stress (Haslam & Ryan, 2008). The next section will touch on further implicit biases that lead to discrimination between women and men.

Explaining the glass cliff: implementing organisational change

A second explanation for the glass cliff is that companies in crisis are willing to instigate change by appointing an atypical manager (Haslam & Ryan, 2008; Ryan et al., 2007). Past research in a Japanese context showed that difficult times are antecedents of an endeavour to change leadership by choosing an outsider as manager (Kaplan & Minton, 1994). Moreover, experimental research revealed that female leaders are associated with change (Brown, Diekman, & Schneider, 2011), and that glass cliffs only occurred following a male leader's failure, but not when the past leader was a woman (Bruckmüller & Branscombe, 2010). Thus, implementing or at least signalling organisational change may drive an ailing company's motivation to appoint a woman.

This change assumption led Kulich et al. (in press, Study 1) to hypothesise that a glass cliff should only be observed when a crisis is considered to have been caused by faulty management. In this case, the situation can be controlled by the company by changing its leadership. In contrast, if a crisis occurred as a consequence of less controllable factors, such as a global economic crisis, a change in leadership may not be the optimal strategy. An experiment supported this argument. It revealed that when (allegedly male, as assessed by a pre-test) management was held responsible for company performance, participants favoured a woman in the poorly performing company compared to the strongly performing company. In contrast, when an uncontrollable factor (a global economic crisis) was the source of company outcomes, no differences occurred for the choice of the female manager. Thus, these results give initial support to the idea that a motivation to change the situation may be, at least in part, responsible for glass-cliff choices. However, another interpretation in the sense of the above discussed scapegoating conjecture could be that the position associated with poor leadership is the one most associated with blame, and thus a feminine leader (i.e., a woman) is preferred (Ryan et al., 2011). In the uncontrollable conditions, no one can be blamed or rewarded. Hence, other mechanisms should be at play in the selection of a new leader.

In the view that change is likely to play a role, one wonders about the exact nature of the change that is envisioned. During the financial crisis in 2008, the choice of female directors for Icelandic banks was justified by the fact that irresponsible risky male leadership had to be replaced and that the choice of women would signal change (O'Connor, 2008; Sunderland, 2009). The desire to change the situation may thus stem from two different, though not mutually exclusive, motivations. The first motivation consists of a strategic and symbolic type of change. Here, the aim is to take advantage of the fact that women are considered as non-traditional leaders in order to *signal* or *symbolise change* in a visible way to investors and the outside world (Haslam & Ryan, 2008; Ryan et al., 2007). The second motivation consists in implementing an *actual change* and breaking with the traditional agentic leadership style by appointing a woman who adopts, or is stereotypically perceived to adopt, a more communal leadership style. As we will see, this communal style does not necessarily replace but rather adds to an agentic leadership style. Both mentioned motivations may effectively lead to a change in corporate performance: The implementation of *actual change* in leadership may impact accounting performance (i.e., sales and profits). Conversely, *signalling change* by selecting an atypical leader may result in a change of investors' reactions, and thus of the market performance of a company (i.e., share prices). Thus, both motivations may fuel the company's performance, but in different ways. In the Icelandic example, actual and symbolic change motivations were simultaneously aroused. In order to disentangle the role of the two types of motivations for the glass cliff, we recommend studying them separately. Below, we will provide some evidence for and a discussion of both change motivations.

Female appointment in times of crisis: a symbolic change?

One way of implementing change may consist of signalling change to the company's outside world (i.e., investors, rivals, consumers, etc.) by the substitution of a male for a female leader (Haslam & Ryan, 2008). Hereby, the company communicates that action has been taken in order to mark a departure from past unsuccessful leadership. Appointing a woman may thus be a highly visible signal of change, telling investors and clients that the company is active and develops strategies to cope with the adverse situation. The company's hope is to create positive reactions in stock-holders, who may, in turn, push the market performance by investing in the company.

Initial evidence of the signalling change motivation comes from Ryan et al. (2011, Study 3) where participants rated the desirability of several traits for a new manager in an unsuccessful company, depending on the mission that would be assigned to the manager. Participants ascribed more communal than agentic traits to the manager whose mission was to put up with the crisis without necessarily changing the actual situation (i.e., endure the crisis, take responsibility for the failure, or manage personnel issues). In contrast, participants ascribed both communal and agentic traits to the manager whose mission was to actively change the situation (i.e., be a spokesperson or improve performance). This suggests that female leaders, who are stereotypically associated with feminine characteristics, may be deemed suitable when a more symbolic and passive leadership is expected, rather than an active improvement of performance. Kulich et al. (2015, Study 2) tested more directly whether women were selected to signal change and whether this was specific to a poor (as compared to a strong) company's performance. They asked participants to choose a candidate and to indicate to what degree their choice reflected a symbolic change. Findings demonstrated the classic glass-cliff pattern in candidate choice. Moreover, participants who chose the female (compared to the male) candidate were more likely to assume that the company was pressed to show a change of leadership to the outside world. A closer inspection of these findings revealed that the preferential choice of the female candidate in the poorly performing company (following bad leadership), compared to the strongly performing company (following good leadership), was accounted for by the company's motivation to signal change.

Taken together, the two above studies support the idea that a company may appoint a non-prototypical leader in order to signal change to the outside world during crisis times. However, this research only informs about the intentions that decision makers express with their choices. Little is known about the psychological impact of the signal emitted to the outside world. An archival study suggest that investors are particularly sensitive to female director appointments (Haslam, Ryan, Kulich, Trojanowski, & Atkins, 2010). And indeed, female appointments seem to be interpreted as signals of *decline*, as market performance (i.e., stock-prices) tends to drop following the announcement of a new female chief executive director (Lee & James, 2007). Thus, although decision makers may assume that the appointment of a woman would be judged as an active and visible initiative of the company to change their situation, this may not be interpreted in the same way by observers of the company.

Female appointment in times of crisis: an actual change?

The appointment of a woman in times of crisis may also be motivated by the company's willingness to *actually* change *how* a company is led. Indeed, women are assumed to display different ways of leading compared to men. In line with this idea, Ryan et al. (2007) observed that participants suggested that glass cliffs occur because gender stereotypes of women's communal abilities are consistent with what is needed for a leader in times of crisis. The literature shows that agentic, task-oriented, or "transactional" leadership, as well as communal, relationship-oriented, or "transformational" leadership, are indeed the most effective leadership styles (see a meta-analysis by Judge & Piccolo, 2004). Traditionally, descriptions of leaders show more overlap with descriptions of men than of women (*think manager-think male* metaphor by Schein, 2001; see also Ryan et al., 2011, Study 1). In addition, research has demonstrated that women are associated with change and transformational leadership, whereas men are typically associated with stability and a transactional leadership (Brown et al., 2011; Eagly & Johnson, 1990; Guimond, Chatard, & Lorenzi-Cioldi, 2013). And, evidence from field research shows that, as compared with male leaders, female leaders state that they employ a more democratic and participative style, and that they are better equipped to face a crisis (Mano-Negrin & Sheaffer, 2004). Overall, it seems that women are ascribed relational skills that are needed to face a crisis (e.g., Eagly, Makhijani, & Klonsky, 1992). Accordingly, one could assume that they should be more likely to be hired by a company facing a crisis. Ryan et al. (2011, Study 2) systematically assessed the desirability of an ideal manager's characteristics in the context of successful and unsuccessful companies. Findings suggest that an *ideal* manager of a poorly performing company is indeed attributed more feminine than masculine traits. However, as illustrated in the section on signalling change, Study 3 of Ryan et al. (2011) showed that this pattern was specific to crisis contexts where the mission of the manager was to stay passive and act as a symbol of change. When the mission was to be a spokesperson or to improve performance, thus to actually change the situation, communal and agentic traits were judged as equally desirable. Similarly, Gartzia et al. (2012) demonstrated that in a crisis context where effective leadership was portrayed as agentic, both sexes and both gendered characteristics were equally selected.

Based on these findings it seems that crisis contexts where managerial deficiencies are held responsible call for organisational change. An actual improvement of performance may be achieved through a combination of a traditional agentic leadership and a communal style of leading. Lacking communality can indeed be a disadvantage in such a context. When Bruckmüller and Branscombe (2010) explored trait attributions and its relation to the preferential choice of a female candidate in a glass cliff scenario, they found that less communal traits were assigned to the male candidate in an unsuccessful (versus successful) company, as well as compared to the female candidate in an unsuccessful company. This perceived lack of communality of the man explained why the woman was more likely to be chosen in the crisis context. Conversely, no difference in the ascription of agentic traits was observed. Hence, both communal and agentic traits seem to make up the ideal leadership style in the most challenging contexts. And agentic women may have an advantage over men who lack communality.

The choice of a competent woman with traditional leadership abilities may prompt a change in the very nature of leadership because, in addition, she is expected to enact a communal style. In order to systematically investigate the whole impact of the preference of sex and gendered characteristics in different organisational contexts, Kulich, Iacoviello, and Lorenzi-Cioldi (2015, Study 1) presented to participants two male and two female candidates whose descriptions varied in gender stereotypicality (agentic versus communal). Participants read about a target company that had either a strong or a poor performance resulting from past management. They then rated the leadership ability of each of the four candidates. Results showed that company performance had an impact on the perception of candidates' leadership ability depending on their gendered ascriptions (but not their sex). No differences in leadership ability of agentic candidates were observed between the strongly and the poorly performing companies. However, the leadership ability of the communal candidates was rated higher in the strongly than in the poorly performing company. Moreover, in the poorly performing company, the leadership ability of the agentic candidates was rated higher than the leadership ability of the communal candidates, while for the strongly performing company, no differences between the agentic and the communal candidates were observed. These results suggest that in a successful context, both communal and agentic leadership styles are rated as equally suitable. However, in a crisis context, a purely agentic style is considered superior to a purely communal leadership style. Working in a poorly performing company is particularly challenging for a manager, and thus if choices can only be made between extremes of agentic versus communal leadership styles, excellent leadership competences in the prototypical sense are more strongly valued.

Against our initial expectation, sex did not play a role, but this might be due to presenting all candidates simultaneously to participants. Bohnet, van Geen and Bazerman (2012) demonstrated that when candidates for posts or promotions were simultaneously evaluated, interviewers relied less on stereotypes than when assessments were made separately. In view of this finding, sex was probably highly salient to participants in Study 1. Moreover, participants were able to ignore sex information as gendered ascriptions were also available. Thus, they may have paid less attention to sex in order to avoid decisions which could eventually be blamed for sexism. Correcting for this potential bias, we conducted a second study which examined the role of gender-stereotypicality more in depth. In order to make our sex and gendered characteristics manipulations less obvious to participants, we presented either a male or a female candidate who had been allegedly administered an assessment test revealing that s/he possessed either stronger agentic or stronger communal traits (Kulich et al., 2015, Study 2). Participants then imagined that they had to make a suggestion to a head-hunter who searched for candidates for director positions in two companies. Specifically, they had to decide whether to appoint the candidate in a strongly or in a poorly performing company. Paralleling the findings from Study 1, the agentic candidates were more likely than the communal ones to be chosen for the unsuccessful company. However, this effect was mainly due to a preference for the agentic female for the unsuccessful company, while the communal female was preferred for the successful company. Thus, overall, the agentic (male and female) candidates and the communal male were more often chosen for the poorly performing company compared to the communal female.

These results suggest, in line with Study 1, a preference for traditional leadership in a crisis context. But this tendency was more pronounced for the female candidates. Hence, gender ascriptions seem to matter more strongly for women. In particular, a woman should not be too communal in a crisis context. The communal woman was probably least preferred in the crisis context because the combination of female sex and communal ascriptions, which are typically "feminine", may appear as a guarantee of this candidate's *lack of fit* (Heilman, 2001) with a particularly demanding managerial position. Apparently, a woman needs to compensate for her biological sex by proving her agentic abilities. A woman who has proven in an assessment test that she possesses agentic traits can overcome this lack of fit and become a preferred choice because she combines both communal traits – automatically associated to a woman through her sex – and agentic traits – assigned to her through gendered descriptions. These findings are in line with previous research suggesting that female managers are scrutinised more closely than men when evaluating them in a non-stereotypical context (see research on "double standard", Foschi, 1996; see also Kulich, Trojanowski, Ryan, Haslam, & Renneboog, 2011).

Claims on modern leaders suggest an androgynous leader as the ideal (Koenig, Eagly, Mitchell, & Ristikari, 2011; Sargent, 1983) and particularly in crisis contexts that demand actual change (Ryan et al., 2011, Study 3). The best leaders are needed in a crisis, thus, the combination of sex with gender characteristics which are typical of the other sex may correspond to this leadership ideal. The agentic woman and the communal man were both amongst the preferred candidates in the poor performance condition. This suggests that a man (woman) ascribed with communal (agentic) traits is spontaneously attributed agentic (communal) characteristics because of the stereotypes ascribed to candidates through their sex. But why was then the agentic man also amongst the most preferred candidates? Here one may argue that although the androgynous leadership is highly praised nowadays, the traditional agentic leader-prototype has not yet been completely overridden. Following this, the two studies' findings of the choice of a communal person in the strongly performing company may be justified by the fact that agentic traits are less important in a flourishing company, where change and thus "strong" traditional leadership is not mandatory.

Overall, as the above literature shows, the interplay of sex and gendered characteristics is complex and highly dependent on context (i.e., company performance, type of mission of a leader, and simultaneous versus separate presentation of candidates). Future research should take a combination of these dynamics into account. Moreover, different degrees of integration of agentic and communal traits (in our studies candidates were strong on either one or the other dimension) should be addressed which should help to better integrate the literature presented here.

Finally, in this chapter, we mainly talked about companies' choices of women in order to signal change or implement real change. However, little is known about the direction and the quality of female leaders' impact on companies' performance. Future research should investigate the mediators of women's impact on company performance. For example, one should ask in what way the change from a traditionally agentic to a more communal or androgynous leadership impacts on employees' and investors' attitudes and behaviours. And what role these mediating forces play in changes to corporate performance.

Practical implementations

Our research documents that women are more likely to become leaders in adverse circumstances resulting from bad management. Moreover, this is particularly the case when a company looks for a passive leader who takes the blame. Women and recruiters should be informed about these unfavourable conditions of female careers in order to not blame women for negative outcomes that are predictable by a discriminatory selection context, rather than women's competences. Another important implication is that when selecting women as leaders under such precarious circumstances, companies should ascertain that these women get social support so that they can work under the best possible conditions in these challenging positions (Bruckmüller et al., 2014). Moreover, the research on the actual change motivation indicates that women, although described by the same gendered characteristics as men, are treated differently to men. This shows that traits may be differently perceived if associated with men or women. Recruitment practices should take into account such biases and seek to create evaluation schemes that are unaffected by the sex of the candidate.

Conclusions

The glass-cliff phenomenon is not simply a hostile act but, more likely, the outcome of more complex mechanisms linked to gender stereotypes. Our research suggests that glass cliffs are specific to controllable types of crisis due to the need to signal change. They may not be applicable to broader, hardly controllable, and enduring economic crisis contexts. The motivation to change can be signalled by choosing a non-traditional person (i.e., a woman). Moreover, actual change motivations in a crisis lead to preferences of agentic or androgynous leaders (high in both agentic and communal traits). This can also be a woman who combines her female sex with agentic traits, or a man who combines his male sex with communal traits.

If we look more closely at the context of the appointments of Angela Merkel, Marissa Mayer, and Karin Bergmann to their respective positions, one realises that all three were appointed during a crisis and all three replaced men. Thus, their pioneering ascents in the gender hierarchy may just be further indication of the unequal conditions that men and women encounter. However, the motivation to select them was probably not hostility against women, but more likely subtle gender biases that portrayed these women as most suitable leaders. In these cases, the initial aim may have been to signal change. But these leaders have proved to be good examples of women who are not only symbols of change but that they actually developed effective leadership agency and handled the crises. Both Merkel and Bergmann have been re-elected for their positions. Thus, a female leader may actually be a choice that leads to real and positive change.

References

Barreto, M., Ryan, M. K., & Schmitt, M. T. (2009). *The Glass Ceiling in the 21st Century: Understanding barriers to gender equality.* Washington, DC: American Psychological Association.

Bohnet, I., van Geen, A., & Bazerman, M. (2012). *When Performance Trumps Gender Bias: Joint versus separate evaluation,* Working Paper, Havard Business School.

Brown, E. R., Diekman, A. B., & Schneider, M. C. (2011). A change will do us good: Threats diminish typical preferences for male leaders. *Personality and Social Psychology Bulletin, 37,* 930–941. doi:10.1177/0146167211403322

Bruckmüller, S., & Branscombe, N. R. (2010). The glass cliff: when and why women are selected as leaders in crisis contexts. *The British Journal of Social Psychology / The British Psychological Society, 49,* 433–51. doi:10.1348/014466609X466594

Bruckmüller, S., Ryan, M. K., Rink, F., & Haslam, S. A. (2014). Beyond the glass ceiling: The glass cliff and its lessons for organizational policy. *Social Issue and Policy Review, 8,* 202–232. doi:10.1111/sipr.12006

Cook, A., & Glass, C. (2013). Above the glass ceiling: When are women and racial/ ethnic minorities promoted to CEO? *Strategic Management Journal, 35,* 1080–1089. doi:10.1002/smj2161

Eagly, A. H., & Johnson, B. T. (1990). Gender and leadership style: A meta-analysis. *Psychological Bulletin, 108,* 233–256. doi:0033-2909/90/S00.75

Eagly, A. H., Karau, S. J., & Makhijani, M. G. (1995). Gender and the effectiveness of leaders: A meta-analysis. *Psychological Bulletin, 117,* 125–145. doi:10.1037/0033-2909.117.1.125

Eagly, A. H., Makhijani, M. G., & Klonsky, B. G. (1992). Gender and the evaluation of leaders: A meta-analysis. *Psychological Bulletin, 111*, 3–22. doi: 10.1037/0033-2909.111.1.3

Foschi, M. (1996). Double standards in the evaluation of men and women. *Social Psychology, 59*, 237–254. http://www.jstor.org/stable/2787021

Gartzia, L., Ryan, M. K., Balluerka, N., & Aritzeta, A. (2012). Think crisis–think female: Further evidence. *European Journal of Work and Organizational Psychology, 21*, 603–628. do i:10.1080/1359432X.2011.591572

Guimond, S., Chatard, A. & Lorenzi-Cioldi, F. (2013). The social psychology of gender across cultures. In M. K. Ryan & N. R. Branscombe (Eds.), *The SAGE Handbook of Gender and Psychology* (pp. 216–233). London: Sage.

Haslam, S. A., & Ryan, M. K. (2008). The road to the glass cliff: Differences in the perceived suitability of men and women for leadership positions in succeeding and failing organizations. *The Leadership Quarterly, 19*, 530–546. doi:10.1016/j.leaqua.2008.07.011

Haslam, S. A., Ryan, M. K., Kulich, C., Trojanowski, G., & Atkins, C. (2010). Investing with prejudice: The presence of women on company boards is associated with lower stock performance but not with lower financial returns. *British Journal of Management, 21*, 484–497. doi:10.1111/j.1467-8551.2009.00670.x

Heilman, M. E. (2001). Description and prescription – How gender stereotypes prevent women's ascent up the organisational ladder. *Journal of Social Issues, 57*, 657–674. doi:10.1111/0022-4537.00234

Hymowitz, C., & Schellhardt, T. D. (1986, March 24). The corporate woman (a special report): The glass ceiling: Why women can't seem to break the invisible barrier that blocks them from the top jobs. *The Wall Street Journal*, pp.1D, 4D, 5D.

Judge, E. (2003, November 11). 'Women on board: Help or hindrance?', *The Times*, p. 21.

Judge, T. A, & Piccolo, R. F. (2004). Transformational and transactional leadership: A meta-analytic test of their relative validity. *The Journal of Applied Psychology, 89*, 755–68. doi:10.1037/0021-9010.89.5.755

Kaplan, S. N., & Minton, B. A. (1994). Appointment of outsiders to Japanese boards: Determinants and implications for managers. *Journal of Financial Economics, 36*, 225–258. doi:0304-405X/94/S07.00

Koenig, A. M., Eagly, A. H., Mitchell, A. A., & Ristikari, T. (2011). Are leader stereotypes masculine? A meta-analysis of three research paradigms. *Psychological Bulletin, 137*, 616–642. doi:10.1037/a0023557

Kulich, C., Iacoviello, V., & Lorenzi-Cioldi, F. (2015). *Implementing Actual Change During a Crisis: Gender, sex, and the glass cliff.* Manuscript in preparation.

Kulich, C., Ryan, M. K., & Haslam, S. A. (2014). The political glass cliff: Understanding how seat selection contributes to the under-performance of ethnic minority candidates. *Political Research Quarterly, 67*, 84–95. doi:10.1177/1065912913495740

Kulich, C., Lorenzi-Cioldi, F., Iacoviello, V., Faniko, K., & Ryan, M. K. (2012, March). *Minority groups in high-status contexts: Beware of the glass cliff.* Invited talk at University of Lausanne, Seminar of Social Psychology laboratory.

Kulich, C., Lorenzi-Cioldi, F., Iacoviello, V., Faniko, K., & Ryan, M. K. (in press). Signaling change during a crisis: Refining conditions for the glass cliff. *Journal of Experimental Social Psychology.*

Kulich, C., Trojanowski, G., Ryan, M. K., Haslam, S. A., & Renneboog, L. D. R. (2011). Who gets the carrot and who gets the stick? Evidence of gender disparities in executive remuneration. *Strategic Management Journal, 32*, 301–321. doi:10.1002/smj.878

Lee, P. M., & James, E. H. (2007). She'-e-os: Gender effects and investor reactions to the announcement of top executive appointments. *Strategic Management Journal, 28*, 227–241. doi:10.1002/smj.575

Mano-Negrin, R. & Sheaffer, Z. (2004). Are women "cooler" than men during crises? Exploring gender differences in perceiving organisational crisis preparedness proneness. *Women in Management Review, 19*, 109–122. doi:10.1108/09649420410525315

O'Connor, S. (2008, October 14). Iceland calls in women bankers to clean up 'young men's mess', *Financial Times*. Retrieved from http://www.ft.com

Rink, F., Ryan, M. K., & Stoker, J. I. (2013). Influence in times of crisis: How social and financial resources affect men's and women's evaluations of glass-cliff positions. *Psychological Science, 23*, 1306–1313. doi:10.1177/0956797612453115

Ryan, M. K., & Haslam, S. A. (2005). The glass cliff: Evidence that women are over-represented in precarious leadership positions. *British Journal of Management, 16*, 81–90. doi:10.1111/j.1467-8551.2005.00433.x

Ryan, M. K., & Haslam, S. A. (2007). The glass cliff: Exploring the dynamics surrounding women's appointment to precarious leadership positions. *The Academy of Management Review, 32*, 549–572. doi:10.5465/AMR.2007.24351856

Ryan, M. K., Haslam, A. S., & Kulich, C. (2010). Politics and the glass cliff: Evidence that women are preferentially selected to contest hard-to-win seats. *Psychology of Women Quarterly, 34*, 56–64. doi:0361-6843/10

Ryan, M. K., Haslam, A. S., & Postmes, T. (2007). Reactions to the glass cliff: Gender differences in the explanations for the precariousness of women's leadership positions. *Journal of Organizational Change Management, 20*, 182–197. doi:10.1108/09534810710724748

Ryan, M. K., Haslam, S. A., Hersby, M. D., & Bongiorno, R. (2011). Think crisis–think female: Glass cliffs and contextual variation in the think manager–think male stereotype. *Journal of Applied Psychology, 96*, 470–484. doi:10.1037/a0022133

Ryan, M. K., Haslam, S. A., Wilson-Kovacs, M. D., Hersby, M., & Kulich, C. (2007). *Managing Diversity and the Glass Cliff*. London: CIPD.

Sargent, A. G. (1983). *The Androgynous Manager*. New York: Amacom.

Schein, V. E. (2001). A global look at psychological barriers to women's progress in management. *Journal of Social Issues, 57*, 675–688. doi: 10.1111/0022-4537.00235

Sunderland, R. (2009, February 22). After the crash, Iceland's women lead the rescue. *The Observer*, Retrieved from http://www.guardian.co.uk

8

WORK–LIFE BALANCE VULNERABILITIES AND RESOURCES FOR WOMEN IN SWITZERLAND

Results from a national study

Sarah D. Stauffer, Christian Maggiori, Claire S. Johnston, Shékina Rochat, and Jérôme Rossier

Work and family are two important life domains, and women, especially, struggle to balance work and family in mid-life (Emslie & Hunt, 2009). This is also true for Switzerland, where women represent 45 per cent of employees (Graf et al., 2007). A national longitudinal study, Professional Transitions and Pathways, measures the impact of individual characteristics, resources, and culture on career paths. It is embedded within the Swiss National Centre of Competence in Research on vulnerability across the life course (NCCR-LIVES: Overcoming Vulnerabilities), which considers vulnerability from the following four perspectives: resources, stressors, outcomes, and contexts. Spini, Hanapi, Bernardi, Oris, and Bickel (2013) defined vulnerability as a lack of resources within a specific context that places individuals or groups at risk for experiencing negative consequences across their life course. Vulnerability studies are useful in describing difficulties and resilience processes – the resources and stressors faced – within individual and contextual dimensions (Spini et al., 2013). As career counseling and work psychology researchers, we focus our discussion on issues pertaining to the cumulative effects of vulnerability and work–family conflict from psychological and sociological perspectives.

Work–family imbalance and women's responsibilities

Researchers have long identified vulnerabilities for working women/mothers. Eagly (1987) posited that women are socialized to take childrearing and homemaking roles from an early age. Current economic conditions often require that women work for families to meet their needs, although housework remains within their scope of responsibility (Glick & Fiske, 1996). Women in Switzerland are particularly disadvantaged by the unequal distribution of domestic tasks (Swiss Federal Statistics Office, FSO, 2013). Although modern feminist ascriptions suggest that housework and childcare should be evenly divided when both partners in a couple work, this is not often the case (e.g. Higgins, Duxbury, & Lyons, 2010; Hochschild & Machung, 1989/2012). Additionally, single mothers do not have this choice, and work full-time more often (77.1 per cent) than their married counterparts (68.7 per cent; Tomlinson, 2008). Hochschild and Machung (1989/2012) described the increased energy expense in working the "second shift", or women taking on more of the housework and childcare than their partners after a full-day's work.

Regarding the interplay between career and family responsibilities, a series of studies conducted in Switzerland found, first, that women and men showed different professional trajectories (e.g. Levy, Gauthier, & Widmer, 2007; Widmer, Levy, Pollien, Hammer, & Gauthier, 2003) and, second, that men's professional trajectories were more homogeneous and women's more varied (cf., Sapin, Spini, & Widmer, 2007). Sapin et al. (2007) identified four different trajectories for women: reducing work percentage or leaving the workforce for only a few years to care for children, then reintegrating into the workforce part-time (30 per cent) or full-time afterwards (34 per cent); or spending more years caring for children, then reintegrating into the workforce part-time (13 per cent), or quitting altogether after having children (23 per cent). Given that Swiss cultural parameters – formally or informally – prescribe the unequal distribution of domestic tasks to women (FSO, 2013), women often must juggle the logistics of their working lives in order to better accommodate family responsibilities (Sapin et al., 2007).

Juggling work and family logistics is key. Researchers have demonstrated that work is more likely to create a negative spillover effect on family life than family life is on work (e.g. Forma, 2008; Sultana, 2012). Higgins et al. (2010) indicated that many women cope by reducing time they would otherwise take for themselves before cutting or restructuring family or work obligations, which may threaten their well-being. Women are more likely to sacrifice this self-time because they have to simultaneously attend to children's needs and to prove that they're serious at work (Hochschild & Machung, 1989/2012).

Job insecurity and job strain as work stressors

Researchers have identified two other important work-related factors that may exacerbate felt work stress and decrease professional well-being: job insecurity and job strain (Forma, 2008; Karasek, 1979; Lyons, 2002). The current professional landscape is characterized by increased job insecurity due to economic changes in Western society over the last two decades. De Witte (2005) defined job insecurity as the perceived threat of job loss and the worry related to that threat. Job insecurity is considered as one of the most important professional stressors, and it affects employees' well-being and health, both in the short and long term (de Witte, 2005; Sverke, Hellgren, & Näswall, 2002). Adverse professional situations have been associated with a higher divorce rate and have impacted decisions about having a child (e.g. Charles & Stephens, 2004; del Bono, Weber, & Winter-Ebmer, 2012), showing the effect of job insecurity in other life domains.

Karasek's (1979) job demand-control model identified central aspects of the professional context that are important determinants of work-related well-being: job demand and decision latitude (or job control). Job demands reflect professional aspects that require coping responses and involve psychological and/or physiological costs for the employee (Jones & Fletcher, 1996). Decision latitude indicates potential for and perceived control over a job activity, for example, in terms of managing and organizing the tasks (Karasek, 1979). According to the job strain hypothesis, low employee decision latitude and high psychological demands facilitate negative reactions of psychological strain. Consequently, it is not simply the presence of the demands that affects an individual's job satisfaction, but the balance between job demands and personal control. For example, a manager may have high job demands, but these are matched with high levels of control, allowing for active coping with demands and reducing the likelihood of experiencing job strain. By contrast, a salesperson also has high demands (e.g. sales targets and significant interpersonal interaction), but s/he lacks the required control and decision latitude to decide how and when the work is complete, therefore, increasing the likelihood of experiencing job strain.

Job demands and control refer to broad categories that represent both stressors and resources in the workplace. According to the matching hypothesis, for resources to mitigate the effects of stressors, an optimal match needs to exist between stressors and resources (de Jonge & Dormann, 2006). For resources to reduce the possibility of experiencing job strain, they need to correspond to the *functional value* of the stressor to alleviate the strain and enable the person to better restore balance. For example, cognitive and emotional resources provided by team members may contribute to the successful completion of a big project.

Social support as a moderator of job strain

Social support is an essential resource, frequently cited in addressing and managing work strain and adverse professional conditions. Resources, such as social support from family members (e.g. Lyons, 2002), colleagues (e.g. Mesmer-Magnus & Viswesvaran, 2009) and supervisors (e.g. Ernst Kossek, Pichler, Bodner, & Hammer, 2011) may help in this process. By contrast, a lack of such support may hinder achieving this balance. Social support may also be an important resource to mitigate the potential negative effects of job strain. Johnson and Hall (1988) extended the job demands-control theory and proposed social support as a buffer. This would suggest that even in the presence of job strain, social support may reduce the potential negative effects of job strain and thus serve to maintain well-being. Herein, we did not ask women to specify the type of social support they receive, but rather to assess the general functional support that they call upon in meeting their stressors.

Hypotheses

Based on these considerations, family context (having children or not and being single or in a couple), work characteristics (working part- or full-time, number of jobs worked, and management responsibilities) should impact work stressors and social support resources. Subsequently, these vulnerabilities, resources and stressors are expected to have an impact on work-related and general well-being. In order to assess women's situation in Switzerland, these exploratory hypotheses will be tested. Limiting this discussion to the vulnerabilities, resources, stressors, and outcomes for women allowed us to avoid sex comparisons in order to promote a meaningful discourse on working women's issues.

Method

Participants

Based on a random sample drawn from the national register of residents by the FSO, a sample of 960 employed women, 25 to 55 years old (M_{age} = 41.87; SD = 8.71), living in Switzerland participated in the study. Participants were part of the first data collection wave (January–April, 2012) of a larger national longitudinal project on professional trajectories and career paths (e.g. Maggiori, Rossier, Krings, Johnston, & Massoudi, in press). A large majority (84 per cent) were Swiss (see Table 8.1). The majority of the participants were in a couple with one or more children (44.9 per cent); about 10 per cent were single with one or more children. Approximately one-third were managers; 43 per cent worked full-time. Participants most frequently indicated caring for children, assuming housework (42.6 per cent), and the desire to not work full-time (32.7 per cent) as their reasons for working part-time. Furthermore, about 12 per cent had two or more jobs, and slightly more than 11 per cent were actively seeking a new job. Finally, about 18 per cent perceived job insecurity, and more than half of the participants indicated that it would be *difficult* to *very difficult* for them to find a similar job.

Instruments

Job strain

Job strain was assessed with a 14-item version of the Job Content Questionnaire (Karasek, Brisson, Kawakami, & Amick, 1998), including psychological demands (5 items; e.g. "My job is fast-paced and hectic"; α=.69) and decision latitude (9 items, e.g. "I have considerable influence over things at work"; α=.82). Each item was rated on a four-point Likert-type scale (*1=strongly disagree, 4=strongly agree*). The ratio between psychological demands and decision latitude was calculated to obtain a job strain value (Li, Yang, & Cho, 2006).

TABLE 8.1 Family and professional characteristics of the employed women sample (N = 960)

Characteristics	n	Valid %
Nationality		
Swiss nationality	810	84.4
Family structure		
Single without children	164	17.2
Single with children	88	9.2
Couple without children	274	28.7
Couple with children	429	44.9
Work rate		
Full-time	412	42.9
Part-time	548	57.1
Part-time reasons		
To study	44	4.6
Health problems	33	3.4
Impossible to find another job	24	2.5
Do not wish to work more	314	32.7
Domestic tasks, children, etc.	409	42.6
Other	94	9.8
Professional position		
Management position	321	33.4

Job satisfaction

Job satisfaction was measured using six items from Rolland's (1995, as cited in Massoudi, 2009) JobSat Inventory. These items captured satisfaction appraisals of different aspects of work (i.e. boss's attitudes, colleague relationships, salary, work conditions, and job security). Satisfaction was indicated on a four-point Likert-type scale (*1=not at all satisfied, 4=very satisfied*; $\alpha=.76$).

Job insecurity

Past and present job insecurity was assessed using 2 single items developed for the LIVES research project. The first asked participants how many times they faced the risk of losing their job over the last year (*1=never, 5=constantly*). The second asked how they would evaluate the risk of losing their current job in the coming 12 months (*1=very low, 4=very high*).

Work stress

The nine-item General Work Stress Scale (GWSS; de Bruin & Taylor, 2005) provided a measure of the level of felt stress caused by work on a five-point Likert-type scale (*1=never, 5=always*; e.g. "Do you spend time worrying about your work?" α=.88).

Functional social support

The eight-item Duke-UNC Functional Social Support Questionnaire (DUFSS; Broadhead, Gehlbach, DeGruy, & Kaplan, 1988) was used to measure individuals' perceptions of the amount and type of personal support available. Participants responded on a five-point Likert-type scale (*1=much less than I would like, 5=as much as I would like*; e.g. "I have people who care about what happens to me," α=.92).

Life satisfaction

Participants' overall judgment of their satisfaction with life was captured by the Satisfaction With Life Scale (SWLS; Diener, Emmons, Larsen, & Griffin, 1985). Five items are assessed on a seven-point Likert-type scale (*1=strongly disagree, 7=strongly agree*; e.g. "I am satisfied with my life," α=.89).

Self-rated health and quality of life

Two single items used in the World Health Organization Quality of Life (WHOQOL)-Group (e.g. WHOQOL-Skevington, Lotfy, & O'Connell, 2004) were used to assess general quality of life and self-rated health on a five-point Likert-type scale (*1=very poor, 5=very good*; e.g. "How is your health in general?").

Demographic and additional professional variables

Age, household income, nationality (*Swiss, non-Swiss*), spoken language (*German, French*), work percentage (*part-, full-time*), and number of current jobs (*one, two or more*) were assessed. Furthermore, participants were asked whether they were actively looking for a job (*yes, no*). Finally, professional position was determined by being responsible for collaborators and the budget or not (*manager, subordinate*).

Data analyses

To assess the possible differences on social support and job strain, with reference to personal situation (i.e. living with a child, family structure) and professional situation (i.e. work rate, professional position, job search, and number of jobs), six analyses of covariance were conducted. Control variables (age, nationality, language, and household income) were included due to significant correlations with social support and job strain. To predict professional (i.e. job satisfaction, work stress) and general (i.e. life satisfaction, self-rated health, quality of life) well-being, a multiple hierarchical regression analysis (enter method) was applied. For each of the five dependent variables, in Step 1, control variables were entered. In Step 2, family situation was included, using "single with children" as a dummy variable for a baseline against the other three conditions. In Step 3, work characteristics (i.e. work rate, number of jobs, management position, job search, perceived job insecurity, and discrimination) were included. In Step 4, job strain and social support were added. Finally, in Step 5, the moderator effect of social support on the job strain–well-being relationship was included.

Results

Overall, working women reported high levels of professional and general well-being (see Table 8.2). They indicated high self-rated health and good quality of life. Moreover, they perceived life as highly satisfying and social support as highly adequate. Professionally, they reported high levels of job satisfaction, low levels of work stress, and low levels of job strain.

Regarding women's personal situation, the ANCOVAs showed no differences between participants with and without children, $F(1, 951) = 1.17$, $p > .05$, $\eta^2 < .01$ and $F(1, 951) = 0.74$, $p > .05$, $\eta^2 < .01$ respectively for job strain and social support. Regarding family structure, analyses highlighted no differences on job strain, $F(1, 951) = 2.43$, $p > .05$, $\eta^2 = .01$. However, analyses emphasized differences on perceived social support, $F(1, 951) = 8.28$,

TABLE 8.2 Psychometric properties of key outcome variables (N=960)

	n	M	SD
Self-rated health	954	4.19	.75
Quality of life	954	4.24	.65
Satisfaction with life	951	5.28	1.12
Social support	952	4.28	.75
Job satisfaction	960	3.21	.45
Job strain[a]	959	.88	.24
Job demands	959	2.57	.46
Job control	959	6.02	.49
Work-related stress	958	1.85	.59

Note
[a] Job strain is a calculated ratio ranking from .12 to 2.00

$p < .001$, $\eta^2 = .03$, wherein post-hoc analyses revealed that single women reported less social support than women in couples, irrespective of motherhood status. Furthermore, single women with at least one child reported having less support than women in a couple without children. Other comparisons were not statistically significant.

Concerning professional situations, ANCOVA results indicated that women in a management position reported a lower level of job strain than those with subordinate positions, $F(1, 951) = 8.81$, $p < .01$, $\eta^2 = .01$. However, the effect size is modest. Managers reported more job demands, $F(1, 956) = 12.71$, $p < .001$ and more job control, $F(1, 956) = 61.87$, $p < .001$, than subordinates. The differences for job control were larger than for job demands, suggesting that it is job control that is important for reducing job strain in managers.

The effect on social support was not significant, $F(1, 951) = 2.91$, $p > .05$, $\eta^2 = .00$. Furthermore, the analyses emphasized a main effect of job search both on job strain, $F(1, 952) = 12.31$, $p < .001$, $\eta^2 = .02$ and perceived social support, $F(1, 952) = 10.23$, $p < .001$, $\eta^2 = .01$. More precisely, participants looking actively for a new job reported more professional strain and, furthermore, they indicated a lower level of social support. Finally, it is interesting to note that the results highlighted no differences in terms of job strain and functional social support, with regard to the work percentage (full- or part-time) and the number of jobs (one or more). In fact, regarding work percentage, we found $F(1, 951) = 1.17$, $p > .05$, $\eta^2 < .01$ and $F(1, 951) = 0.29$, $p > .05$, $\eta^2 < .01$ respectively for job strain and social support; regarding the number of jobs, we found $F(1, 950) = 2.82$, $p > .05$, $\eta^2 < .01$ and $F(1, 951) = 0.15$, $p > .05$, $\eta^2 < .01$ respectively for job strain and social support.

With regard to the regression analyses conducted to predict general well-being-related outcomes (see Table 8.3), the final model explained 38 per cent of the total variance of satisfaction with life, $F(17, 881) = 32.80$, $p < .001$. Satisfaction with life was positively predicted by income and social support, and negatively by job insecurity and job strain. Self-rated health was negatively predicted by age, perceived discrimination at work and job strain and positively predicted by social support. The final model accounted for about 10 per cent of self-rated health: Total $R^2 = .09$, $F(17, 888) = 5.92$, $p < .001$. Regarding quality of life, the final model explained 23 per cent of the total variance, $F(17, 888) = 16.64$, $p < .001$. This outcome was positively predicted by the household income and the functional social support, but negatively by perceived difficulties of finding a similar job, perceived discrimination at work, and job strain. Moreover, the analyses indicated that women in couples without children reported a greater general quality of life than single women with children.

Concerning the work-related outcomes (see Table 8.3), work stress was positively predicted by age, perceived job insecurity, perceived work-place discrimination and job strain, and negatively by social support and not actively seeking new employment. The final model explained 17 per cent of the work stress, $F(17, 889) = 11.83$, $p < .001$. Finally, the final model accounted

TABLE 8.3 Hierarchical multiple regression analyses predicting general and professional well-being from family and professional situations – final models ($N=960$)

Entered	Predictors	General well-being			Professional well-being	
		Satisfaction with life	Self-rated health	Quality of life	Work stress	Job satisfaction
Step 1	Age	-.02	-.12*	.02	.08*	.00
	Nationality	.00	-.04	-.03	-.02	-.01
	Language	.07*	-.02	-.02	.19*	-.04
	Household income	.13*	.04	.16***	.06	.12***
Step 2	Single with children vs. single without children	.04	-.05	.09	.02	.08
	Single with children vs. couple without children	.05	-.11	.11*	-.00	-.01
	Single with children vs. couple with children	.12*	-.03	.05	-.10	.04
Step 3	Work rate (part-, full-time)	-.02	.05	-.04	.02	.00
	Number of jobs (one, more)	.01	-.01	-.00	-.04	.02
	Management position (no, yes)	.04	.03	-.03	.06	.03
	Job search (no, yes)	-.04	.04	.02	.08*	-.16***
	Job insecurity (no, yes)	-.08**	-.02	-.06	.07*	-.22***
	Difficulties in finding similar job (no, yes)	-.05	-.02	-.08*	.02	.01
	Perceived discrimination (no, yes)	-.03	-.10**	-.07*	.10**	-.12***
Step 4	Job strain	-.16***	-.10**	-.14***	.28***	-.29***
Step 5	Social support	.47***	.20***	.33***	-.10**	.13***
Step 6	Job strain × social support	-.03	-.01	-.03	.02	-.08**
Total R^2		.38	.09	.23	.17	.30

Notes

For each predictor variable the standardized β values of the final model are presented.

Control variables included age, nationality, language, and household income.

* p < .05. ** p < .01. *** p < .001

30 per cent of the total variance regarding job satisfaction $F(17, 889) = 24.03$, $p < .001$). More precisely, job satisfaction was positively predicted by household income, not seeking a new job, and social support and negatively predicted by job insecurity, perceived discrimination at work and job strain.

Regarding the moderation effect, a significant interaction effect was found only between job strain and social support in predicting job satisfaction. However, this effect was quite modest and indicated that the greater the job strain, the less likely the impact of social support. This implies that no amount of social support could overcome a certain high amount of job strain. Nevertheless, independent of job strain level, women in this sample who indicated having higher social support reported being more satisfied with their job. Finally, it is interesting to note that nationality, work rate, number of jobs, and management position were not important predictors for either general or professional well-being outcomes.

Discussion

Our results indicate that differences in perceived resources and stressors, as well as differences in both general and professional well-being exist as a function of women's personal and professional situations. First, concerning the effect of personal characteristics on job strain, family situation (e.g. marital status and children) showed no effect on job strain. This implies that researchers cannot make assumptions about women's perceived job strain based on their motherhood status. It could be that constraints related to family life can set more strict limits on work life, especially regarding time management. Or a conscious decision to maintain a distinct separation between worker and mother identities may be in play. Working women aim to be psychologically and emotionally accessible to their children when they are with them and, thus, strive to give them their full attention (Johnston & Swanson, 2006). Differences emerged in social support levels for women who do and do not have children. Single women reported lower levels of social support. This could be explained by the relevant and personal support that is provided by a partner.

Professional characteristics, notably holding a management position, corresponded with less strain. Though counterintuitive, it may be explained by the correspondence between job demands and job control in these positions. Consistent with Karasek's (1979) job demand-control framework, the balance between job demands and personal control outweighs the simple presence of job demands. Managers may be faced with higher demands but also have higher control in how they meet those demands.

Turning to the effects of personal and professional characteristics on well-being, we found consistent effects for job strain and social support across all general and professional well-being outcomes. Job strain contributed to reduced well-being, whereas social support contributed to higher levels of well-being. This underscored the importance of stressors and resources for well-being. Globally, job strain, a work-specific stressor, has larger effects on work specific outcomes, whereas social support is more important for general well-being. This may suggest that stressors and resources have the most potential to contribute to negative and positive outcomes within the same domain, respectively, and implies the necessity of having resources that match the stressors in a particular domain (de Jonge & Dormann, 2006). Correspondingly, effects of both work-specific (job strain) and general (social support) aspects on both professional and general outcomes suggest that there is an interaction between life domains and the potential for negative and positive spillover.

We also tested the possibility that social support may moderate the effect of job strain on well-being. This effect was seen only for job satisfaction, suggesting that social support may provide some buffer and reduce the effect of job strain on job satisfaction. However, at higher levels of job strain, the impact of perceived support on women's job satisfaction was less important, implying that when things are too stressful at work, perceived social support is no longer able to balance the effect of job strain on work-related satisfaction. To explain this – and the lack of significant moderating effects for other outcomes – culturally speaking, in Switzerland, one's job is mainly considered a private matter rather than a collective one (Hofstede, Hofstede, & Minkov, 2010). Therefore, women reporting high levels of job strain are likely to consider their social environments as powerless in helping them cope with the acute difficulties arising from the professional sphere. It could be that the resource (social support) did not have functional value in reducing the stressor (the imbalance between job demands and control). Other researchers also demonstrated that targeted types of support, given by specific people, are more effective for certain problems (e.g. Albino Gilbert & Rader, 2008; Ernst Kossek et al., 2011).

Finally, other predictors of well-being included seeking a new job, perceived difficulty in finding a similar job, job insecurity, and perceived discrimination at work. This suggests that other risk factors may be present that could threaten well-being and contribute to a situation of vulnerability. This may be especially dangerous when various risk factors or stressors accumulate (Spini et al., 2013). However, in this study, these effects tended to be small, and no clear patterns emerged.

Practical implications

On a practical level, although personal juggling and management of time and tasks can be one answer to maintaining well-being, social policy may also offer more systemic solutions. Johnston and Swanson (2007) called for cultural changes in which both workers and workplaces share family care responsibilities, such as the creation of and participation in flexible employment programs, community facilities, and support for caregiving. However, the development of childcare facilities in the workplace becomes more important.

Interestingly, developing childcare facilities is also likely to contribute to young women's career development. Girls in Switzerland overwhelmingly preferred more caregiving and teaching occupational domains, in which there are few apprenticeship positions (e.g. Falter & Wendelspiess Chávez Juárez, 2012). Increasing the number of childcare facilities, therefore, is likely to create job and training positions in these domains and to facilitate entry for Swiss girls in their preferred career choices.

Moreover, Ernst Kossek et al. (2011) suggested that workplaces could be more supportive in providing the *right type* of support to workers, such as training supervisors to recognize and appropriately respond to individuals expressing difficulty with work–family conflict demands. Workers who perceive greater work–family support from their supervisors will be more likely to report difficulties and seek flexibility in dealing with them, therefore, feeling in greater control over both domains and that they have resources for managing the conflicts (Ernst Kossek et al., 2011).

Limitations and future directions

This study was conducted on the first wave of a longitudinal data, providing a snapshot of the lives of the women sampled. It is possible that we found no differences in job strain because these women were already employed and already may have made job trajectory choices concomitant with their family constraints. Or they have learned how to manage the demands and obtain balance. Furthermore, regarding results related to work stress and job strain, it is important to consider their relatively low variance because it represents a ratio term. It will be interesting to see how this could evolve in future waves of data collection.

We chose to focus solely on variables related to women's vulnerability in mitigating work–life balance because it is often women placed in the dual role of childcare or housework *and* work for economic advantage to the family, more so than men (Eagly, 1987; Glick & Fiske, 1996). Due to partial percentages and social roles, women are often responsible for restructuring hours to accommodate family needs (Higgins et al., 2010). However, we didn't consider specific coping strategies or other resources women use to reconcile work and family, which could be an interesting qualitative follow up.

To conclude, even if working conditions are good in Switzerland overall, women in Switzerland are also tasked with the greatest part of family and household responsibilities, coinciding with whatever percentage of work time they hold. There is evidence that the second shift described by Hochschild and Machung (1989/2012) is in effect. Not surprisingly, women who seek and receive social support are happier with their jobs and with their lives. The types of resources available and sought by women and the people from whom these resources are offered can make a difference in how a particular vulnerability is addressed or overcome. For example, our data showed that beyond a certain point of job strain, social support is of little help, giving us reason to call into question the ultimate buffering effects of social support. Is there a cutoff point after which a high number of resources will not help? Does that cutoff depend on other factors as well, such as worker personality or other individual characteristics? These are questions that warrant further research.

Acknowledgement

This publication is part of the research work conducted at the Swiss National Centre of Competence in Research LIVES – Overcoming vulnerability: life course perspectives, which is financed by the Swiss National Science Foundation.

References

Albino Gilbert, L., & Rader, J. (2008). Work, family, and dual-earner couples: Implications for research and practice. In S. D. Brown & R. W. Lent (Eds.), *Handbook of Counseling Psychology* (4th ed., pp. 426–443). New York: Wiley.

Broadhead, W. E., Gehlbach, S. H., DeGruy, F. V., & Kaplan, B. H. (1988). The Duke-UNC Functional Social Support Questionnaire: Measurement of social support in family medicine patients. *Medical Care, 26*, 709–723. doi:10.1097/00005650-198807000-00006

Charles, K. K., & Stephens, M., Jr. (2004). Job displacement, disability, and divorce. *Journal of Labor Economics, 22*, 489–522. doi:10.3386/w8578

de Bruin, G. P., & Taylor, N. (2005). Development of the Sources of Work Stress Inventory. *South African Journal of Psychology, 35*, 748–765. doi:10.1177/008124630503500408.

de Jonge, J., & Dormann, C. (2006). Stressors, resources, and strains at work: A longitudinal test of the triple match principle. *Journal of Applied Psychology, 91*, 1359–1374. doi:10.1037/0021-9010.91.5.1359

de Witte, H. (2005). Job insecurity: Review of the international literature on definitions, prevalence, antecedents and consequences. *SA Journal of Industrial Psychology, 31*(4), 1–6. doi:10.4102/sajip.v31i4.200

del Bono, E., Weber, A., & Winter-Ebmer, R. (2012). Clash of career and family: Fertility decisions after job displacement. *Journal of the European Economic Association, 10*, 659–683. doi:10.1111/j.1542-4774.2012.01074.x

Diener, E., Emmons, R. A., Larsen, R. J., & Griffin, S. (1985). The Satisfaction with Life Scale. *Journal of Personality Assessment, 49*, 71–75. doi:10.1207/s15327752jpa4901_13

Eagly, A. H. (1987). *Sex Differences in Social Behavior: A social-role interpretation*. Hillsdale, NJ: Erlbaum.

Emslie, C., & Hunt, K. (2009). Live to work or work to live? A qualitative study of gender and work-life balance among men and women in mid-life. *Gender, Work & Organization, 16*, 151–172. doi:10.1111/j.1468-0432.2008.00434.x

Ernst Kossek, E., Pichler, S., Bodner, T., & Hammer, L. B. (2011). Workplace social support and work-family conflict: A meta-analysis clarifying the influence of general and work-family specific supervisor and organizational support. *Personnel Psychology, 64*, 289–313. doi:10.1111/J.1744-6570.2011.01211.X

Falter, J.-M. & Wendelspiess Chávez Juárez, F. (2012). Can gender traits explain job aspiration segregation? *Social Science Electronic Publishing, Inc.* Retrieved from http://www.educationeconomics.unige.ch/Recherches/Projet-Falter/Falterwendel_Gender_Study_revised2012.pdf

Forma, P. (2008). Work, family and intentions to withdraw from the workplace. *Journal of Social Welfare, 18*, 183–192. doi:10.1111/J.1468-2397.2008.00585.X

Glick, P., & Fiske, S. T. (1996). The Ambivalent Sexism Inventory: Differentiating hostile and benevolent sexism. *Journal of Personality and Social Psychology, 70*, 491–512. doi:10.1037/0022-3514.70.3.491

Graf, M., Pekruhl, U., Korn, K., Krieger, R., Mücke, A., & Zölch, M. (2007). Quatrième enquête européenne sur les conditions de travail en 2005: Résultats choisis du point de vue de la Suisse [Fourth European survey on working conditions 2005: Selected results from the point of view of Switzerland]. Bern, Switzerland: Secrétariat d'État à l'Économie.

Higgins, C. A., Duxbury, L. E., & Lyons, S. T. (2010). Coping with overload and stress: Men and women in dual-earner families. *Journal of Marriage and Family, 72*, 847–859. doi:10.1111/j.1741-3737.2010.00734.x

Hochschild, A., & Machung, A. (2012). *The "second shift": Working parents and the revolution at home.* New York: Penguin. (Original work published 1989).

Hofstede, G., Hofstede, G. J., & Minkov, M. (2010). *Cultures and Organizations: Software on the mind.* New York: McGraw-Hill.

Johnson, J. V., & Hall, E. M. (1988). Job strain, work place social support, and cardiovascular disease: A cross-sectional study of a random sample of the Swedish working population. *American Journal of Public Health, 78*, 1336–1342. doi:10.2105/AJPH.78.10.1336

Johnston, D. D., & Swanson, D. H. (2006). Constructing the "good mother": The experience of mothering ideologies by work status. *Sex Roles, 54*, 509–519. doi:10.1007/S11199-006-9021-3

Johnston, D. D., & Swanson, D. H. (2007). Cognitive acrobatics in the construction of worker-mother identity. *Sex Roles, 57*, 447–459. doi:10.1007/s11199-007-9267-4

Jones, F., & Fletcher, B. C. (1996). Taking work home: A study of daily fluctuations in work stressors, effects on moods and impacts on marital partners. *Journal of Occupational and Organizational Psychology, 69*, 89–106. doi:10.1111/j.2044-8325.1996.tb00602.x

Karasek, R. A., Jr. (1979). Job demands, job decision latitude, and mental strain: Implications for job redesign. *Administrative Science Quarterly, 24*, 285–308. doi:10.2307/2392498

Karasek, R. A., Jr., Brisson, C., Kawakami, N., & Amick, B. (1998). The Job Content Questionnaire (JCQ): An instrument for internationally comparative assessments of psychosocial job characteristics. *Journal of Occupational Health Psychology, 3*, 322–355. doi:10.1037/1076-8998.3.4.322

Levy, R., Gauthier, J.-A., & Widmer, E. (2007). Entre contraintes institutionnelle et domestique: Les parcours de vie masculins et féminins en Suisse [Between institutional and domestic constraints: Masculine and feminine life courses in Switzerland]. *Canadian Journal of Sociology/Cahiers Canadiens de Sociologie, 31*, 461–489. doi:10.1353/csj.2006.0070

Li, J., Yang, W., & Cho, S.-I. (2006). Gender differences in job strain, effort-reward imbalance, and health functioning among Chinese physicians. *Social Sciences and Medecine, 62*, 1066–1077. doi:10.1016/j.socscimed.2005.07.011

Lyons, E. (2002). Psychosocial factors related to job stress and women in management. *Work, 18*(1), 89–93.

Maggiori, C., Rossier, J., Krings, F., Johnston, C. S., & Massoudi, K. (in press). Career pathways and professional transitions: Preliminary results from the 1st wave of a 7-year longitudinal study. In M. Ernst-Staehli, D. Joye, M. Oris, & C. Roberts (Eds.), *Surveying vulnerabilities*. Dordrecht: Springer.

Massoudi, K. (2009). *Le Stress Professionnel: Une analyse des vulnérabilités individuelles et des facteurs de risque environnementaux* [Professional stress: Analysis of individual vulnerabilities and environmental risk factors]. Bern: Peter Lang.

Mesmer-Magnus, J., & Viswesvaran, C. (2009). The role of the coworker in reducing work-family conflict: A review and directions for future research. *Pratiques Psychologiques, 15*, 213–224. doi:10.1016/j.prps.2008.09.009

Sapin, M., Spini, D., & Widmer, E. (2007). *Les parcours de vie: De l'adolescence au grand âge* [Life trajectories: From adolescence to old age]. Lausanne: Presses Polytechniques et Universitaires Romandes.

Skevington, S. M., Lotfy, M., & O'Connell, K. A. (2004). The World Health Organization's WHOQOL-BREF quality of life assessment: Psychometric properties and results of the international field trial. A report from the WHOQOL group. *Quality of life Research, 13*, 299–310. doi:10.1023/B:Qure.0000018486.91360.00

Spini, D., Hanapi, D., Bernardi, L., Oris, M., & Bickel, J.-F. (2013). Vulnerability across the life course: A theoretical framework and research directions. *LIVES Working Papers*. Lausanne: LIVES Swiss National Centre of Competence in Research. doi:10.12682/lives.2296-1658.2013.27

Sultana, A. M. (2012). A study on stress and work family conflict among married women in their families. *Advances in Natural and Applied Sciences, 6*, 1319–1324.

Sverke, M., Hellgren, J., & Näswall, K. (2002). No security: A meta-analysis and review of job insecurity and its consequences. *Journal of Occupational Health Psychology, 7*, 242–264. doi:10.1037//1076-8998.7.3.242

Swiss Fedral Statistics Office. (2013). *On the Way to Gender Equality: Current situation and developments* (Publication No. 619-1300). Retrieved from http://www.bfs.admin.ch/bfs/portal/en/index/themen/20/22/publ.html?publicationID=5215

Tomlinson, J. (2008). Causes and consequences of the divergent working-time patterns of employed mothers in the UK and the US: Developing a comparative analysis. *Gender Issues, 25*, 246–266. doi:10.1007/s12147-008-9064-6

Widmer, E., Levy, R., Pollien, A., Hammer, R., & Gauthier, J.-A. (2003). Entre standardisation, individualisation et sexuation: Une analyse des trajectoires personnelles en Suisse [Between standardization, individualization, and gendering: An analysis of personal life courses in Switzerland]. *Schweizerische Zeitschrift für Soziologie, 29*, 35–67.

PART III

Gender-related prejudice

9

A MODEL OF GENDER PREJUDICE, POWER, AND DISCRIMINATION

How hierarchy-enhancing factors predominate over hierarchy-attenuating factors

Emmanuelle P. Kleinlogel and Joerg Dietz

Gender inequalities remain an issue in our society and particularly in the workplace (Morrison & von Glinow, 1990; Pratto, Sidanius, & Levin, 2006). For instance, whereas women represent almost half of the workforce, they occupy fewer than 5 per cent of executive manager positions in public listed companies (International Labour Organization, 2015). Several factors can explain this gender difference in top-level managerial positions such as career ambitions but also biases against women (Morrison & von Glinow, 1990).

In this chapter, we propose a model explaining why gender inequalities and particularly workplace discrimination against women is still present in our societies despite social norms and existing legislation on gender equality (Treviño & Nelson, 2003). To this purpose, we review research on discrimination through two different approaches, that is (a) prejudice through the justification-suppression model developed by Crandall and Eshleman (2003) and (b) power through the social dominance theory (Pratto, Sidanius, Stallworth, & Malle, 1994; Sidanius & Pratto, 1999). We then propose a model integrating these two approaches, namely the model of gender prejudice, power, and discrimination. The integration of these two approaches contributes to a better understanding of how discrimination against women is formed and maintained over time. Indeed, whereas the first approach helps to understand processes through which prejudice is expressed, the second helps to understand the sustainable dominance of men over women through a multi-level approach and a power and behaviour asymmetry.

The chapter is organized as follows. In the two first sections, we introduce the theoretical background related to the two approaches, namely the justification-suppression model (Crandall & Eshleman, 2003) and the social dominance theory (Sidanius & Pratto, 1999). We then present our model and explain how these approaches are complementary. Finally, before concluding we discuss the implications of our model.

Psychology of prejudice and discrimination

Definition of prejudice and discrimination

Prejudice can be defined as "a negative evaluation of a social group or a negative evaluation of an individual that is significantly based on the individual's group membership" (Crandall & Eshleman, 2003, p. 414; see also Brigham, 1971; Paluck & Green, 2009). A social group refers, for instance, to age, disability, gender, national origin, culture, race, ethnicity, sexual orientation, social class, and religion. In this chapter, we adopt the view of Crandall and Eshleman (2003) who presented prejudice as a motivational variable such that when individuals are confronted with a target of their prejudice, they are motivated to express it. However, if this motivation cannot be fulfilled, dissatisfaction might result. The behavioural expression of prejudice leads to discriminatory behaviour.

Discrimination can be defined as unfair treatment of the members of a group (e.g., social class and gender) due to their membership in this group (Dietz, Kleinlogel, & Chui, 2012). In the workplace context, discrimination occurs when employees are treated differently based on factors not related to their qualifications, such as their ethnicity or gender (Pratto et al., 2006; Treviño & Nelson, 2003). However, discrimination does not always occur through a simple expression of prejudice. Instead, it is most often the result of processes, which are a function of social and personal factors. These factors act as a motivational force in favour either of the suppression or the release of prejudice (Crandall & Eshleman, 2003; Pratto et al., 2006). These factors are presented in the next section.

The justification-suppression model of prejudice

Crandall and Eshleman (2003) proposed a model to explain how prejudice is expressed, namely the justification-suppression model (JSM) of the expression and experience of prejudice. The JSM finds its foundation in the two-factor theories of racial prejudice (e.g., Allport, 1954; Gaertner & Dovidio, 1986; Katz & Hass, 1988; Rogers & Prentice-Dunn, 1981). These theories state that individuals are confronted with two competing motivations, (a) prejudice and (b) the motivation to control it. Accordingly and through the JSM, Crandall and Eshleman proposed that individuals face motivational force attempting to either refrain or foster the expression of prejudice, namely suppression factors and justification factors. Whereas suppression factors restrain individuals' prejudice expression, justification factors allow individuals to release their prejudice without experiencing (or experiencing to a low extent) internal or external sanction (Crandall & Eshleman, 2003). Suppressors can take several forms such as social norms promoting tolerance, and personal values such as empathy and egalitarianism. Justifiers can be grouped into three categories; those stemming from individual differences (e.g., belief in a just world, Lerner, 1980; right-wing authoritarianism, Altemeyer, 1981), those that are situation-specific (e.g., situational ambiguity), and those stemming from intergroup processes (e.g., intergroup contact, Amir, 1976).

Through their model, Crandall and Eshleman (2003) proposed that at the first stage the expression of prejudice is prevented through suppression factors whereas at the second stage it is fostered by the presence of justification factors. They argued that the presence of suppression factors fosters individuals' motivation and need to seek justification factors, which then would allow individuals to express their prejudice. These processes imply that "prejudice itself is usually not directly expressed, but rather is modified and manipulated to meet social and personal goals" (Crandall & Eshleman, 2003, p. 416).

The JSM contributes to the literature on discrimination by explaining how prejudice can still be expressed through motivational forces despite the presence of counterbalancing forces (i.e., suppression factors). However, this model does not provide theoretical explanations for why discrimination is maintained over time. In the next sections, we briefly review social dominance theory (Sidanius & Pratto, 1999) and explain how this theory is complementary to the model developed by Crandall and Eshleman (2003). We then present the model of gender prejudice, power, and discrimination in which we integrate social dominance theory in the JSM and apply it to discrimination against women.

Social dominance theory

Social dominance theory (SDT) was developed to explain how discrimination through group-based inequalities is formed and maintained by focusing on the notion of power (Sidanius, Pratto, van Laar, & Levin, 2004; Pratto et al., 2006). Social dominance can be defined as the desire for individuals to live in a hierarchically group-based structured society (Pratto et al., 1994). According to this theory, each society should be organized based on three distinct systems to be able to reach a stable economic level, namely an age system, a gender system, and an arbitrary-set system (i.e., a system in which groups are organized on an arbitrary basis such as nationality, origin, and religion). In each of these systems, members of dominant groups have disproportionate social power over the members of subordinate groups (O'Brien & Dietz, 2011; Pratto et al., 2006). Social power refers to "the ability to impose one's will on others, despite resistance" as opposed to social status which refers to "the amount of prestige one possesses along some evaluative dimension" (Sidanius et al., 2004, p. 865). For instance, adults, men, and locals have more social power than children, women, and immigrants. As a consequence, this trimorphic structure leads to discrimination through unfair inequalities between members of dominant groups and subordinate groups.

In this approach, discrimination is conceptualized as a means of forming and maintaining a group-based social hierarchy (Sidanius et al., 2004) and prejudice is conceptualized as partly motivated by social dominance in terms of individuals' desire to acquire power for their own group at the detriment of the other groups (McDonald, Navarette, & Sidanius, 2011). Central to SDT is the notion of legitimizing myths. Legitimizing myths are "attitudes, values, beliefs, stereotypes, and ideologies that provide moral and intellectual justification for the social practices that distribute social value within the social system" (Sidanius & Pratto, 1999, p. 45). The theory distinguishes between two types of legitimizing myths; those enhancing group-based inequalities and those attenuating group-based inequalities, namely Hierarchy-Enhancing (HE) legitimizing myths and Hierarchy-Attenuating (HA) legitimizing myths. HE legitimizing myths provide a rational explanation for group-based inequalities and justify the practices that maintain them (e.g., stereotypes, just world beliefs) whereas HA legitimizing myths tend to reduce group dominance by "delegitimizing inequality or the practices that sustain it, or by suggesting values that contradict hierarchy" (e.g., egalitarian values and democratic political doctrine, Sidanius & Pratto, 1999, p. 104; see also Pratto et al., 2006).

In addition to legitimizing myths, at the upper level in societies SDT distinguishes between HE and HA institutions. HE institutions are institutions which "promote and sustain inequality by allocating disproportionately more positive social value or less negative social value to dominant groups than to subordinate groups" whereas HA institutions are institutions which "disproportionately aid members of subordinate social groups (e.g., the poor, ethnic and religious minorities) and attempt to open access to resources otherwise restricted to dominants (e.g., public services)" (Pratto et al., 2006, pp. 276–277).

A model of gender prejudice, power, and discrimination

In our research, we draw on the JSM and extend it by integrating SDT. Figure 9.1 is a graphical depiction of our model of gender prejudice, power, and discrimination. Integrating SDT in the JSM allows for a more complete understanding of how gender inequalities and particularly workplace discrimination is formed and maintained over time for two main reasons. First, the JSM and SDT share some common aspects. Both views argue for discrimination as a function of prejudice and other motivational forces conceptualized as justification and suppression factors through the JSM and as HE and HA legitimizing myths through SDT. However, SDT is complementary to the JSM through its multi-level approach by helping to understand how discrimination is formed and maintained at, and across, different levels of the society.

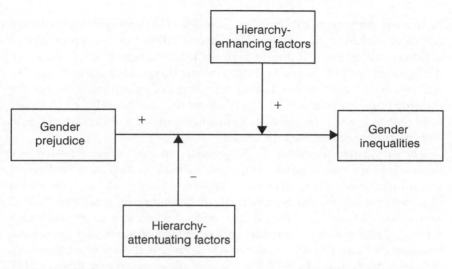

FIGURE 9.1 The model of gender prejudice, power, and discrimination

Second, whereas the JSM and SDT share some common aspects, they contribute uniquely to understanding processes of discrimination and its maintenance. On one hand, as described previously, the JSM contributes to a better understanding of the process through which prejudice is expressed. On the other hand, SDT contributes to the understanding of discrimination through power and behavioural asymmetry. In the following sections, we first introduce our model and then present the uniqueness of SDT in more detail and how it helps to understand gender-based inequalities through our model.

Presentation of the model

The model we propose is an adaptation of the JSM developed by Crandall and Eshleman (2003) for discrimination against women, and in which we integrate elements of SDT (Sidanius & Pratto, 1999) (see Figure 9.1). Our work implies three main changes in the initial JSM. First, we focus on prejudice related to gender and particularly prejudice targeting women. Second, we focus on gender inequalities as an outcome of gender prejudice. Finally, we rename suppression and justification factors as HA and HE factors. This label change aims at integrating the notion of power and behavioural asymmetry unique to SDT through the term *hierarchy*.

Our model is thus composed of four elements, namely gender prejudice, gender inequalities, HA and HE factors. However, contrary to Crandall and Eshleman (2003) who drew a figure to illustrate how these four elements work together, our model is a depiction of a structural equation model (see Figure 9.1). First, gender prejudice is represented as a predictor of gender inequalities. Second, HA and HE factors are represented as moderators in the relationship between gender prejudice and gender inequalities. HA factors are conceptualized as factors weakening this relationship whereas HE factors are conceptualized as factors strengthening it. In line with the JSM, we represent HE factors on the right side of HA factors to emphasize the theoretical argument that HE factors occur after HA factors. Indeed, according to Crandall and Eshleman the presence of prejudice and HA factors calls for the need to seek for HE factors to be able to express the prejudice individuals harbour and thus to engage in discriminatory behaviour against women.

The integration of SDT in our model has two implications. These implications are related to the uniqueness of SDT in helping to understand group-based inequalities, namely its multi-level approach, and its notion of power and behavioural asymmetry. First, it implies adopting a multi-level approach of HA and HE factors in our model. Second, this integration adds a theoretical explanation to the model on how gender inequalities are formed and sustained over time through a consensual acceptance of these gender inequalities by both gender groups. In the following sections, we present elements of SDT that we integrate in our model and explain in more detail the implications of this integration on our understanding of discrimination against women.

Multi-level approach

Contrary to the JSM, SDT has a multi-level approach of factors that either attenuate or enhance discrimination and argues for the coordination of these factors across the different levels contributing to forming and maintaining group-based hierarchy (Pratto et al., 2006). SDT distinguishes between three distinct levels, the individual level, the group level, and the institutional level, respectively. At the individual level, HA and HE factors are composed of individual differences reducing (e.g., egalitarian values) or providing the rationale for the expression of prejudice (e.g., stereotypes). At the group level, they are mainly composed of processes justifying prejudice (e.g., stereotypes threat). Finally, at the institutional level HA and HE factors are composed of institutions acting either in favour of equality of treatment between groups (e.g., welfare organizations) or in favour of group-based inequalities (e.g., criminal justice systems).

We propose to add this multi-level approach to our model. To this purpose, we classify HA and HE factors into the three levels defined by SDT. Table 9.1 reports this classification in which we combine HA and HE factors listed by Crandall and Eshleman (2003) and by Pratto et al. (2006) (see for a detailed description of these factors, Crandall & Eshleman, 2003; Pratto et al., 2006). As displayed by Table 9.1, some factors are common to the two categories of HA and HE factors such as religious organizations and political value systems at the institutional level because these factors can either weaken or foster the expression of gender prejudice depending on their content. For instance, some religious organizations can promote tolerance whereas others can disapprove

TABLE 9.1 Classification of hierarchy-attenuating factors and hierarchy-enhancing factors at the individual, group, and institutional levels

Level	Hierarchy-attenuating factors	Hierarchy-enhancing factors
Institutional	• Human rights, civil rights, and civil liberties groups • Welfare organizations • Religious organizations • Social norms • Political value systems	• Profit-maximizing financial institutions • Transnational corporations • Internal security organizations • Criminal justice systems • Religious organizations • Social norms • Political value systems
Group	• Intergroup contact	• Intergroup contact • Perceived threat • Justification of group rights • Intergroup anxiety
Individual	• Empathy • Moral and humanitarian values • Cognitive abilities • Political orientation	• Social status beliefs • Political orientation • Attributional processes • Covering processes • Stereotypes • Group-based beliefs and values

and thus sanction certain types of behaviours and people, such as single mothers (Crandall & Eshleman, 2003; Jackson & Esses, 1997). At the individual level, social status beliefs and values include beliefs supporting the status quo and social hierarchy, such as Protestant work ethic (Katz & Hass, 1988), social dominance orientation (Pratto et al., 1994), and sexism (Glick & Fiske, 1996). Attributional and covering processes refer to factors allowing individuals to blame the targets of prejudice for their fate (e.g., attributional scapegoating) or to justify the expression of their prejudice through seemingly legitimate explanations (e.g., situational ambiguity) (see Crandall & Eshleman, 2003). Apart from its multi-level approach, the uniqueness of SDT in explaining how discrimination is formed and maintained resides in its notion of power and behavioural asymmetry.

Power asymmetry

SDT argues for an asymmetry in power between HE and HA institutions, in which HA institutions are disadvantaged leading to the maintenance of group-based hierarchy (Pratto et al., 2006). According to SDT, HE institutions have more power than HA institutions because whereas the former usually allocate both positive social value to dominant groups and negative social value to subordinate groups, the latter tend to only allocate positive value to subordinate groups. As a result, the net effect of these two types of institutions favours dominant groups over subordinate groups which then contribute to maintain group-based inequalities.

For instance, due to their gender role women are penalized when they take a maternity leave, that is, women applicants are less likely to be hired than men applicants because they have less professional experience (O'Brien & Dietz, 2011; Treviño & Nelson, 2003). This institutional gender discrimination provides both a negative social value to women and a positive social value to men who have increased chances of being hired. Regarding HA institutions such as organizations helping women to find a job after a maternity leave, they allocate only a positive social value to women. As a consequence, men keep their advantage over women. The maintenance of these gender inequalities is also due to the power asymmetry between the two gender groups. Indeed, it is easier for men, as dominant group members and occupying top-level positions in society, to protect their social dominance by maintaining gender inequalities than for women, as subordinate group members, to change their well-accepted gender role. For instance, it is easy for a male human resources manager to favour members of his gender group by hiring only male applicants into managerial positions as compared to female applicants seeking access to such positions.

Behavioural asymmetry

Apart from the power asymmetry, SDT argues for a behavioural asymmetry between members of different groups such that dominant group members and subordinate group members collaborate in an effort to maintain a group-based hierarchy. SDT distinguishes between three different types of behavioural asymmetry, namely the asymmetrical ingroup bias, self-debilitating behaviours among subordinates, and ideological asymmetry. First, through the asymmetrical ingroup bias, the theory states that ingroup favouritism differs between members of distinct groups such that in a stable group-based system individuals tend to favour dominant groups by endorsing HE legitimizing myths and by accepting group-based hierarchy over HA legitimizing myths independently of their group membership. As a result, dominant groups engage in ingroup favouritism whereas subordinate groups do so to a lesser extent or contribute to their oppression by engaging in outgroup favouritism (O'Brien & Dietz, 2011; Pratto et al., 2006; Sidanius & Pratto, 1999; Sidanius et al., 2004).

Second, self-debilitating behaviours refer to self-destructive and self-damaging behaviours (e.g., stereotype threat leading women to poorly perform in male-typed tasks, Spencer, Steel, & Quinn, 1999) perpetuated by members of subordinate groups (O'Brien & Dietz, 2011; Pratto et al., 2006; Sidanius & Pratto, 1999; Sidanius et al., 2004). Self-debilitation is the result of self-fulfilling prophecies among subordinate group members stemming from HE legitimizing myths. Finally, the notion of ideological asymmetry refers to the greater compatibility of HE legitimizing myths with dominant group members than with subordinate group members, thus favouring the dominance of the former over the latter (Pratto et al., 2006). For instance, a successful leader tends to be perceived as a person with agentic attributes such as competitive and ambitious (Eagly & Karau, 2002). This view contributes to the underrepresentation of women in leadership positions given that women tend to be perceived as having less agentic attributes than men and more communal attributes such as helpful and sensitive.

This asymmetry in behaviour between members of different groups provides additional explanations for gender discrimination by arguing (a) for a consensual preference for the dominant group members, men, and (b) for a consensual acceptance of gender-based hierarchy. As a result, both men and women collaborate to achieve and maintain gender inequalities thus rendering HA factors powerless. As an example, legislations on gender equality are created to reduce gender discrimination and particularly to reduce the treatment difference between men and women in organizations (Treviño & Nelson, 2003). Despite these legislations, most top-management positions are occupied by men (International Labour Organization, 2015). One of the HE legitimizing myths providing the rationale for this gender segregation is the gender role stereotype in which men are perceived as having "breadwinner and higher status roles" whereas women are perceived as having "homemaker and lower status roles" (Eagly & Karau, 2002, p. 574). Men are thus favoured to occupy managerial and particularly leadership positions as opposed to women who are favoured for jobs such as child care. This myth tends to be endorsed by both men and women and has become the norm (Dennerlein, Kleinlogel, Dietz, & Gabarrot, 2013; Eagly, 1987; Eagly & Karau, 2002).

Maintenance of gender inequalities through a self-reinforcing spiral

The integration of SDT in the JSM allows for a better understanding of gender inequalities and its maintenance for two reasons. First, through a multi-level approach it allows for a more complete picture of attenuating and enhancing factors of gender inequalities by including the institutional level, which was missing in the JSM. Second, the multi-level approach allows an understanding of the maintenance of gender inequalities by connecting factors at different levels. Indeed and according to SDT, factors at the institutional level, group level, and individual level contribute interactively to the maintenance of gender inequalities forming a self-reinforcing spiral. For instance, at the individual level gender stereotypes contribute to the expression of prejudice, but also contribute to discriminatory group-level processes, such as stereotype threat, and institution-level discrimination, such as female under-representation in top-level positions. At the same time, at the institutional level this gender segregation reinforces stereotypes at the individual level as well as at the group level through self-fulfilling prophecies. As a result, gender inequalities are maintained by the interaction of HE factors at different levels in society. However, this self-reinforcing spiral would not exist without the notion of power and behavioural asymmetry.

Indeed, the presence of HA factors should counteract the effect of HE factors leading to a zero-sum game. However, we observe a disproportionate allocation of power to HE factors as compared to HA factors leading HA factors to be powerless when confronted with HE factors. In addition, this effect is strengthened by a power difference and a behavioural asymmetry between groups. The disproportionate allocation of power to dominant group members (i.e., men) makes subordinate group members (i.e., women) defenceless when faced with inequalities and the behavioural asymmetry acts in support of these inequalities through which both groups favour the dominant group. As a consequence, HE factors at each level of society tend to be stable which then allow the spiral to be continuously self-reinforced and gender inequalities to remain over time.

Discussion

In this chapter, we propose a model explaining how discrimination against women is achieved and maintained over time, namely the model of gender prejudice, power, and discrimination. We draw on two complementary approaches, namely prejudice and power. First, we draw on the work by Crandall and Eshleman (2003) and particularly on the justification-suppression model of the expression and experience of prejudice to explain how gender prejudice is expressed leading to gender inequalities through discrimination against women. Second, we draw on social dominance theory to explain how these gender inequalities are maintained over time (Sidanius & Pratto, 1999). Our model is thus an adaptation to discrimination against women of the justification-suppression model integrating elements of social dominance theory (i.e., its multi-level approach and its notion of power and behavioural asymmetry).

Theoretical contributions

The integration of these two approaches theoretically contributes to a better understanding of gender inequalities by providing a more complete picture of how discrimination against women is formed and maintained. These two approaches of discrimination share common aspects because they both argue for a "win-lose game" between factors enhancing and attenuating group-based inequalities. However, the arguments of these two approaches are unique because they focus on two distinct explanations, the powerful effect of prejudice, and power and behavioural asymmetry, respectively. On one hand, through their model Crandall and Eshleman (2003) argue that individuals are motivated to express their prejudice while at the same time, they are also motivated to refrain from doing so due to situational and personal factors (e.g., political value systems, empathetic feeling). These two motivations are conflicting, which leads to "ambivalent emotions, behavioural instability, and cognitive inconsistency" among individuals (Crandall & Eshleman, 2003, p. 415).

However, whereas situational and personal factors prevent prejudice expression, they also create the need for individuals to seek justifiers. As a result, the presence of justification factors leads individuals to express their prejudice and thus to engage in discriminatory behaviour against women. On the other hand, the social dominance theory argues for a power and behavioural asymmetry in which both members of dominant (i.e., men) and subordinate (i.e., women) groups contribute to the maintenance of gender inequalities through gender-based hierarchy acceptance (Sidanius & Pratto, 1999). Through its multi-level approach, this theory also argues that this power and behavioural asymmetry is strengthened by the coordination of hierarchy-enhancing factors across the different levels of society (i.e., individual, group, and institutional level).

Practical implementations

Our model allows reflection on how gender inequalities can be reduced. According to our model, gender inequalities are a function of gender prejudice, HA factors, and HE factors. We propose to focus on the processes by which prejudice is expressed to discover potential interventions to reduce gender inequalities. Particularly, we focus on the interactive effects of HE factors at different levels in society. Potential interventions would be to weaken the self-reinforcing spiral by breaking the effect of one of its components. Whereas it seems difficult to act at the individual and group levels in which processes are mostly influenced by prejudice, we suggest a top-down approach by acting at the institutional level.

Potential interventions would include introducing HA factors within HE institutions such as new legislation targeting institutional selection processes. As a concrete example, legislation introducing gender quotas within firms and reflecting the actual population might be one possible way to remedy the situation. For instance, if women represent 40 per cent of the top-qualified workforce, firm top-management board composition should reflect this percentage. In the short term, such intervention would allow allocation of both a positive social value to women by favouring the employment of female applicants in top-level positions and a negative social value to men by hiring fewer male applicants in these positions. In the long term, this intervention would have an effect on HE factors at the individual and group levels by, for instance, changing gender role stereotypes towards a less biased view of gender role in societies.

Future research

To conclude, we suggest that future research should use our model to empirically investigate the conflicting effect of gender prejudice, hierarchy-attenuating, and hierarchy-enhancing factors on individuals' propensity to engage in discriminatory behaviour against women. For instance, it would be interesting to study the effect of prejudice, hierarchy-attenuating factors, and hierarchy-enhancing factors on employment discrimination against women. As a concrete example, one might test the interactive effect of gender prejudice, organizational norms promoting gender equality treatment, and situational ambiguity on individuals' propensity to hire female applicants for top-level positions.

We expect prejudiced individuals to be less likely to hire female applicants for top-level positions in cases of situational ambiguity (e.g., male and female applicants equally qualified for the positions) than in the absence of situational ambiguity (e.g., female applicants more qualified than male applicants). We also expect gender equality norms to moderate the relationship between prejudice, situational ambiguity, and individuals' employment decisions. For instance, we expect that when there is no situational ambiguity prejudiced individuals are less likely to hire female applicants for top-level positions in absence of equality treatment norms than in presence of such norms. Such empirical evidence would allow for a better understanding of processes leading to discrimination against women and thus maintaining gender inequalities, which then would ultimately allow reflection on how to counteract hierarchy-enhancing factors.

References

Allport, G. H. (1954). *The nature of prejudice*. Cambridge, MA: Addison-Wesley.

Altemeyer, R. (1981). *Right-wing authoritarianism*. Winnipeg: University of Manitoba Press.

Amir, Y. (1976). The role of intergroup contact in change of prejudice and ethnic relations. In P. A. Katz (Ed.), *Towards the elimination of racism* (pp. 245–308). New York: Pergamon.

Brigham, J. C. (1971). Ethnic stereotypes. *Psychological Bulletin, 76*, 15–38. doi: 10.1037/h0031446

Crandall, C. S., & Eshleman, A. (2003). A justification-suppression model of the expression and experience of prejudice. *Psychological Bulletin, 129*, 414–446. doi: 10.1037/0033-2909.129.3.414

Dennerlein, T., Kleinlogel, E. P., Dietz, J., & Gabarrot, F. (2013, April). *Gender ingroup prototypicality and manager prototypes*. Paper presented at the 28th Annual Conference of the Society for Industrial and Organizational Psychology, Houston, Texas, USA.

Dietz, J., Kleinlogel, E. P., & Chui, C. W. S. (2012). Research on intergroup conflict: Implications for diversity management. In G. K. Stahl, I. Björkman, & S. Morris (Ed.), *Handbook of research in international human resource management* (pp. 253–270). Cheltenham: Edward Elgar Publications.

Eagly, A. H. (1987). *Sex differences in social behavior: A social-role interpretation*. Hillsdale, NJ: Erlbaum.

Eagly, A. H., & Karau, S. J. (2002). Role congruity theory of prejudice toward female leaders. *Psychological Review, 109*, 573–598. doi: 10.1037//0033-295X.109.3.573

Gaertner, S. L., & Dovidio, J. F. (1986). The aversive form of racism. In J. F. Dovidio & S. L. Gaertner (Eds.), *Prejudice, discrimination, and racism* (pp. 61–89). New York: Academic Press.

Glick, P., & Fiske, S. T. (1996). The Ambivalent Sexism Inventory: Differentiating hostile and benevolent sexism. *Journal of Personality and Social Psychology, 70,* 491–512. doi: 10.1037/0022-3514.70.3.491

International Labour Organization (2015). *Women in business and management: Gaining momentum.* Retrieved from http://www.ilo.org/global/publications/ilo-bookstore/order-online/books/WCMS_316450/lang--ja/index.htm

Jackson, L. M., & Esses, V. M. (1997). Of scripture and ascription: The relation between religious fundamentalism and intergroup helping. *Personality and Social Psychology Bulletin, 23,* 893–906. doi: 10.1177/0146167297238009

Katz, I., & Hass, R. G. (1988). Racial ambivalence and American value conflict: Correlational and priming studies of dual cognitive structures. *Journal of Personality and Social Psychology, 55,* 893–905. doi: 10.1037/0022-3514.55.6.893

Lerner, M. J. (1980). *Belief in a just world: A fundamental delusion.* New York: Plenum Press.

McDonald, M. M., Navarette, C. D., & Sidanius, J. (2011). Developing a theory of gendered prejudice: An evolutionary and social dominance perspective. In R. M. Kramer, G. J. Leonardelli, & R. W. Livingston (Ed.), *Social cognition, social identity, and intergroup relations: A festschrift in honor of Marilynn B. Brewer* (pp. 189–220). London: Psychology Press.

Morrison, A. M., & von Glinow, M. A. (1990). Women and minorities in management. *American Psychologist, 45,* 200–208. doi: 10.1037/0003-066X.45.2.200

O'Brien, J., & Dietz, J. (2011). Maintaining but also changing hierarchies: What social dominance theory has to say. In J. L. Pearce (Ed.), *Status in management and organizations* (pp. 55–84). Cambridge: Cambridge University Press.

Paluck, E. L., & Green, D. P. (2009). Prejudices reduction: What works? A review and assessment of research and practice. *Annual Review of Psychology, 60,* 339–367. doi: 10.1146/annurev.psych.60.110707.163607

Pratto, F., Sidanius, J., & Levin, S. (2006). Social dominance theory and the dynamics of intergroup relations: Taking stock and looking forward. *European Review of Social Psychology, 17,* 271–320.doi: 10.1080/10463280601055772

Pratto, F., Sidanius, J., Stallworth, L. M., & Malle, B. F. (1994). Social dominance orientation: A personality variable predicting social and political attitudes. *Journal of Personality and Social Psychology, 67,* 741–763. doi: 10.1037/0022-3514.67.4.741

Rogers, R. W., & Prentice-Dunn, S. (1981). Deindividuation and anger-mediated interracial aggression: Unmasking regressive racism. *Journal of Personality and Social Psychology, 41,* 63–73. doi: 10.1037/0022-3514.41.1.63

Sidanius, J., & Pratto, F. (1999). *Social dominance: An intergroup theory of social hierarchy and oppression.* New York: Cambridge University Press.

Sidanius, J., Pratto, F., van Laar, C., & Levin, S. (2004). Social dominance theory: Its agenda and method. *Political Psychology, 25,* 845–880. doi: 10.1111/j.1467-9221.2004.00401.x

Spencer, S. J., Steele, C. M., & Quinn, D. M. (1999). Stereotype threat and women's math performance. *Journal of Experimental Social Psychology, 35,* 4–28. doi: 10.1006/jesp.1998.1373

Treviño, L. K., & Nelson, K. A. (2003). *Managing business ethics: Straight talk about how to do it right* (3rd Ed.). New York: Wiley.

10

WOMEN'S ENDORSEMENT OF SEXIST BELIEFS DIRECTED TOWARDS THE SELF AND TOWARDS WOMEN IN GENERAL

Regula Zimmermann and Pascal M. Gygax

Introduction

Even though some nations have progressed enormously with regard to gender equality there is strong evidence that virtually no society has reached a state of true equality between men and women (Hausmann, Tyson, Bekhouche, & Zahidi, 2011). In Switzerland, where the present research was conducted, women earn on average less than men for equal work and hold lower professional positions (Swiss Federal Statistical Office, 2008). More generally, labour is still statistically gender segregated, reinforcing the wage gap between men and women (Strub, Gerfin, & Buetikofer, 2008). Beside these statistical indications of segregation, there is increasing empirical evidence for multiple manifestations of sexism and sexist attitudes, in turn negatively affecting women's psychological well-being and identity development (e.g. Matteson & Moradi, 2005; Swim, Hyers, Cohen, & Ferguson, 2001).

Though sexism is undeniably negatively affecting a substantial proportion of women and virtually all women report that they have been targets of sexist discrimination (Klonoff & Landrine, 1995; Matteson & Moradi, 2005 for US data), some women have been shown to endorse sexist beliefs directed towards their own gender (e.g. Glick et. al., 2000; Sarrasin, Gabriel, & Gygax, 2012, for Swiss-French and Swiss-German samples). In light of the continuous struggle for the implementation of gender equal policies (Hausmann et al., 2011), the endorsement of sexist beliefs by women can be considered as problematic, as it undeniably contributes to the maintenance of gender inequalities (e.g. Brandt, 2011).

Research on these issues, yet sparse, has focused either on the internalization (i.e. accepting social norms and values as one's own) of sexism to explain the hostility of women towards women (Cowan & Ullman, 2006), or on a combination of internalization and subtyping (i.e. the tendency to divide a group into different categories) to account for women's endorsement of sexist beliefs (Becker, 2010). In the present paper, we suggest that the tendency that some socially shared norms are interpreted as inevitable may complement these accounts for women's endorsement of sexist beliefs.

Ambivalent sexism

Any explanation for the hostility of women towards women, though, has to take into account that sexism is an ambivalent prejudice (Glick & Fiske, 1996). The actual concept of ambivalent sexism was developed by Glick and Fiske (1996), who defined overt negative attitudes as hostile sexism (HS) yet argued that sexism could also consist of subjectively positive attitudes towards women. Those positive attitudes mainly refer to those that assume women to be "morally more sensible", "men as protectors of women" and/or "women as incomplete without men" and were defined under the umbrella of benevolent sexism (BS). Whereas individuals seldom fail to recognize hostile sexism as discriminatory, benevolent sexism, due to its subjectively positive tone, is often not recognized as sexism (Barreto & Ellemers, 2005). Although BS appears as subjectively positive, it nonetheless undermines women's participation in collective action fighting gender inequalities or reduces their cognitive performances (Becker & Wright, 2011; Dardenne, Dumont, & Bollier, 2007). According to Glick and Fiske (1996), HS and BS have the same underlying components, namely, paternalism, gender differentiation and heterosexuality. Based on this concept, the authors developed the ambivalent sexism inventory (ASI), a self-report measure to assess sexist attitudes, the very measure used in this paper, focused on women's endorsement of sexist beliefs.

Internalization and subtyping

As mentioned above, previous research analysing reasons for women's endorsement of sexist beliefs focused on the role of *internalization* and *subtyping* (Becker, 2010; Cowan & Ullman, 2006). Cowan and Ullman (2006), for example, explained women's hostility towards women in terms of *internalization* and *social projection*. Internalization is a process which occurs when a person accepts social norms and values as their own (Kelman, 1958). They might then project these norms and values onto others, assuming that they are similar to them. Such a so-called social projection most often allows a person to quickly and effortlessly evaluate others' behaviour (Krueger, 2007). Combined with a tendency to stereotype, an internalized negative self-view (i.e. low self-esteem, pessimism and low perceived control) may result in some women's hostility towards women (Cowan & Ullman, 2006). Note that in their study, Cowan and Ullman (2006), measuring hostility with the hostile Sexism Scale from Glick and Fiske (1996), found a higher level of sexism in their participants than in other studies (e.g. Glick et al., 2000).

In two different studies, Becker (2010), using the Ambivalent Sexism Inventory (ASI) (Glick & Fiske, 1996), tried to explain women's agreement with sexist statements not only in terms of internalization, but also in terms of subtyping. Following previous literature, Becker (2010) was most interested in three types of prevalent subtypes of women: traditional women (e.g. housewives), non-traditional women (e.g. career women), and a sexual subtype (e.g. temptresses; Becker, 2010; Glick, Diebold, Bailey-Werner, & Zhu, 1997). Glick et al. (1997) found that men's hostile sexism predicted a negative evaluation of non-traditional subtypes, yet benevolent sexism was positively correlated to the evaluation of traditional subtypes. Female participants showed a similar, but somehow attenuated pattern for hostile sexism.

Taking these results into account, Becker (2010), in her first study, examined the influence of subtyping as well as internalization on women's agreement with sexist statements. Female participants filled in both the hostile and benevolent sexism scales, and after completing each item of the scales, they were asked if they had thought of a specific subtype when answering, and if they did, which subtype. Participants were given several possibilities to choose from: "women in general", "career women", "feminists", "housewives", "temptresses", or were asked to write down other subtypes. Participants were also asked, for each item, whether they considered the statement as an accurate description of themselves (i.e. internalization). The results revealed that women thought mostly of "women in general" when answering (in 66.5 per cent when answering the HS scale, in 84 per cent when answering the BS scale). However, when they thought of "feminists" or "career women", hostile sexist beliefs were more likely to be endorsed, and when they had "housewives" in mind benevolent sexist beliefs were more likely to be endorsed. Internalization also had an influence on the way participants responded. The more they considered sexist statements as an accurate description of themselves, the more likely they were to endorse them. Although this was true for hostile as well as for benevolent sexism, benevolent sexist statements were generally more internalized.

In the second study, Becker (2010) focused more closely on the issue of subtyping. She modified the German version of the ASI (Eckes & Six-Materna, 1999) to create three versions focused specifically on one of three subtypes ("feminists", "career women", "housewives") and one focused on the self (i.e. presenting all statements with the pronoun "I"). Each participant completed only one of the four possible versions. The results revealed that hostile sexism scores were significantly higher when the statements were directed towards "feminists" or "career women" than towards "housewives", and were in turn numerically higher than when they were directed towards the self. However, benevolent sexism scores were higher when directed towards the self than when directed towards "career women", "feminists" or "housewives". Becker (2010) concluded that when women endorsed hostile sexist beliefs, the beliefs were not really directed towards their gender ingroup but rather towards women who may not match their traditional role conception (i.e. "norm-deviant women").

Becker (2010) explained the observed subtyping as grounded in what Jost and Banaji (1994) or Jost and Kay (2005) defined as *system justification*. System justification is defined as the "process by which existing social arrangements are legitimized, even at the expense of personal and group interest" (Jost & Banaji, 1994, p. 2) and is based on empirical evidence showing that members of low status groups sometimes support an existing societal status quo, even to their own disadvantage. For example, financially disadvantaged people may at times contest financial redistribution from which they would benefit (Kluegel & Smith, 1986).

Consequently, Becker (2010) argued that her participants stereotyped sub-groups of women and directed their sexist attitudes towards the norm-deviant subtypes (e.g. career women), therefore maintaining gender stereotypes, consequently power differences between women and men, as imposed by the system. Although this is a fair interpretation, we argue that system justification goes further than subtyping: it predicts that members of disadvantaged groups see the world through the dominant cultural lens and, therefore, ascribe to others' traits that are consonant with their social position (Jost & Banaji, 1994). This means that under a system justifying perspective, women would adopt the dominant ideology in order to have a positive image not only of themselves (ego justification) and their ingroup (ingroup justification), but also of the social system in which they live (Jost & Hunyady, 2003).

Current study

Based on this hypothesis we tested whether women not only agree with sexism when it is internalized or when it is directed towards norm-deviant subtypes, but also when it is directed towards *women* in general. As Becker (2010) only compared sexism directed towards the self and sexism directed towards female subtypes, one cannot draw definitive conclusions as to whether the same effect would occur when comparing sexism (1) directed towards the self to (2) that directed towards women in general. In essence, one could argue that the condition "women" was lacking for Becker (2010).

In this paper, we put this idea to the test. We used Becker's (2010) version of the ASI with the personal pronoun condition ("I") measuring the internalization of the statement and compared it to the standard "women" condition (German version of the ASI, Eckes & Six-Materna, 1999). To ensure the most direct comparison and to avoid any cohort effects, we also decided to run the experiment with version as a repeated measure, with each participant completing both questionnaires (completions separated by at least 7 days, as explained in the Procedure section below).

Method

Participants

Twenty-five female psychology students from the University of Fribourg (Switzerland) took part in this study and received course credits in return. One participant had to be excluded, as she did not complete the questionnaire. Sixteen participants were native Swiss German speakers, eight stated that their first language was standard German, twenty-two participants self-identified as heterosexual, two as bisexual. Their age ranged from 19 to 24 years ($M = 21.2$, $SD = 1.5$).

Measure

Becker's (2010) slightly adapted version of the German translation of the Ambivalent Sexism Inventory (Eckes & Six-Materna, 1999) was used. The scale consisted of eleven hostile sexism (HS) and eleven benevolent sexism (BS) items.

Each scale was used in a *general* and in a *self* condition (e.g. for HS: "Women/I interpret innocent remarks or acts as being sexist", for BS: "Women/I should be cherished and protected by men"). Participants could answer on a six-point rating scale from 1 (*disagree strongly*) to 6 (*agree strongly*).

For a complete list of HS statements, see Table 10.1; for BS items and the German translations of the two scales, see Becker (2010). As we tested a sample of students, who possibly do not have (permanent) jobs, the HS item "Women/I exaggerate problems at work" was changed to "Women/I exaggerate problems at university". The reliability for the 22 HS items (11 from the personal and 11 from the general condition) was $\alpha = .63$. The reliability for all BS items was $\alpha = .88$. The HS and the BS items were presented in a mixed order.

Procedure

All participants were tested individually in two sessions. They were randomly assigned either to a questionnaire with the general or with the self condition items (half of the participants received the self condition first). After a waiting period of between 7 and 22 days, the same participants received the other questionnaire in a second session. The interruption was chosen to ensure that the answers from the first questionnaire would not influence those of the second questionnaire. To test for an effect arising from the order of questions, two versions of the questionnaire with diametrically opposed question layouts were created.

To control for potential order effects, we ran an initial 2 (order of the questions) x 2 (order of the condition) mixed ANOVA on HS and BS scores, with the order of questions as a between-participant factor and order of conditions as a within-participant factor. As there were no significant effects, all subsequent analyses are presented without order as a factor.

Results

Mean scores on the benevolent sexism scale revealed no significant difference between the self ($M = 2.80, SD = 0.91$) and the general conditions ($M = 3.00, SD = 0.92$), t (23) $= -1.60, p = .12$. Although Becker's (2010) sample was different (i.e. "a convenience sample of German women"), we replicated her findings of the self-version of the BS questionnaire. It is interesting to see our results agreeing with Becker's (2010), showing that when it comes to benevolent sexism, women participants tend to treat "I", "women" and "housewives" similarly.

As found by Becker (2010), the picture was quite different when looking at hostile sexism. Mean scores on the hostile sexism scale revealed that participants were more likely to reject hostile sexist statements when they were directed at the self ($M = 2.11, SD = 0.55$) than when they were directed towards women in general ($M = 3.00, SD = 0.53$), t (23) $= -6.82, p < .001, \eta^2 = .33$. This difference, although based on a different sample, resembles that of Becker's difference between sexism directed towards norm-deviant subtypes and that directed towards the self. Together, these results show a stronger adherence to sexist beliefs when directed towards norm-deviant subtypes (at least towards the ones tested by Becker, 2010) *and* women in general than when directed towards the self.

To further examine the differences between the self and the general conditions of the hostile sexism scale, separate analyses of each statement were conducted.[1] The analysis of the HS scale revealed that all items of the questionnaire were rejected more significantly if directed at the self than towards women in general (see Table 10.1). The highest score in the general condition was for the statement "Women are too easily offended", with a mean of 4.04 ($SD = 0.95$), the only item higher than the centre of the scale.

The item with the largest difference between the two conditions was "When women/I lose to men in a fair competition, they/I typically complain about being discriminated against." This statement, explicating competition between men and women, and part of the "Competitive Gender Differentiation" factor (Glick & Fiske, 1996), was the most rejected in the self condition ($M = 1.38, SD = 0.65$). This shows that women may not only deny being discriminated against (Crosby, 1984), but may also reject the idea of complaining about being discriminated against.

Discussion

The core issue here remains, as unfolded early in this paper, as to the reason why some women seem to hold sexist beliefs against women. If our data seem to suggest that this issue is highly relevant as far as hostile sexism is concerned (and we will come back to this), it does not seem to be the case for benevolent sexism. Benevolent sexism, being formulated as subjectively positive and in part promising women certain benefits, is sometimes not considered to be sexism (Barreto & Ellemers, 2005), which explains why it is more internalized

TABLE 10.1 Means and standard deviations (in brackets) of endorsement of hostile and benevolent sexist beliefs as a function of the target of sexism in this present study (globally, and for each item separately for the hostile Sexism scale)

	General condition ("women")		Self condition ("I")		t (23)	p
	M	(SD)	M	(SD)		
Entire scales						
Hostile sexism	3.00	(0.53)	2.11	(0.55)	−6.82	<.001
Benevolent sexism	3.00	(0.92)	2.80	(0.91)	−1.60	ns
Questions of the Hostile Sexism Scale						
When women/I lose to men in a fair competition, they/I typically complain about being discriminated against.	3.17	(1.09)	1.38	(0.65)	−7.96	<.001
Once a woman/I get a man to commit to her/me, she/I usually tries/try to put him on a tight leash.	2.54	(1.22)	1.67	(0.92)	−3.23	.004
Women are/I am making reasonable demands of men.[a,b]	3.88	(0.95)	3.08	(1.18)	−3.02	.006
Many women/I get a kick out of teasing men by seeming sexually available and then refusing male advances.	3.25	(1.51)	2.13	(1.51)	−2.87	.009
Women/I seek to gain power by getting control over men.[d]	2.17	(1.09)	1.42	(0.78)	−2.64	.015
Many women actually seek/I actually seek special favors, such as hiring policies that favor them/me over men, under the guise of asking for "equality".	2.58	(1.25)	1.71	(0.86)	−2.60	.016
Women/I am too easily offended.	4.04	(0.95)	3.29	(1.33)	−2.43	.023
Women/I interpret innocent remarks or acts as being sexist.	2.67	(1.34)	1.83	(1.05)	−2.35	.028
Women/I exaggerate problems they/I have at university.[c]	3.13	(1.42)	2.38	(1.10)	−2.23	.036
Women/I seek more power than men.[b,d]	2.29	(0.86)	1.79	(0.88)	−2.15	.043
Most women/I fail to appreciate fully all that men do for them/me.	3.25	(1.29)	2.58	(1.02)	−2.11	.046

Notes: [a] Reversed Item. [b] "Feminists" (from the original version of the ASI) was changed into "Women". [c] The original ASI uses "Problems at work". [d] The German version of the ASI distinguishes these two questions more clearly: "Women/I seek to gain power by getting control over men" is translated with "Frauen versuchen, Macht zu erlangen, indem sie Männer immer mehr beherrschen" and "Women/I seeking more power than men" with "Was Frauen wirklich wollen, ist, dass sie mehr Macht bekommen als Männer".

than hostile sexism. Participants may have considered the self and the women conditions as equivalent.

As internalization is weaker for hostile sexism, Becker (2010) suggested that subtyping was the process to explain women's agreement with hostile sexist statements. It seems to us that this idea relies on the premise that when answering the hostile sexism questionnaire with the pronoun "I", participants might have answered as "I = Women in general (without the deviant ones)". Our results, based on a female student sample, seem somehow difficult to reconcile with this idea.[2] As ambivalent sexism has been shown to be an ideology legitimizing the status quo (e.g. Glick & Fiske, 2001), we suggest that higher scores on the hostile sexism scale combined with the benevolent sexism scale patterns, illustrate system justification. We even argue that they exemplify the notion that some socially shared norms (e.g. "Once a woman gets a man to commit to her, she usually tries to put him on a tight leash.") are interpreted as inevitable (or even fair).

When looking at the results of the self condition, we would like to suggest that they illustrate the fact that people, here women, need to maintain an advantageous self-image (i.e. ego justification), as being a target of discrimination is socially undesirable (Jost & Banaji, 1994). This reasoning is in line with research showing that stereotype threat can cause low status groups to disengage from a system (Steele, 1997), consequently supporting positive self-esteem (e.g. Crocker & Major, 1989).

In essence, our data support the idea that for members of disadvantaged groups (here women), justification motives can typically conflict (Jost & Banaji, 1994). We suggest that our results for the hostile sexism scale illustrate a conflict between ego-justification (the lower scores on the personal scale) and system justification (the higher scores on the women in general scale). Importantly, and despite the fact that we did not directly test system justification motives (e.g. outgroup favoritism), system justification theory predicts that members of disadvantaged groups would not engage in social change if their system justification motives were stronger than their ego and group justification motives (Jost & Hunyady, 2005). Policies intended to promote social change should, therefore, take into account that men and women contribute to the maintenance of women's subjugation.

More globally, results of this study, along with those of Becker (2010), demonstrate that women (both from convenience and student samples) responding to sexism scales can be influenced by the phrasing of the items (e.g. Women are…, I am…, Career women are…), suggesting different underlying responding processes (e.g. subtyping, internalization, system justification). This should motivate future research in this domain to understand not only the processes at stake when women respond to sexism scales, but also their triggering factors. A shortcoming of the present study is that we had no true access to the reasoning processes of our participants as well as their triggering factors. This is probably true of most of the studies investigating possible effects of, and on, sexism. As such, and in light of the results of the present study, some findings in the literature might have to be considered with caution, as the way participants consider sexism scales, and maybe even individual items of the sexism scales, is never fully clear-cut.

Finally, this study, as well as those conducted by Julia Becker, should impel researchers to more closely examine the effects of women endorsing sexist beliefs on men's endorsement of these beliefs. Previous research suggests that women's endorsement of sexist beliefs directs men towards thinking that, in fact, as women also hold sexist beliefs, they might not actually be so problematic (e.g. DeKeseredy, 1999).

Practical implementations

On a more practical side, the processes that were discussed in this paper may be alarming in terms of societal progress, inasmuch as the implementation of interventions to balance power differences between women and men may be disrupted by members considering these differences as legitimate. Of course, when belonging to the high power group, such a consideration is not really astonishing, but when belonging to the low power one, it may seem somehow surprising. Even more surprising may be that, irrelevant of the exact nature of the mental processes at stake, these processes illustrate the extent to which some people go to legitimize the system in place.

Ironically, interventions to promote changes in stereotypes may actually reinforce them, as those trying to oppose gender stereotypes may simply be considered as part of norm-deviant subtypes (Becker, 2010). Crucially, the success of an intervention may well depend on its perceived norm deviance. Put simply, a proposal for social change that is not perceived as norm deviant is more likely to be accepted (Gaucher & Jost, 2011). For example, some experiments have shown that women's interest in political participation increased when participants perceived women as more highly represented in politics (e.g. Friesen, Gaucher, & Kay as cited in Gaucher & Jost, 2011).

Alternatively, constructive interventions may be possible at young ages, to prevent gender stereotypes (or even biased system structures) to creep into young children's representations of the world, allowing both girls and boys to construct representations independent of gender. Although such a claim goes beyond the scope of this paper, interventions aiming at children's construct of gender stereotypes may have to be implemented very early, as previous research has shown that toddlers of 24 months are already sensitive to gender stereotypes (Zosuls et al., 2009).

Notes

1 Since BS items showed no difference, they were not analysed separately.
2 Note that although the scores on the hostile Sexism Scale were higher when *women* was included in the items than when *I* was (by .89 on a six-point scale), they were still under the mid-point (3.5) (yet similar to an equivalent male population in Sarrasin et al., 2012).

References

Barreto, M., & Ellemers, N. (2005). The burden of benevolent sexism: How it contributes to the maintenance of gender inequalities. *European Journal of Social Psychology, 35*, 633–642. doi:10.1002/ejsp.270

Becker, J. C. (2010). Why do women endorse hostile and benevolent sexism? The role of salient female subtypes and internalization of sexist contents. *Sex Roles, 62*, 453–467. doi:10.1007/s11199-009-9707-4

Becker, J. C., & Wright, S. C. (2011). Yet another dark side of chivalry: Benevolent sexism undermines and hostile sexism motivates collective action for social change. *Journal of Personality and Social Psychology, 101*, 62–77. doi:10.1037/a0022615

Brandt, M. J. (2011). Sexism and gender inequality across 57 societies. *Psychological Science, 22*, 1413–1418. doi:10.1177/0956797611420445

Cowan, G., & Ullman, J. B. (2006). Ingroup rejection among women: The role of personal inadequacy. *Psychology of Women Quarterly, 30*, 399–409. doi:10.1111/j.1471-6402.2006.00315.x

Crocker, J., & Major, B. (1989). Social stigma and self-esteem: The self-protective properties of stigma. *Psychological Review, 96*, 608–630. doi: 10.1037/0033-295x.96.4.608

Crosby, F. (1984). The denial of personal discrimination. *American Behavioral Scientist, 27*, 371–386.

Dardenne, B., Dumont, M., & Bollier, T. (2007). Insidious dangers of benevolent sexism: Consequences for women's performance. *Journal of Personality and Social Psychology, 93*, 764–779. doi:10.1037/0022-3514.93.5.764

DeKeseredy, W. S. (1999). Tactics of the antifeminist backlash against Canadian national woman abuse surveys. *Violence Against Women, 5*, 1258–1276. doi:10.1177/10778019922183363

Eckes, T., & Six-Materna, I. (1999). Hostilität und Benevolenz: Eine Skala zur Erfassung des ambivalenten Sexismus. [Hostility and benevolence: A scale measuring ambivalent sexism]. *Zeitschrift für Sozialpsychologie, 30*, 211–228. doi:10.1024//0044-3514.30.4.211

Gaucher, D., & Jost, J. T. (2011). Difficulties awakening the sense of injustice and overcoming oppression: On the soporific effects of system justification. In P. T. Coleman (Ed.), *Conflict, Interdependence, and Justice* (pp. 227–246). New York: Springer. doi:10.1007/978-1-4419-9994-8_10

Glick, P., & Fiske, S. T. (1996). The Ambivalent Sexism Inventory: Differentiating hostile and benevolent sexism. *Journal of Personality and Social Psychology, 70*, 491–512. doi:10.1037/0022-3514.70.3.491

Glick, P., & Fiske, S. T. (2001). Ambivalent stereotypes as legitimizing ideologies. In J. T. Jost & B. Major (Eds.), *The Psychology of Legitimacy: Emerging perspectives on ideology, justice, and intergroup relations* (pp. 278–306). Cambridge: Cambridge University Press.

Glick, P., Diebold, J., Bailey-Werner, B., & Zhu, L. (1997). The two faces of Adam: Ambivalent sexism and polarized attitudes toward women. *Personality and Social Psychology Bulletin, 23*, 1323–1334. doi:10.1177/01461672972312009

Glick, P., Fiske, S. T., Mladinic, A., Saiz, J. L., Abrams, D., Masser, B., . . . López López, W. (2000). Beyond prejudice as simple antipathy: Hostile and benevolent sexism across cultures. *Journal of Personality and Social Psychology, 79*, 763–775. doi:10.1037/10022-3514.79.5.763

Good, J., & Rudman, L. (2010). When female applicants meet sexist interviewers: The costs of being a target of benevolent sexism. *Sex Roles, 62*, 481–493. doi:10.1007/s11199-009-9685-6

Hausmann, R., Tyson, L. D., Bekhouche, Y., & Zahidi, S. (2011). *The Global Gender Gap Index* 2011. Cologny/Geneva: World Economic Forum Retrieved from http://www. weforum.org/issues/global-gender-gap.

Jost, J. T., & Banaji, M. R. (1994). The role of stereotyping in system-justification and the production of false consciousness. *British Journal of Social Psychology, 33*, 1–27. doi:10.1111/j.2044-8309.1994.tb01008.x

Jost, J. T., & Hunyady, O. (2003). The psychology of system justification and the palliative function of ideology. *European Review of Social Psychology, 13*, 111–153. doi:10.1080/10463280240000046

Jost, J. T., & Hunyady, O. (2005). Antecedents and consequences of system-justifying ideologies. *Current Directions in Psychological Science, 14*, 260–265. doi:10.1111/j.0963-7214.2005.00377.x

Jost, J. T., & Kay, A. C. (2005). Exposure to benevolent sexism and complementary gender stereotypes: consequences for specific and diffuse forms of system justification. *Journal of Personality and Social Psychology, 88*, 498–509. doi:10.1037/0022-3514.88.3.498

Kelman, H. C. (1958). Compliance, identification, and internalization: Three processes of attitude change. *The Journal of Conflict Resolution, 2*, 51–60.

Klonoff, E. A., & Landrine, H. (1995). The schedule of sexist events. A measure of lifetime and recent sexist discrimination in women's lives. *Psychology of Women Quarterly, 19*, 439–470. doi:10.1111/j.1471-6402.1995.tb00086.x

Kluegel, J. R., & Smith, E. R. (1986). *Beliefs about Inequality: Americans' views of what is and what ought to be*. Piscataway, NJ: AldineTransaction.

Krueger, J. I. (2007). From social projection to social behaviour. *European Review of Social Psychology, 18*, 1–35. doi:10.1080/10463280701284645

Matteson, A. V., & Moradi, B. (2005). Examining the structure of the Schedule of Sexist Events: Replication and extension. *Psychology of Women Quarterly, 29*, 47–57. doi:10.1111/j.0361-6843.2005.00167.x

Sarrasin, O., Gabriel, U., & Gygax, P. (2012). Sexism and attitudes toward gender-neutral language: The case of English, French and German. *Swiss Journal of Psychology, 71*, 113–124. doi:10.1024/1421-0185/a000078

Steele, C. M. (1997). A threat in the air: How stereotypes shape intellectual identity and performance. *American Psychologist, 52*, 613–629. doi:10.1037/0003-066X.52.6.613

Strub, S., Gerfin, M., & Buetikofer, A. (2008). *Vergleichende* Analyse der Löhne von Frauen und Männern anhand der Lohnstrukturerhebungen 1998 bis 2006. Untersuchung im Rahmen der Evaluation der Wirksamkeit des Gleichstellungsgesetzes. [Comparative analysis of women's and men's wages based on the Swiss wage structure survey from 1998 to 2006. Study within the evaluation of the gender equality act] Bern: Büro BASS/Universität Bern.

Swim, J. K., Hyers, L. L., Cohen, L. L., & Ferguson, M. J. (2001). Everyday sexism: Evidence for its incidence, nature, and psychological impact from three daily diary studies. *Journal of Social Issues, 57*, 31–53. doi:10.1111/0022-4537.00200

Swiss Federal Statistical Office. (2008). *On the Way to Gender Equality. Current situation and developments*. Neuchâtel: Swiss Federal Statistical Office. Retrieved from http://www. bfs.admin.ch/bfs/portal/en/index/themen/20/22/press.Document.121343.pdf.

Zosuls, K. M., Ruble, D. N., Tamis-LeMonda, C. S., Shrout, P. E., Bornstein, M. H., & Greulich, F. K. (2009). The acquisition of gender labels in infancy: Implications for sex-typed play. *Developmental Psychology, 45*, 688–701. doi:10.1037/a0014053

11

GENDER DIFFERENCES IN THE ACCEPTANCE OF THE MUSLIM HEADSCARF

Oriane Sarrasin, Nicole Fasel, and Eva G. T. Green

Introduction

Negative attitudes toward Muslim minorities are widespread in many Western countries (Strabac & Listhaug, 2008). Stereotypical views of Muslims commonly include associating Islam with terrorism and religious extremism, and perceiving Muslims' cultural practices as incompatible with the local customs (Chakraborti & Zempi, 2012). Indeed, Islamic practices seen as contrary to gender equality receive extensive media and political attention (Aly & Walker, 2007). The headscarf worn by some Muslim women, in particular, has provoked fierce legal and political battles in several European countries (Amiraux, 2013). In the name of gender equality and secularism, Belgium banned the public wearing of face-covering headscarves (e.g. niqabs, burkas) in 2010. The same year, all types of face-covering headgears were banned from public spaces in France. In Switzerland, the canton of Ticino was the first to accept banning face-covering headscarves in a referendum in September 2013, while the population of a municipality in St Gallen has recently decided to ban wearing headscarves in primary school.

While some of the opposition toward the headscarf may be due to a general dislike of Muslims, because of the gendered aspect of the headscarf, these two phenomena are distinct (van der Noll, 2014). Indeed, often Muslim women not only face negative attitudes from the national majority because of their religious membership, but are also perceived by members of this majority as suffering from gender discrimination by male members of their own religious community. For this reason, women and men from the majority are likely to differ in the way they accept the headscarf. On the one hand, women are known to generally express more positive attitudes toward ethnic and cultural diversity (Ceobanu & Escandell, 2010) and toward Muslims (Strabac & Listhaug, 2008) than men. Following the argument that opposition to the headscarf is, above all, rooted in negative attitudes toward cultural diversity (e.g. Roux, Gianettoni, & Perrin, 2006), women's greater support for multiculturalism may translate into positive attitudes toward the headscarf as an expression of tolerance towards diversity. On the other hand, women may not approve of a garment often presented as a symbol of patriarchal oppression. The evidence gathered so far—with respondents' gender used as a control variable—is rather inconclusive. While some studies report no gender differences in attitudes toward the headscarf (e.g. in Switzerland: Fasel, Green, & Sarrasin, 2013; Gianettoni, 2011; in different European countries: van der Noll, 2010), women have sometimes been found to hold more positive attitudes (Helbling, 2014; Saroglou, Lamkaddem, Van Pachterbeke, & Buxant, 2009). Moreover, there is, to our knowledge, no systematic examination of the factors that may cause men and women to differ in their reactions to the Muslim headscarf.

To fill this gap, the present study examines ideologies that are expected to explain gender differences in acceptance of the headscarf. We start this undertaking by defining political ideology in general. Then, since attitudes towards the headscarf involve two crosscutting categorizations—Muslims vs. non-Muslims and women vs. men, we take into account two operational ideologies relevant to the organization of intergroup relations: *Support for multiculturalism* and *support for gender equality*. At each step, we report known gender differences, and discuss whether they are likely to explain gender differences in acceptance of the headscarf. Finally, we test our predictions in Switzerland with data from the 2011 Swiss post-electoral survey Selects.

Political ideology

As a "set of beliefs about the proper order of society and how it can be achieved" (Erikson & Tedin, 2003; p. 64), political ideology is often conceptualized as a left-to-right continuum. According to Jost and colleagues (e.g. Jost, Federico, & Napier, 2009), political ideology contains, in fact, two interrelated dimensions: supporting vs. resisting social change, and rejecting vs. accepting inequality. However, as these two dimensions are rooted in the same motives—the needs to create order and minimize insecurity, in this study we consider only a left-right dimension to measure political ideology.

During the last few decades, women from Western countries have tended to endorse a more left-oriented and egalitarian political ideology than men, and this gap has grown wider (Inglehart & Norris, 2000). This gender gap in ideology as an abstract form of thinking about societal matters results from several mechanisms, such as traditional gender roles (e.g. women being raised to care for others) and women's greater dependency on welfare services, which make them approve more of left-wing politics (e.g. Howell & Day, 2000). This gender gap in political ideology is likely to be expressed in more operational ideologies (i.e. referring to more concrete issues; see Jost et al., 2009), such as support for multiculturalism and support for gender equality.

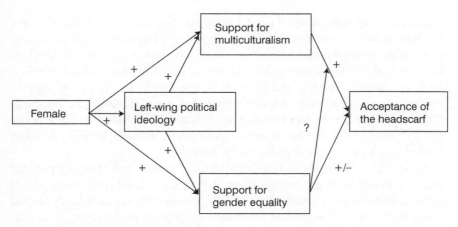

FIGURE 11.1 Summary of predictions

Support for multiculturalism

"Multiculturalism" can refer to the demographic make-up of a society where individuals with different cultural and ethnic origins live together, to public policies that promote ethnic and cultural diversity (in opposition to policies that seek for the assimilation of migrants), and to an ideology (Berry, Kalin, & Taylor, 1977). Indeed, *support for multiculturalism* describes the majority's attitudes toward multicultural policies, and, more generally, their opinion towards ethnic and migrant minorities as a cultural enrichment to society.[1]

Individuals supporting multiculturalism generally feel less threatened by immigration (Ward & Masgoret, 2006), and express more positive attitudes toward ethnic minorities (Verkuyten, 2005). Support for multiculturalism was for instance found to relate to stronger support for Muslims' freedom to practise their religion (van der Noll, 2012). Moreover, some argue that opposition to the headscarf is above all rooted in negative attitudes toward ethnic and cultural diversity (Roux et al., 2006), which explains why support for multiculturalism has been found to relate to positive attitudes toward the headscarf (van der Noll, 2014). Since women tend to be more favourable towards multiculturalism than men (in general; Dandy & Pe-Pua, 2010; regarding Muslim immigrants; Verkuyten, 2009), we put forward the following hypothesis: Women express a higher acceptance of the headscarf because of their stronger support for multiculturalism (see Figure 11.1).

Support for gender equality

Individuals differ greatly in the way they believe that gender relationships should play out. Some *support gender equality* by encouraging equal opportunities for men and women. For instance, they think everyone, men as well as women, should be able to pursue a professional career if they wish to. Women tend to be more supportive than men of equal gender opportunities. Studies conducted in the US have shown that women support women's employment to a greater extent and traditional family arrangements to a lesser extent than men (e.g. Bolzendahl & Myers, 2004). These trends have been confirmed in cross-national studies. In Great Britain, Sweden and Norway, women were also found to support traditional gender roles to a lesser extent than men (Knudsen & Waerness, 2001). In a similar vein, in their analysis of data from 33 countries, Yu and Lee (2013) found women to be more positive toward mothers' employment and toward men's greater participation in the household.

While the relationship between individuals' gender and their support for gender equality has been extensively studied, how the latter relates to gendered political attitudes such as toward the Muslim headscarf has attracted only limited research attention. This is all the more surprising, given the frequent association between gender (in)equality and the Muslim headscarf in the political discourse and the media (Aly & Walker, 2007; Chakraborti & Zempi, 2012). Moreover, the scarce empirical evidence for such a link among the population is inconclusive. In Switzerland, using different measures related to the concept of gender equality, Roux et al. (2006) and Gianettoni (2011) found no direct relationship between these measures and attitudes toward the headscarf. In contrast, in Australia, those who showed prejudice against Muslims were found to express concerns that Islam is contrary to gender equality (Pedersen & Hartley, 2012). However, their attitudes toward gender equality in general—that is, independent of concerns related to Islam—were not assessed.

To shed light on the relationship between support for gender equality and attitudes toward the headscarf, here we make two alternative predictions. On the one hand, individuals who support gender equality may oppose the headscarf because they perceive it as contrary to gender equality. On the other hand, because individuals who support gender equality are also more tolerant and egalitarian in general, they may also more readily support ethnic minorities' cultural and religious practices (see Figure 11.1). Finally, Roux et al. (2006) found in Switzerland that those who supported gender equality but also the expelling of undocumented immigrants were the ones who most strongly opposed the headscarf. We thus examine how support for gender equality and support for multiculturalism interact to predict attitudes toward the headscarf.

Current study

We tested our predictions with data collected in Switzerland. Since the country has recently witnessed hostile public reactions to Muslims, as reflected in recent federal (e.g. the ban of building minarets) and local (e.g. the ban of 'full face' headscarves in Ticino) votes, it is a relevant context to study attitudes toward the headscarf.

In addition to ideologies, we included in our analysis a number of factors known to impact attitudes toward ethnic minorities and/or reactions to the

Muslim headscarf. First, older individuals generally express more negative attitudes toward ethnic minorities and their practices, such as the Muslim headscarf (e.g. Fasel et al., 2013). Moreover, those with a lower economic status are more likely to feel threatened by ethnic minorities, and in turn, to reject Muslims (Savelkoul, Scheepers, Tolsma, & Hagendoorn, 2011). Because antireligious stances relate to a lower support for the headscarf (Saroglou et al., 2009), we also accounted for having no religion and not being involved in religious activities. Finally, because individuals with a migration background generally express more positive attitudes toward cultural diversity (Sarrasin, Green, Fasel, & Davidov, 2014), we controlled for being born Swiss vs. having been granted Swiss citizenship.

Method

Data and sample

To examine our research questions, we relied on the data from the 2011 Swiss post-electoral survey Selects.[2] Among the Swiss citizens who were asked to give their opinion on the Muslim headscarf,[3] we retained data of those who provided an answer to all variables of interest. We then excluded those who declared to be Muslims ($N = 10$). Among the remaining 1531 respondents, there were 756 women and 775 men, ranging in age from 18 to 92 ($M = 52.18$, $SD = 16.51$). The majority of them declared themselves to be Christians (664 Catholics and 502 Protestants; no further specification was provided), 72 had another religion, and 293 reported having no religious affiliation. Slightly less than half of the respondents ($N = 607$) reported not being engaged in at least one religious activity (e.g. being a member of, or donating to, a religious association). The great majority of the respondents ($N = 1377$) held Swiss citizenship at birth. Finally, when asked to compare their household's income to the average household on a scale from 1 = *much below* to 5 = *much above*, respondents reported an income situated on average in the middle of the scale ($M = 3.33$, $SD = 1.07$).

Attitudes and ideologies

Acceptance of the Muslim headscarf was measured with agreement with the following item: "Muslim women should have the right to wear a religious headscarf". On a scale from 1 (totally disagree) to 5 (totally agree), the average attitude seems to be slightly disapproving ($M = 2.54$, $SD = 1.44$).

Political ideology was measured with a self-declared political orientation scale, from 0 (left) to 10 (right—reversed such that high scores indicate left or egalitarian political ideology; $M = 4.91$, $SD = 2.22$). We assessed respondents' support for multiculturalism ($M = 3.30$, $SD = 1.06$) with agreement to the two following items (α = .71), both ranging from 1 (totally disagree) to 5 (totally agree): "Cultural life is enriched by people coming from other countries", and "Immigrants have the right to keep their traditions when they come to live in Switzerland". Finally, support for gender equality was measured with a question regarding childcare ("The state should provide affordable childcare to all parents", from 1 = in no case to 4 = in all cases; $M = 2.64$, $SD = 0.95$). In Switzerland, there is a severe shortage of day care places, and many women are home carers or work part time. In such a context, supporting day care for all parents implies supporting equal opportunities for men and women.[4] Unsurprisingly, individuals reporting a left-wing political ideology were more likely to support multiculturalism ($r = .43$, $p < .001$) and gender equality ($r = .35$, $p < .001$).

Results

The data used in this study were collected in all the 26 Swiss (half-) cantons. Although we are not interested in testing the impact of canton-level factors, this nested structure is likely to bias the standard errors of the estimates if not taken into account.[5] For this reason, we tested our predictions with multilevel regressions (performed with Mplus 5.1). All models were conducted using maximum likelihood estimation. When additional predictors were entered in the model, we estimated whether they significantly improved the model through a significant difference in chi-square between the two models. All continuous variables were centred at the grand mean.

In a first step, we examined the impact of gender (1 = female) on our variables of interest. We tested whether, as expected, women held a more left-wing political ideology and expressed stronger support for multiculturalism and gender equality than men when controlled for other socio-demographic variables. In a second step, we examined whether gender and ideologies (i.e. political ideology, support for multiculturalism and support for gender equality) predicted acceptance of the headscarf. In accordance with our hypotheses, we tested whether gender was indirectly related to acceptance of the headscarf through ideologies. Finally, we tested whether ideologies interacted in predicting acceptance of the headscarf.

Gender differences in ideologies

In accordance with our expectations, when controlling for age, religious affiliation, religious activities, and perceived household financial situation, women were more left-wing than men ($b = 0.48$, $SE = 0.11$, $p < .001$). Similar models but including political ideology as a predictor in addition to socio-demographics were used to examine support for multiculturalism and support for gender equality: While there was no significant gender difference in multiculturalism ($b = -0.02$, $SE = 0.05$, $p = .72$),[6] women expressed a stronger support for gender equality than men ($b = 0.13$, $SE = 0.05$, $p = .003$). Gender had an indirect impact on the two intergroup ideologies: Women expressed a stronger support for both multiculturalism (b = 0.10, SE = 0.02, p < .001) and gender equality (b = 0.11, SE = 0.02, p < .001) through a stronger left-wing political ideology.

Regarding the impact of the control variables, results revealed some significant effects. Older respondents were more right-wing (b =–0.01, SE = 0.00, p = .02) and supported gender equality to a lesser extent (b =–0.01, SE = 0.00, p < .001), but were also more supportive of multiculturalism (b = 0.01, SE = 0.00, p = .001). Both Catholics (b =–0.74, SE = 0.17, p < .001) and Protestants (b =–0.65, SE = 0.17, p < .001) were more right-wing, and supported multiculturalism (C: b =–0.22, SE = 0.07, p = .002; P: b =–0.18, SE = 0.07, p = .01) and gender equality (C: b =–0.17, SE = 0.07, p = .01; P: b =–0.12, SE = 0.07, p = .08) less than respondents who reported no religion. Those who were not engaged in religious activities were more supportive of multiculturalism (b = 0.19, SE = 0.05, p < .001) than those who were. Respondents who were Swiss citizens at birth supported to a lesser extent both multiculturalism (b =–0.27, SE = 0.08, p = .001) and gender equality (b =–0.41, SE = 0.08, p < .001) than those who were not. Finally, the perceived financial situation of a household was positively related to support for multiculturalism (b = 0.08, SE = 0.02, p < .001).

Gender differences in the acceptance of the headscarf

Results are presented in Table 11.1. When controlling for the other socio-demographic variables, female respondents expressed more tolerant views toward the headscarf than men (Model 1). Entered in Model 2, a left-wing political ideology was significantly and positively related to acceptance of the headscarf. The impact of gender became non-significant (p = .38). In Model 3, both multiculturalism and support for gender equality predicted higher acceptance of the headscarf.

Indirect paths were estimated in a path model ($\chi^2(10)$ = 95.48, p < .001, CFI = .93, RMSEA = .08). Results showed that while female respondents expressed a higher acceptance of the headscarf through a stronger support for gender equality (b = 0.02, SE = 0.01, p = .03), the indirect path through multiculturalism was not significant (b =–0.01, SE = 0.03, p = .74). However, when political ideology was considered as an additional mediator, both the indirect paths from gender via political ideology and multiculturalism to acceptance of the headscarf (b = 0.05, SE = 0.01, p < .001) and from gender via political ideology and support to gender equality to acceptance of the headscarf (b = 0.01, SE = 0.00, p = .01) were significant.

Interaction between intergroup ideologies

We tested for the interactive role of support for multiculturalism (MC) and support for gender equality (GE). Because their impact may also be moderated

TABLE 11.1 Multilevel regressions predicting acceptance of the headscarf (unstandardized coefficients and standard errors are displayed)

	Model 1		Model 2		Model 3		Model 4		Model 5	
	b	SE	b	SE	b	SE	b	SE	b	SE
Intercept	2.56	(0.15)***	2.45	(0.14)***	2.23	(0.13)***	2.19	(0.13)***	2.18	(0.13)***
Gender	0.17	(0.07)*	0.06	(0.07)	0.06	(0.06)	0.06	(0.06)	0.12	(0.07)
Age	-0.01	(0.00)*	-0.00	(0.00)†	-0.01	(0.00)**	-0.01	(0.00)**	-0.01	(0.00)*
Being born Swiss	0.04	(0.12)	0.09	(0.12)	0.29	(0.11)**	0.29	(0.11)**	0.28	(0.11)*
Household situation	0.03	(0.04)	0.02	(0.03)	-0.02	(0.03)	-0.02	(0.03)	-0.03	(0.03)
Protestant (ref: no religion)	-0.20	(0.11)†	-0.06	(0.10)	0.05	(0.10)	0.07	(0.10)	0.07	(0.10)
Catholic (ref: no religion)	-0.42	(0.11)***	-0.26	(0.10)*	-0.13	(0.09)	-0.11	(0.09)	-0.11	(0.09)
Other (ref: no religion)	-0.31	(0.19)	-0.26	(0.18)	-0.21	(0.17)	-0.20	(0.17)	-0.21	(0.17)
No religious activities	0.26	(0.08)*	0.26	(0.08)***	0.16	(0.07)*	0.15	(0.07)*	0.15	(0.07)*
Left vs. right ideology			0.22	(0.02)***	0.10	(0.02)***	0.09	(0.02)***	0.09	(0.02)***
Multiculturalism (MC)					0.54	(0.03)***	0.52	(0.05)***	0.53	(0.05)***
Gender equality (GE)					0.12	(0.04)***	0.14	(0.05)***	0.14	(0.05)***

MC X GE				0.08 (0.03)**	0.17 (0.04)***
MC X Gender				0.08 (0.06)	0.07 (0.06)
GE X Gender				−0.03 (0.07)	−0.05 0.07
MC X GE X Gender					−0.18 (0.06)**
R²	1.91%	13.01%	27.09%	27.53%	27.92%
Δdeviance (Δdf)	33.86 (8)***	185.29 (1)***	273.96 (2)***	8.39 (3)*	8.44 (1)*

***$p < .001$ **$p < .01$ *$p < .05$ †$p < .10$

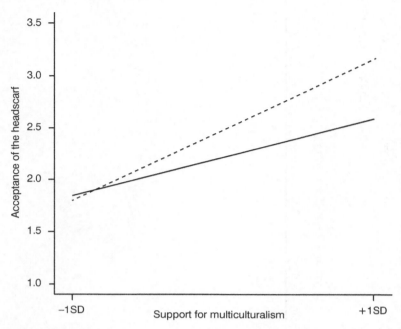

FIGURE 11.2   Impact of support for multiculturalism on acceptance of the headscarf as a function of support for gender equality among male respondents

by gender, we also added the two other two-way interactions (MC X Gender and GE X Gender). As shown in Model 4, only the MC X GE interaction yielded a significant impact. This impact was, however, further moderated by gender (Model 5). Decomposition of the simple slopes showed that in all cases (among male and female respondents, independent of their support for gender equality) support for multiculturalism was significantly related to a stronger acceptance of the headscarf.[7] Support for gender equality moderated this relationship, but only among male respondents (see Figure 11.2). Among men supporting multiculturalism, those scoring high on support for gender equality expressed a significantly higher acceptance of the headscarf than those scoring low on support for gender equality ($b = 0.33$, $SE = 0.07$, $p < .001$). In contrast, among men who did not support multiculturalism, there was no significant difference between men scoring low and men scoring high on support for gender equality ($b =-0.04$, $SE = 0.07$, $p = .56$). No similar pattern was revealed in the case of female respondents. Both, among women who did not support multiculturalism, ($b = 0.10$, $SE = 0.06$, $p = .13$) and those who did ($b = 0.09$, $SE = 0.07$, $p = .24$), there was no significant difference between those expressing low and high support for gender equality.

Discussion

The present study showed that Swiss women more readily accept the Muslim headscarf than Swiss men. This gender gap was explained by women holding a stronger left-wing political ideology, which in turn translated into more positive stances toward multiculturalism and gender equality. Finally, while support for multiculturalism and support for gender equality had independent effects among female respondents, their impacts were multiplicative in the case of male respondents.

Gendered aspects of the headscarf

Our results revealed that Swiss nationals supporting gender equality expressed a higher acceptance of the headscarf. However, because the Muslim headscarf is frequently portrayed as contrary to the principle of gender equality, one may have expected individuals who support gender equality to oppose the wearing of the headscarf. It cannot be ruled out that in some circumstances it may be so, and future research on the topic should explore at least three different directions. First, gender equality arguments can be used by those opposed to the headscarf for reasons other than gender concerns (e.g. negative attitudes toward cultural minorities) to justify their opinions. In the political arena, gender equality rhetoric may be a successful strategy to mobilize individuals who do not have a firm opinion on the headscarf. Indeed, while it is unlikely that strongly left-oriented individuals are mobilized against the public wearing of the headscarf simply on equality grounds, those in the middle of the left-right spectrum may be more easily convinced (Danaci, 2009).

Second, our result may be due to the measure of attitudes toward the headscarf we used in the present study. Indeed, when asked whether Muslim women should have the *right* to wear a headscarf as was the case in the present study, left-oriented egalitarian individuals are likely to express their support. In contrast, they may feel torn when asked whether the headscarf should be banned because it is contrary to gender equality. In line with this argument, Gianettoni (2011) found no relationship between such a question and support for gender equality.

Finally, we used a single item measure, tapping support for affordable childcare. This may reflect attitudes toward the welfare state, which we attempted to account for in additional analyses by including another item measuring support for a greater state intervention. For this reason, future studies should include a multi-item gender equality measure distinct from other ideological stances. Moreover, beyond limitations of the measure used in the present study, the specific type of gender-related ideology we examined may also have played a role. Indeed, support for non-traditional gender roles can take different forms (Braun, 2008). A distinction that very likely plays a crucial role when predicting acceptance of the Muslim headscarf is the one between support for gender equality and willingness to enforce it (Sarrasin, 2015). While the former involves supporting equal opportunities and freedom of choice for both men and women, the latter implies that gender equality should be achieved by all means. As revealed in the present study, those supporting gender equality are likely to support the public wearing of the headscarf in the name of equality, that is, via granting equal rights to all groups to uphold their customs and traditions. In contrast, those willing to enforce gender equality by all means may support banning headscarves with the intention to "free" Muslim women from practices they perceive to be sexist.

Multiplicative effect of intergroup ideologies

We found that among Swiss men, but not Swiss women, support for multiculturalism and support for gender equality had multiplicative effects on the acceptance of the headscarf. Swiss men—the dominant group in immigrant-Swiss as well as gender relationships—expressing the strongest acceptance were those who scored high on both measures of intergroup ideologies. This may be due to the fact that in Switzerland, as in many other places, supporting day care for all parents means supporting the independence of those who are subordinate in the gender relations, women. Thus, supporting childcare for all parents may denote, among men, a desire to help and support a disadvantaged group and thus reflect stronger egalitarian views than among women for which the latter is partially motivated by self-interest. In combination with support for multiculturalism, such men are likely to express strong support of equal opportunities for all ethnic and cultural groups, and thus least oppose the wearing of the headscarf. In the same vein, it has been shown that both, feminist and multiculturalist ideologies were necessary for members of the dominant ethnic group to counteract sexist attitudes towards ethnic minorities such as Muslims (Gianettoni & Roux, 2010). Our findings suggest that this may be especially true for members of a double majority—Swiss men—who are aware of their belonging to both dominant groups to express positive attitudes towards a double subordinate group (Muslim women).

Tolerance and ambivalent emotions

Our results showed that women, and more generally left-wing individuals, expressed a higher acceptance of the headscarf. However, with the measure of attitudes we used, we cannot conclude that left-oriented individuals truly welcome the presence of Muslim immigrants and their practices, but instead, merely choose to tolerate them (e.g. the public wearing of the headscarf) as an expression of their general support for ethnic and cultural minorities' rights.

Indeed, a dislike of Muslims or the perception that Muslims are a particularly problematic immigrant group have been shown to predict attitudes towards the ban of headscarves over and above support for equality and multiculturalism (van der Noll, 2014). This indicates that individuals favouring equality may experience ambivalent feelings towards the concerned minority group. Theorizing of modern forms of racism underscores that equality concerns drive attitudes especially when normative cues are salient. Yet in an everyday context, attitudes often conflict with more individualistic values, leading to ambivalent emotions towards minority groups (Gaertner & Dovidio, 1986). For this reason, future research should include not only nuanced equality and gender-related ideologies, but also assess more fine-grained measures of reactions toward the headscarf and dislike of Muslims, including emotions.

Practical implications

Many Muslims report facing abuse and discrimination on a daily basis. To design interventions and policies to tackle anti-Muslim prejudices efficiently, it is thus important to underpin their exact causes. The present study showed that negative attitudes toward the headscarf seem, above all, rooted in individuals' lack of support for ethnic and cultural diversity. On a practical level, these results indicate that tolerance of Muslim religious and cultural practices among men and women could be increased by measures targeting xenophobia in general. This could be achieved by interventions promoting intercultural understanding through intergroup contact between Muslims and non-Muslims. Indeed, regular encounters between Muslims and non-Muslims have been related to more positive attitudes towards Muslims in the same vein as multicultural ideologies (Velasco González, Verkuyten, Weesie, & Poppe, 2008). In addition, our findings also indicate that opposition to the headscarf justified by concerns for gender equality does not necessarily reflect endorsement of gender equality in general. To raise awareness, this finding should be brought forward in the political arena as well as the media when bans of headscarves are proposed in the name of gender equality.

Notes

1 Note that the focus here is on the majority perspective. Obviously, minority group members also support multiculturalism at different degrees
2 Selects is a representative survey of Swiss citizens of voting age, with an oversampling of the small Swiss cantons. For detailed information see http://www2.unil.ch/selects/spip.php?lang=en
3 The Selects survey combines data from a telephone survey, and data from a reduced sample which answered to an additional postal/online questionnaire ($N = 1786$). The question pertaining the headscarf, to which 89 respondents did not provide an answer, was included in the postal/online questionnaire.
4 Because this item also taps support for a greater State intervention, we performed additional analyses controlling for another type of State support (e.g. the State should help poor students and apprentices; correlation with support for gender equality, $r = .36, p < .001$). Results are similar to those presented in Table 11.1.
5 Indeed, a small but significant portion of the variance of the variables of interest was due to the clustering structure (acceptance of the headscarf: 2.1 per cent; multiculturalism: 2.1 per cent; support for gender equality: 5.2 per cent).

6 This is also the case when political ideology is not controlled for ($b = 0.08$, $SE = 0.05$, $p = .14$).
7 Female respondents: low support for gender equality, $b = 0.61$, $SE = 0.06$, $p < .001$; high support for gender equality, $b = 0.60$, $SE = 0.06$, $p < .001$. Male respondents: low support for gender equality, $b = 0.40$, $SE = 0.06$, $p < .001$; high support for gender equality, $b = 0.70$, $SE = 0.07$, $p < .001$.

References

Aly, A., & Walker, D. (2007). Veiled threats: Recurrent cultural anxieties in Australia. *Journal of Muslim Minority Affairs, 27*, 203–214. doi:10.1080/13602000701536141

Amiraux, V. (2013). 'The ,illegal covering' saga: What's next? Sociological perspectives. *Social Identities, 19*, 794–806. doi:10.1080/13504630.2013.842678

Berry, J. W., Kalin, R., & Taylor, D. (1977). *Multiculturalism and Ethnic Attitudes in Canada.* Ottawa: Ministry of Supply and Services.

Bolzendahl, C. I., & Myers, D. J. (2004). Feminist attitudes and support for gender equality: Opinion change in women and men, 1974–1998. *Social Forces, 83*, 759–789. doi:10.1353/sof.2005.0005

Braun, M. (2008). Using egalitarian items to measure men's and women's family roles. *Sex Roles, 59*, 644–656. doi:10.1007/s11199-008-9468-5

Ceobanu, A. M., & Escandell, X. (2010). Comparative analyses of public attitudes toward immigrants and immigration using multinational survey data: A review of theories and research. *Annual Review of Sociology, 36*, 309–328. doi:10.1146/annurev. soc.012809.102651

Chakraborti, N., & Zempi, I. (2012). The veil under attack: Gendered dimensions of Islamophobic victimization. *International Review of Victimology, 18*, 269–284. doi:10.1177/0269758012446983

Danaci, D. (2009). When two worlds collide: Does cultural liberalism of Swiss citizen guarantee tolerance for Islamic minorities? *Working Paper, Institute for Political Science.* Zurich: University of Zurich.

Dandy, J., & Pe-Pua, R. (2010). Attitudes to multiculturalism, immigration and cultural diversity: Comparison of dominant and non-dominant groups in three Australian states. *International Journal of Intercultural Relations, 34*, 34–46. doi:10.1016/j. ijintrel.2009.10.003

Erikson, R. S., & Tedin, K. L. (2003). *American Public Opinion [6th edition].* New York: Longman.

Fasel, N., Green, E. G. T., & Sarrasin, O. (2013). Unveiling naturalization: A multilevel study on minority proportion, conservative ideologies and attitudes towards the Muslim veil. *Zeitschrift für Psychologie, 221*, 242–251. doi:10.1027/2151-2604/a000154

Gaertner, S. L., & Dovidio, J. F. (1986). The aversive form of racism. In J. F. Dovidio & S. L. Gaertner (Eds.), *Prejudice, Discrimination, and Racism* (pp. 61–89). Orlando, FL: Academic Press.

Gianettoni, L. (2011). Egalité des sexes et régulation institutionnelle de l'altérité racisée: Une analyse psychosociale des attitudes politiques envers les musulmans en Suisse [Gender equality and institutional regulation of racialized otherness: A social psychological analysis of political attitudes toward Muslims living in Switzerland]. *Swiss Journal of Sociology, 37,* 507–524.

Gianettoni, L., & Roux, P. (2010). Interconnecting race and gender relations: Racism, sexism and the attribution of sexism to the racialized other. *Sex Roles, 62*, 374–386. doi:10.1007/s11199-010-9755-9

Helbling, M. (2014). Opposing Muslims and the Muslim headscarf in Western Europe. *European Sociological Review, advance online publication.* doi:10.1093/esr/jct038

Howell, S. E., & Day, C. L. (2000). Complexities of the gender gap. *The Journal of Politics, 62,* 858–874. doi:10.1111/0022-3816.00036

Inglehart, R., & Norris, P. (2000). The developmental theory of the gender gap: Women's and men's voting behavior in global perspective. *International Political Science Review, 21,* 441–463. doi:10.1177/0192512100214007

Jost, J. T., Federico, C. M., & Napier, J. L. (2009). Political ideology: Its structure, functions, and elective affinities. *Annual Review of Psychology, 60,* 307–337. doi:10.1146/annurev.psych.60.110707.163600

Knudsen, K., & Waerness, K. (2001). National context, individual characteristics and attitudes on mothers' employment: A comparative analysis of Great Britain, Sweden and Norway. *Acta Sociologica, 44,* 67–79. doi:10.1177/000169930104400106

Pedersen, A., & Hartley, L. K. (2012). Prejudice against Muslim Australians: The role of values, gender and consensus. *Journal of Community & Applied Social Psychology, 22,* 239–255. doi:10.1002/casp.1110

Roux, P., Gianettoni, L., & Perrin, C. (2006). Féminisme et racisme. Une recherche exploratoire sur les fondements des divergences relatives au port du foulard [Femininsm and racism. An exploratory study on the divergent attitudes toward the wearing of the headscarf]. *Nouvelles Questions Féministes, 25,* 84–106.

Saroglou, V., Lamkaddem, B., Van Pachterbeke, M., & Buxant, C. (2009). Host society's dislike of the Islamic veil: The role of subtle prejudice, values, and religion. *International Journal of Intercultural Relations, 33,* 419–428. doi:10.1016/j.ijintrel.2009.02.005

Sarrasin, O. (2015). *Attitudes Toward Gender Equality and Opposition to the Muslim Headscarf.* Manuscript in preparation.

Sarrasin, O., Green, E. G., Fasel, N., & Davidov, E. (2014). Does survey respondents' immigrant background affect the measurement and prediction of immigration attitudes? An illustration in two steps. *International Journal of Public Opinion Research, advance online publication.*

Savelkoul, M., Scheepers, P., Tolsma, J., & Hagendoorn, L. (2011). Anti-Muslim attitudes in the Netherlands: Tests of contradictory hypotheses derived from ethnic competition theory and intergroup contact theory. *European Sociological Review, 27,* 741–758. doi:10.1093/esr/jcq035

Strabac, Z., & Listhaug, O. (2008). Anti-Muslim prejudice in Europe: A multilevel analysis of survey data from 30 countries. *Social Science Research, 37,* 268–286. doi:10.1016/j.ssresearch.2007.02.004

van der Noll, J. (2010). Public support for a ban on headscarves: A cross-national perspective. *International Journal of Conflict and Violence, 4,* 191–204.

van der Noll, J. (2012). The aftermath of 9/11: Tolerance toward Muslims, Islamophobia and value orientations. In M. Helbling (Ed.), *Islamophobia in the West. Measuring and explaining individual attitudes* (pp. 124–136). London: Routledge.

van der Noll, J. (2014). Religious toleration of Muslims in the German public sphere. *International Journal of Intercultural Relations, 38,* 60–74. doi:10.1016/j.ijintrel.2013.01.001

Velasco González, K., Verkuyten, M., Weesie, J., & Poppe, E. (2008). Prejudice towards Muslims in the Netherlands: Testing integrated threat theory. *British Journal of Social Psychology, 47,* 667–685. doi:10.1348/014466608X284443

Verkuyten, M. (2005). Ethnic group identification and group evaluation among minority and majority groups: Testing the multiculturalism hypothesis *Journal of Personality and Social Psychology, 88,* 121–138. doi:10.1037/0022-3514.88.1.121

Verkuyten, M. (2009). Support for multiculturalism and minority rights: The role of national identification and out-group threat. *Social Justice Research, 22*, 31–52. doi:10.1007/s11211-008-0087-7

Ward, C., & Masgoret, A.-M. (2006). An integrative model of attitudes toward immigrants. *International Journal of Intercultural Relations, 30*, 671–682. doi:10.1016/j.ijintrel.2006.06.002

Yu, W.-h., & Lee, P.-l. (2013). Decomposing gender beliefs: Cross-national differences in attitudes toward maternal employment and gender equality at home. *Sociological Inquiry, 83*, 591–621. doi:10.1111/soin.12013

12

MASCULINITY AND SEXUAL PREJUDICE

A matter of heterosexual men's need to differentiate themselves from women and gay men

Jacques Berent, Juan M. Falomir-Pichastor, and Marion Chipeaux

About gender norms, and the importance of gender differentiation for heterosexual men

Research on gender stereotypes has shown that men are perceived as more agentic (e.g. independent, self-focused, power-oriented, etc.) than women, whereas women are perceived as more communal (e.g. caring, other-oriented, emotional, modest, etc.; Eagly & Kite, 1987). Importantly, these gender stereotypes not only indicate how men and women are typically perceived, they also create powerful norms and expectations about how men and women should (or should not) behave (Fiske & Stevens, 1993). Thus, in order to be considered as "real" women, women are expected to comply with norms of caretaking, dependency, deference, thinness, purity, modesty, and emotionality amongst others (e.g. Mahalik, Morray, Coonerty-Femiano, Ludlow, Slattery, & Smiler, 2005). In turn, men must conform to norms of dominance, risk-taking, aggression, pursuit of high social status, self-reliance, toughness, emotional control, and avoidance of femininity (Mahalik et al., 2003; Thompson & Pleck, 1986).

Men and women conform to these gender norms because of important identity needs. Indeed, according to social identity theory (Tajfel & Turner, 1986), people are motivated to gain a positive image of themselves (i.e. a positive self-esteem) through their membership in valued and distinctive groups. When group members feel a threat to their group's positive distinctiveness, they try to defend or restore the ingroup's positive distinctiveness. Such defensive reactions may happen when a relevant outgroup challenges one's ingroup value and/or distinctiveness, and results in intergroup differentiation efforts, such as ingroup favouritism or discrimination against the outgroup (Branscombe, Ellemers, Spears, & Doosje, 1999; Jetten & Spears, 2003). Thus, given that gender identity constitutes a powerful criterion for social categorization, men and women who identify the most with their gender group are likely to endorse gender-specific norms and maintain gender differences in an attempt to maintain a positive and distinctive image of their gender category.

That said, gender norms seem to accomplish an especially important identity function for men. Indeed, masculine roles and stereotypes are more socially valued, and contribute to legitimize men's greater status (Jost & Banaji, 1994; Pratto, Sidanius, Stallworth, & Malle, 1994). Furthermore, masculinity norms explicitly oppose to femininity (e.g. Thompson & Pleck, 1986), whereas no such opposition to the other gender exists within femininity norms. Hence, men feel stronger pressures (and are more motivated) than women to adhere to ingroup gender roles (Kite & Whitley, 1996; Whitley, 2001), as well as to maintain and reinforce the gender dichotomy (Bosson & Michniewicz, 2013). This is illustrated by various studies showing for instance that men are more concerned about not appearing feminine than women about not appearing masculine (Herek, 1988; Maccoby, 1987), or that men feel more discomfort during gender role violations (Bosson, Prewitt-Freilino, & Taylor, 2005). Even during adolescence, men perceive themselves as more typical examples of one's gender category and feel more pressure to conform to gender stereotypes (Bem, 1981; Egan & Perry, 2001).

Masculinity and sexual prejudice

Endorsement of masculinity norms and the underlying gender differentiation processes are not without consequences for those group members who deviate from gender norms. Indeed, because deviant members might threaten ingroup's positive image and distinctiveness, they are often the object of negative evaluations and attitudes, and the most harsh reactions are displayed by those individuals to whom it is important to be part of the group (Marques, Abrams, Páez, & Martínez-Taboada, 1998). As a matter of fact, homosexuals (and homosexual men in particular) deviate from the expected sexual preferences (because they are not heterosexual), and might even undermine gender distinctiveness (because they are often perceived as stereotypically effeminate; e.g. Kite & Deaux, 1987). As a consequence, men show more negative attitudes towards homosexuals (in general) than women, but especially towards same-sex homosexuals (Herek, 1988; see also Eagly, Diekman, Johannesen-Schmidt, & Koenig, 2004). In the present section, we review three research domains illustrating the role masculinity plays in heterosexual men's prejudice towards those men who deviate from gender norms (e.g. gay men).

Endorsement of masculinity norms

To the extent that sexual prejudice serves men's motivation to uphold a positive and distinct social identity, social identity theory suggests that those who derive their self-esteem from their belonging to their gender group should show more prejudice than others. In the context of sexual prejudice, several studies have consistently indicated that men's gender self-esteem, but not women's gender self-esteem, is positively correlated to negative attitudes towards homosexuals (Falomir-Pichastor & Mugny, 2009). Moreover, those who strongly adhere to *traditional* masculine roles and norms (i.e. "traditional men") show more sexual prejudice than others (Keller, 2005; Kilianski, 2003; Kite & Whitley, 1996; Smiler, 2004; Whitley, 2001). Interestingly, other studies indicate that sexual prejudice is particularly related to the anti-femininity sub-component of masculinity norms (Martínez, Vázquez, & Falomir-Pichastor, in press; Parrot, Peterson, Vincent, & Bakeman, 2008; Wilkinson, 2004).

Threats to men's masculinity

Additional evidence of the importance of masculinity in sexual prejudice stems from studies focusing on the consequences of threats to men's masculinity. In general, when group members personally fail to meet group norms, or when situational uncertainty prevent them from unambiguously conforming to group norms, they are often motivated to dispel all doubts of deviance by (re-) endorsing group norms (Falomir-Pichastor, Gabarrot, & Mugny, 2009) or by evaluating more negatively ingroup norm violators (Gómez, Morales, Hart, Vázquez, & Swann, 2011). In the case of masculinity, it is to be expected that such threats activate a need for masculinity compensation (or reaffirmation) that can be satisfied through a variety of means. Accordingly, men led to believe their personality was more similar to that of women rather than to that of average men (i.e. that they were not "prototypical" members of their gender-group) subsequently engaged in higher sexual harassment (Maass, Cadinu, Guarnieri, & Grasselli, 2003), or displayed more negative evaluations of (and felt more negative affect towards) effeminate gay targets (Glick, Gangl, Gibb, Klumpner, & Weinberg, 2007). Other studies indicate that such threats increase heterosexual men's aggressiveness towards gay men (Talley & Bettencourt, 2008), especially if the former had previously asserted their heterosexuality (Bosson, Weaver, Caswell, & Burnaford, 2012). Such a defensive reaction not only results from threats to heterosexual men's personal masculinity, but also from threats to heterosexual men's masculinity as a group. For instance, heterosexual men exposed to a "generalized" threat to masculinity (i.e. those led to believe that men's level of masculinity was decreasing over time in society) reported higher levels of personal masculinity and anti-social behaviour (Babl, 1979).

Heterosexual men's motivation to differentiate themselves from homosexual men

Lastly, other studies have confirmed the role of masculinity in the emergence of sexual prejudice by focusing on heterosexual men's motivation to differentiate themselves from ingroup deviant members (e.g. from gay men). Indeed, given that masculinity is intrinsically related to heterosexuality, and that gay men are considered more feminine than heterosexual men (Kite & Deaux, 1987), heterosexual men's sexual prejudice might not only accomplish the function of affirming one's masculinity by differentiating themselves from women, but also from gay men (Herek, 1988). As a matter of fact, a significant body of research illustrates the importance of heterosexual men's motivation to psychologically differentiate themselves from gay men, a motivation which again seems to operate both on an *individual* level and on a *collective* level.

On the individual level

Regarding heterosexual men's motivation to *individually* distance themselves from gay men (i.e. to avoid being perceived as homosexuals), research first indicates that the possibility of such misclassification is aversive and leads heterosexual men to assert their heterosexuality in one way or another. For instance, homophobic insults are common and are sometimes considered as the worst possible affront to heterosexual men (Burn, 2000; Pascoe, 2005; Preston & Stanley, 1987). Moreover, heterosexual men subliminally primed with the homophobic label "fag" were more motivated to assert their heterosexual identity (Carnaghi, Maass, & Fasoli, 2011). These heterosexual men have also been found to shift their descriptions of themselves in order to maximize their differentiation from gay men with whom they might interact (Talley & Bettencourt, 2008), especially when the risk of being misperceived as being gay was high (Bosson et al., 2005). Further, heterosexual men feel discomfort when violating certain gender norms (i.e. when performing stereotypically feminine behaviours) in part because they are aware of a potential misclassification as a homosexual person, and this discomfort is reduced once they can publicly claim their heterosexist identity (Bosson et al., 2005).

Second, heterosexual men's motivation to distinguish themselves from gay men increases other defensive reactions, such as sexual prejudice. Indeed, studies have shown that heterosexual men perceive themselves to be less similar to gay men than to heterosexual men when they are strongly prejudiced (Herek, 1988), and that heterosexual men react negatively toward gay men once they have been exposed to gay erotic materials (Parrott & Zeichner, 2008). Falomir-Pichastor and Mugny (2009; Studies 3 & 4) have shown that heterosexual men's gender self-esteem is related to sexual prejudice, in particular amongst those who are particularly motivated to differentiate themselves from gay men. Further, endorsement of gender roles is significantly related to sexual prejudice, but only amongst those heterosexual men who are strongly motivated to maintain a psychological distance from gay men (Falomir-Pichastor, Martínez, & Paterna, 2010). Finally, perceived psychological distance between oneself and gay men constitutes a reliable mediator of the effect of one's adherence to masculinity norms (and in particular that of anti-femininity) on sexual prejudice (Martínez et al., in press).

On the collective level

Other studies have focused on the importance of heterosexual men's motivation to psychologically differentiate themselves from gay men on a *collective* level (i.e. to maintain clear-cut boundaries between heterosexual and homosexual men as social categories), notably by considering the effects of one's beliefs in biological theories of sexuality. Biological theories of sexuality posit that sexual orientation and identity are genetically determined, rather than a result of environmental factors. As other essentialist beliefs (Verkuyten, 2003), biological theories may have both positive and negative meanings, and may have different consequences for majority and minority groups. On the one hand, the genetic argument has gained in popularity amongst some defendants of homosexual rights (Herek, Gillis, & Cogan, 2009) because it somewhat protects homosexuals (and other sexual minorities) from the denial of their identity by the majority (Morton & Postmes, 2009). On the other hand, biological theories also echo a tendency people and scholars have to reify the stereotype of minority groups by attributing to them inherent and stable characteristics, which may either justify prejudice and discrimination (Keller, 2005) or fulfil intergroup differentiation needs.

Recent research has tested the role played by the biological theory of sexuality both as an outcome of men's need to maintain a positive and distinct social identity (Falomir-Pichastor & Hegarty, 2013) and as a moderator of the effect of this need on sexual prejudice (Falomir-Pichastor & Mugny, 2009). First, biological theories of sexuality establish clear-cut differences between homosexual and heterosexual men, and heterosexual men may endorse them in order to satisfy positive distinctiveness needs on the group level (for ingroup distinctiveness purposes). In support of this reasoning, studies have shown that, compared to women, heterosexual men with a narrower perception of gender identity (i.e. that excludes homosexual people) endorse the biological explanation of sexual orientations to a greater extent (Falomir-Pichastor & Hegarty, 2013). Moreover, heterosexual men with strong distinctiveness needs endorsed the biological theory of sexuality to a greater extent when such needs were threatened by an *equality* social norm (i.e. a social norm suggesting that intergroup differentiation between various social groups is not to be tolerated).

Second, several studies tested the contention that biological beliefs function as a buffer against the effects of threats to heterosexual men's distinctiveness needs. For instance, heterosexual men with higher gender-based self-esteem are motivated to maintain intergroup differences between sexual groups, and show less positive attitudes towards homosexuality (Falomir-Pichastor & Mugny, 2009). However, this pattern disappears when these men are primed with scientific evidence about the existence of biological differences between homosexuals and heterosexuals. Moreover, biological beliefs also moderated the influence of egalitarian social norms, such as these norms only reduce sexual prejudice when biological differences between homo- and heterosexual people are believed to exist (Falomir-Pichastor, Mugny, & Berent, 2015).

Taken together, the studies reviewed in this section strongly support the hypothesis according to which heterosexual men's expression of sexual prejudice serves their motivation to maintain clear-cut boundaries between their ingroup (including themselves) and the two other relevant outgroups (women and gay men). As a matter of fact, the effect of masculinity on sexual prejudice seems to be so consistent that some authors even contend that fear and hatred of homosexuals should be considered as an integral part of masculine norms (Herek, 1986; Keller, 2005; see also Kimmel, 1997; Mahalik et al., 2003).

On the effects of societal changes in sex roles

If sexual prejudice is strongly rooted in heterosexual men's need to differentiate themselves from women (and ultimately from homosexuals), one could be prompted to conclude that a social context encouraging heterosexual men to act in a less traditional and anti-feminine way could reduce gender dichotomization needs as well as sexual prejudice (e.g. Pleck, 1981). However, to date, the role of gender differences on sexual prejudice has mainly been investigated through inter-individual differences (e.g. Falomir-Pichastor et al., 2015), and experimental studies on the influence of more contextual and societal factors are strongly needed. This lack of research is even more striking when considering the fact that what defines masculinity and femininity has dramatically changed over the last decades in Western societies. Indeed, on the one hand, there has been an emergence of pro-equality, non-prejudiced or anti-discriminatory values which have changed the way in which men and women behave and interact with each other. On the other hand, feminist movements' systematic questioning of traditional sex roles and pleading for greater intersex equality have influenced the traditional roles men and women occupy in Western societies. Despite the fact that gender equality is actually far from being reached, and that people in general still hold negative attitudes towards those persons who show cross-gender behaviours, it is worth examining the consequences of the fact that *modern* masculine roles are less opposed to feminine roles than ever before.

Thus, the potential effects of societal changes surrounding gender roles remain to be studied, and we have recently argued that such changes (and in particular the feminization of men) might not straightforwardly relate to sexual prejudice (Falomir-Pichastor, Berent, & Chipeaux, 2014). Rather, the consequences of these changes might depend on the way in which men construe their gender identity and deal with their ingroup distinctiveness needs. Following previous literature, our starting point was that traditional masculinity implies both anti-femininity (gender dichotomization) and heterosexuality (distinction from homosexuality). Thus, we anticipated that heterosexual men can respond to changes in the anti-femininity norm of masculinity in three different ways: first, the feminization of men could reduce the importance of the anti-femininity mandate as a masculinity norm, and, therefore, reduce the expression of sexual prejudice as a way of affirming one's masculinity by re-stating gender differences (Hypothesis 1). Second, such changes in traditional gender roles might rather introduce an additional threat to gender distinctiveness, and, therefore, motivate traditional men to restore gender dichotomy in one way or another (Bosson & Michniewicz, 2013). This could for instance be achieved by expressing greater sexual prejudice (against effeminate gay men in particular; Hypothesis 2). Third, the feminization of men could lead men to reduce the importance attributed to gender differences, but not necessarily to reduce sexual prejudice *per se*. Indeed, given that men cannot affirm their masculinity through anti-femininity, masculinity affirmation would only occur through the affirmation of an alternative masculine characteristic, such as heterosexuality. According to this hypothesis, men's feminization could increase the relative importance of men's heterosexuality affirmation through sexual prejudice, in order to avoid being mislabelled as homosexuals (Hypothesis 3).

We tested these general and alternative hypotheses in a series of experiments (Falomir-Pichastor et al., 2015). In the first two studies, we used a sample of heterosexual men and women, and first assessed the degree to which they endorsed traditional gender norms. Depending on the experimental conditions, participants were then provided with the alleged results of fictitious sociological surveys indicating that, during the last decades, men and women's behaviours remained *stable* (i.e. gender roles remained traditional), or *evolved* in such a way that they tended to become similar to that of the other gender (i.e. feminine for men and masculine for women; see Babl, 1979). A *control* condition was also introduced, in which no information was provided about this topic. We found that adherence to one's own traditional gender norms (to masculinity for men, and to femininity for women) was strongly related to sexual prejudice, irrespective of participants' gender. More importantly, men who endorsed traditional masculinity norms to a greater extent showed more sexual prejudice both in the *stability* and *evolution* conditions, as compared to the *control* condition. Interestingly, this was not the case for women.

In a second set of studies, we focused on heterosexual men and investigated the specific processes related to sexual prejudice in both the *stability* and *evolution* conditions. In one study, we used the same procedure as previously mentioned, and we additionally manipulated the gay prototype: it was described either as effeminate or as masculine (Glick et al., 2007). Results showed that, when gender roles were said to be *stable*, heterosexual men's endorsement of traditional masculinity norms mostly increased sexual prejudice when the prototypical gay was depicted as "feminine" (as compared to a "masculine" gay). However, gay prototypicality did not moderate the effect of masculinity on sexual prejudice in the *evolution* condition. Thus, in line with past findings (see Glick et al., 2007), the *stability* condition appears to reinforce the motivation to maintain gender differences and to reject feminine gay men. However, this dynamic vanished once the importance of gender dichotomization was reduced by the feminization of men (i.e. in the *evolution* condition).

Finally, in another study, we investigated the process underlying the expression of sexual prejudice observed when gender norms are believed to be changing. Here, we considered the possibility that beliefs in the biological theory of sexuality could satisfy the hypothesized increase in one's need for differentiation between heterosexual and gay men (Falomir-Pichastor & Hegarty, 2013; Falomir-Pichastor & Mugny, 2009). The procedure was similar to that of the previous studies. In addition, participants were informed that science either *supports* the existence of biological differences between heterosexual and gay men, or *infirms* the existence of such differences. Results showed that, in the *evolution* condition, traditional heterosexual men displayed greater sexual prejudice when biological differences between heterosexual and gay men were *infirmed* by science, but not when they were *supported* by science. In the *stability* condition, the biological theory of sexuality did not moderate the influence of masculinity on sexual prejudice. Thus, scientific evidence in support of biological intergroup differences seemed to fulfil the need to remove possible confusion between hetero- and homosexual men that social changes might have introduced, and sexual prejudice seems to be less necessary in order to reaffirm one's own masculinity.

Taken together, the results of these studies demonstrate that, amongst the three alternative hypotheses outlined above, only the third one seems to be supported. Indeed, it appears that the evolution of gender norms can increase sexual prejudice (contrary to Hypothesis 1) and lead heterosexual men to discriminate against homosexuals, irrespective of the latter's degree of femininity (contrary to Hypothesis 2). It finally appears that the evolution of gender norms increases men's sexual prejudice because of their heightened motivation to affirm their gender identity through another masculinity norm such as heterosexuality and, eventually, in order to dissociate themselves from gay men (in line with Hypothesis 3).

Summary and concluding thoughts

The aim of this chapter was to illustrate and explain why men (rather than women) display higher levels of sexual prejudice. This phenomenon seems rooted to some extent in men's specific need to affirm and maintain a distinct gender identity through the endorsement of masculinity norms. Indeed, factors increasing men's need to affirm a positive and distinctive masculine identity (e.g. a threat to masculinity, endorsement of traditional gender roles, or gender-based self-esteem) appear to increase sexual prejudice. Furthermore, factors granting clear-cut differences between hetero- and homosexual people (such as biological differences) reduced the impact of the afore-mentioned factors.

Finally, we have shown that either the stability of traditional gender roles or the evolution they have undergone in the past decades might both increase men's sexual prejudice, but for different reasons. In the present section we will address some of the implications of the large body of research we have outlined here.

To begin with, this chapter points to the fact that the relation between masculinity and sexual prejudice is not straightforward. Whereas fear and hatred of homosexuals are often considered as a central and indissociable component of masculinity norms (e.g. Mahalik et al., 2003), we rather suggest that this relationship is complex and varies as a function of different dispositional and contextual factors. Future research could further examine this link, and determine for instance whether the relationship between masculinity and sexual prejudice is bidirectional, or whether men's fear of appearing gay might also lead to an increased motivation to differentiate themselves from (and discriminate against) women. Not only would this help to better understand the very basis of masculine norms and its effects on sexual prejudice, this would also help to understand how other forms of discrimination (e.g. against women) are related to heterosexual men's particular relationship to homosexual men.

One could also wonder about the role of men's motivation to maintain their dominant social status in the investigated processes. Indeed, men's sexual prejudice may also translate as an attempt to exclude deviant ingroup members who threaten the superiority men benefit from within the social hierarchy (Connell & Connell, 2005), and the effects of traditional masculinity on sexual prejudice could in fact be ultimately driven by men's concern over their social status. Although compelling, this hypothesis has not found strong supportive evidence, especially when pitted against the idea that opposition to femininity is the main determinant of men's sexual prejudice (Wilkinson, 2004). Future research should further investigate the central role played by anti-femininity, and if it turns out to be a better predictor than (or a mediator of) the effects of other components of masculinity norms (e.g. emotional control) on men's sexual prejudice.

Another contribution of this chapter to the existent literature on gender and sexual prejudice is the consideration of contextual and societal (rather than inter-individual) factors, namely the evolution of gender roles. Results showed that both the perceived stability and evolution of traditional roles might lead men to express higher sexual prejudice. Therefore, one could be rather pessimistic about the potential reduction in sexual prejudice following changes in gender roles. However, it is worth noting that we initially highlighted three alternative hypotheses regarding the potential effects of men's feminization, and we still believe that all these hypotheses are theoretically grounded. Despite the fact that our studies have rather confirmed the third hypothesis according to which men's feminization overall increases sexual prejudice, they point to important moderators of this effect. For instance, this pattern disappeared when the biological theory of sexual orientation was supported by scientific evidence, which constitutes a moderator of particular relevance to the social context under study. Whereas this theory is upheld and supported by numerous pro-gay movements in an attempt to convey the idea that sexual orientation is not a choice and sexual prejudice illegitimate (Herek et al., 2009), the present findings suggest that this theory can also satisfy one's distinctiveness needs and, again, reduce sexual prejudice. Accordingly, further research is needed in order to investigate conditions under which men's feminization increases rather than decreases sexual prejudice.

Practical implementations

Finally, and more broadly speaking, the considerations raised in this chapter inform us about inter- and intra-group processes leading to everyday life intergroup discrimination. Indeed, heterosexual men's struggle to distinguish themselves both from women and "deviant" gay men is only one of many illustrations of the main function accomplished by prejudice and discrimination: the upholding of a positive and distinctive social identity (Tajfel & Turner, 1986). Thus, it seems possible to reduce sexual prejudice to the extent that one's masculine gender identity is affirmed by other means. Moreover, these considerations might as well possibly inform scholars and practitioners on ways to reduce other forms of intergroup prejudice (e.g. sexism) and pacify the social relationships that take place in a society where structure and hierarchy is of utmost interest to all of its members. Indeed, efforts to build and maintain a harmonious society must acknowledge each and every group's identity needs and avoid as far as possible threatening them, for such threats, evidently, have negative consequences for intergroup relations.

References

Babl, J. D. (1979). Compensatory masculine responding as a function of sex role. *Journal of Consulting and Clinical Psychology, 47*, 252–257. doi:10.1037/0022-006X.47.2.252

Bem, S. L. (1981). *Bem Sex-role Inventory: Professional manual*. Palo Alto, CA: Consulting Psychologists Press.

Bosson, J. K., & Michniewicz, K. S. (2013). Gender dichotomization at the level of ingroup identity: What it is, and why men use it more than women. *Journal of Personality and Social Psychology, 105*, 425–442. doi:10.1037/a0033126

Bosson, J. K., Prewitt-Freilino, J. L., & Taylor, J. N. (2005). Role rigidity: A problem of identity misclassification. *Journal of Personality and Social Psychology, 89*, 552–565. doi:10.1037/0022-3514.89.4.552

Bosson, J. K., Weaver, J. R., Caswell, T. A., & Burnaford, R. M. (2012). Gender threats and men's antigay behaviors: The harmful effects of asserting heterosexuality. *Group Processes & Intergroup Relations, 15*, 471–486. doi:10.1177/1368430211432893

Branscombe, N. R., Ellemers, N., Spears, R., & Doosje, B. (1999). The context and content of social identity threat. In N. Ellemers & R. Spears (Eds.), *Social Identity: Context, commitment, content* (pp. 35–58). Oxford: Blackwell Science.

Burn, S. M. (2000). Heterosexuals' use of "fag" and "queer" to deride one another: A contributor to heterosexism and stigma. *Journal of Homosexuality, 40*, 1–12. doi:10.1300/J082v40n02_01

Carnaghi, A., Maass, A., & Fasoli, F. (2011). Enhancing masculinity by slandering homosexuals: The role of homophobic epithets in heterosexual gender identity. *Personality and Social Psychology Bulletin, 37*, 1655–1665. doi:10.1177/0146167211424167

Connell, R. W., & Connell, R. (2005). *Masculinities*. University of California Press.

Eagly, A. H., Diekman, A. B., Johannesen-Schmidt, M. C., & Koenig, A. M. (2004). Gender gaps in sociopolitical attitudes: A social psychological analysis. *Journal of Personality and Social Psychology, 87*, 796–816. doi: 10.1037/0022-3514.87.6.796

Eagly, A. H., & Kite, M. E. (1987). Are stereotypes of nationalities applied to both women and men? *Journal of Personality and Social Psychology, 53*, 451. doi:10.1037/0022-3514.53.3.451

Egan, S. K., & Perry, D. G. (2001). Gender identity: a multidimensional analysis with implications for psychosocial adjustment. *Developmental Psychology, 37, 4*, 451. doi:10.1037//0012-1649.37.4.451

Falomir, J. M., Berent, J., & Chipeaux, M. (2014, July 9). *Evolution of Gender Identity and Attitudes Towards Homosexuality*. Paper presented at the 17th General Meeting of the European Association of Social Psychology (EASP), Amsterdam, the Netherlands.

Falomir-Pichastor, J. M., & Hegarty, P. (2013). Maintaining distinctions under threat: Heterosexual men endorse the biological theory of sexuality when equality is the norm. *British Journal of Social Psychology, 53*, 731–751.doi:10.1111/bjso.12051

Falomir-Pichastor, J. M., Gabarrot, F., & Mugny, G. (2009). Group motives in threatening contexts: When a loyalty conflict paradoxically reduces the influence of an anti-discrimination ingroup norm. *European Journal of Social Psychology, 39, 2*, 196–206. doi: 10.1002/ejsp.520

Falomir-Pichastor, J. M., & Mugny, G. (2009). "I'm not gay.... I'm a real man!": Heterosexual men's gender self-esteem and sexual prejudice. *Personality and Social Psychology Bulletin, 35*, 1233–1243. doi:10.1177/0146167209338072

Falomir-Pichastor, J. M., Martínez, C., & Paterna, C. (2010). Gender-role's attitude, perceived similarity, and sexual prejudice against gay men. *The Spanish Journal of Psychology, 13*, 841–848. doi:10.1017/S1138741600002493

Falomir-Pichastor, J. M., Mugny, G. & Berent, J. (2015). *Egalitarian Norms and Distinctiveness Threat: The role of the biological theory of sexuality on attitudes towards homosexuality*. Manuscript submitted for publication.

Fiske, S. T., & Stevens, L. E. (1993). What's so special about sex? Gender ste-reotyping and discrimination. In S. Oskamp, & M.Costanzo (Eds.), *Gender is-sues in contemporary society* (pp. 173-196). Thousand Oaks, CA: Sage Publications.

Glick, P., Gangl, C., Gibb, S., Klumpner, S., & Weinberg, E. (2007). Defensive reactions to masculinity threat: More negative affect toward effeminate (but not masculine) gay men. *Sex Roles, 57*, 55–59. doi:10.1007/s11199-007-9195-3

Gómez, Á., Morales, J. F., Hart, S., Vázquez, A., & Swann, W. B. (2011). Rejected and excluded forevermore, but even more devoted irrevocable ostracism intensifies loyalty to the group among identity-fused persons. *Personality and Social Psychology Bulletin, 37, 12*, 1574-1586. doi:10.1177/0146167211424580

Herek, G. M. (1986). On heterosexual masculinity: Some psychical consequences of the social construction of gender and sexuality. *American Behavioral Scientist, 29,* 563–577.

Herek, G. M. (1988). Heterosexuals' attitudes toward lesbians and gay men: Correlates and gender differences. *Journal of Sex Research, 25*, 451–477. doi:10.1080/00224498809551476

Herek, G. M., Gillis, J. R., & Cogan, J. C. (2009). Internalized stigma among sexual minority adults: Insights from a social psychological perspective. *Journal of Counseling Psychology, 56*, 32–43.doi:10.1037/a0014672

Jetten, J., & Spears, R. (2003). The divisive potential of differences and similarities: The role of intergroup distinctiveness in intergroup differentiation. *European Review of Social Psychology, 14*, 203–241. doi:10.1080/10463280340000063

Jost, J. T., & Banaji, M. R. (1994). The role of stereotyping in system-justification and the production of false consciousness. *British Journal of Social Psychology, 33*, 1–27. doi:10.1111/j.2044-8309.1994.tb01008.x

Keller, J. (2005). In genes we trust: The biological component of psychological essentialism and its relationship to mechanisms of motivated social cognition. *Journal of Personality and Social Psychology, 88*, 686–702. doi:10.1037/0022-3514.88.4.686

Kilianski, S. E. (2003). Explaining heterosexual men's attitudes toward women and gay men: The theory of exclusively masculine identity. *Psychology of Men and Masculinity, 4*, 37–56. doi:10.1037/1524-9220.4.1.37

Kimmel, M. (1997). Masculinity as homophobia: Fear, shame, and silence in the construction of gender identity. In M. M. Gergen & S. N. Davis (Eds.), *Toward a New Psychology of Gender* (pp. 223–242). New York: Routledge.

Kite, M. E., & Deaux, K. (1987). Gender belief systems: Homosexuality and the implicit inversion theory. *Psychology of Women Quarterly, 11*, 83–96. doi:10.1111/j.1471-6402.1987.tb00776.x

Kite, M. E., & Whitley, B. E., Jr. (1996). Sex differences in attitudes toward homosexual persons, behaviors, and civil rights: A meta-analysis. *Personality and Social Psychology Bulletin, 22,* 336–353. doi:10.1177/0146167296224002

Maass, A., Cadinu, M., Guarnieri, G., & Grasselli, A. (2003). Sexual harassment under social identity threat: The computer harassment paradigm. *Journal of Personality and Social Psychology, 85*, 853–870. doi:10.1037/0022-3514.85.5.853

Maccoby, E. E. (1987). The varied meanings of "masculine" and "feminine". In J. M. Reinisch, L. A. Rosenblum, & S. A. Sanders (Eds.), *Masculinity/femininity* (pp. 227–239). New York: Oxford University Press.

Mahalik, J. R., Morray, E. B., Coonerty-Femiano, A., Ludlow, L. H., Slattery, S. M., & Smiler, A. (2005). Development of the conformity to feminine norms inventory. *Sex Roles, 52*, 417–435. doi:10.1007/s11199-005-3709-7

Mahalik, J. R., Locke, B. D., Ludlow, L. H., Diemer, M. A., Scott, R. P., Gottfried, M., & Freitas, G. (2003). Development of the conformity to masculine norms inventory. *Psychology of Men & Masculinity, 4*, 3–25. doi:10.1037/1524-9220.4.1.3

Marques, J., Abrams, D., Páez, D., & Martínez-Taboada, C. (1998). The role of categorization and in-group norms in judgments of groups and their members. *Journal of Personality and Social Psychology, 75,* 976–988. doi:10.1037/0022-3514.75.4.976

Martínez, C., Vázquez, C., & Falomir-Pichastor, J. M. (in press). Perceived similarity with gay men mediates the effect of antifemininity on heterosexual men's antigay prejudice. *Journal of Homosexuality*.

Morton, T. A., & Postmes, T. (2009). When differences become essential: Minority essentialism in response to majority treatment. *Personality and Social Psychology Bulletin, 35*, 5, 656-668. doi: 10.1177/0146167208331254

Parrott, D. J., & Zeichner, A. (2008). Determinants of anger and physical aggression based on sexual orientation: An experimental examination of hypermasculinity and exposure to male gender role violations. *Archives of Sexual Behavior, 37*, 891–901. doi:10.1009/s10508-007-9194-z

Parrott, D. J., Peterson, J. L., Vincent, W., & Bakeman, R. (2008). Correlates of anger in response to gay men: Effects of male gender role beliefs, sexual prejudice, and masculine gender role stress. *Psychology of Men & Masculinity, 9,* 167–178. doi:10.1037/1524-9220.9.3.167

Pascoe, C. J. (2005). "Dude, you're a fag": Adolescent masculinity and the fag discourse. *Sexualities, 8,* 329–346. doi:10.1177/1363460705053337

Pleck, J. H. (1981). *The myth of masculinity.* Cambridge, MA: MIT Press.

Pratto, F., Sidanius, J., Stallworth, L. M., & Malle, B. F. (1994). Social dominance orientation: A personality variable predicting social and political attitudes. *Journal of Personality and Social Psychology, 67,* 741–763. doi:10.1037/0022-3514.67.4.741

Preston, K., & Stanley, K. (1987). "What's the worst thing...?" Gender-directed insults. *Sex Roles, 17,* 209–219. doi:10.1007/BF00287626

Smiler, A. P. (2004). Thirty years after the discovery of gender: Psychological concepts and measures of masculinity. *Sex Roles, 50,* 15–26. doi:10.1023/B:SERS.0000011069.02279.4c

Tajfel, H., & Turner, J. C. (1986). The social identity theory of intergroup behavior. In S. Worchel & W. Austin (Eds.), *Psychology of Intergroup Relations* (pp. 7–24). Chicago, IL: Nelson-Hall.

Talley, A. E., & Bettencourt, A. B. (2008). Evaluations and aggression directed at a gay male target: The role of threat and antigay prejudice. *Journal of Applied Social Psychology, 38,* 647–683. doi:10.1111/j.1559-1816.2007.00321.x

Thompson, E. H., & Pleck, J. H. (1986). The structure of male role norms. *American Behavioral Scientist, 29,* 531–543.

Verkuyten, M. (2003). Discourses about ethnic group (de)essentialism: Oppressive and progressive aspects. *British Journal of Social Psychology, 42,* 3, 371–391. Doi:10.1348/014466603322438215

Whitley, B. E. (2001). Gender-role variables and attitudes toward homosexuality. *Sex Roles, 45,* 691–721. doi:10.1023/A:1015640318045

Wilkinson, W. W. (2004). Authoritarian hegemony, dimensions of masculinity, and male antigay attitudes. *Psychology of Men & Masculinity, 5,* 121–131. doi:10.1037/1524-9220.5.2.121

CONCLUSIONS

From research to action

Brigitte Mantilleri

First and foremost, this text tells a story of meetings within the framework of the awareness campaign *Stéréotypes tip tip* launched in 2013 and orchestrated by the Equal Opportunity Office at Geneva University.

It was written by what is termed an "administration", as part of a collective work to be published, moreover, by a prestigious publisher. It was devised for publication by academics – researchers, men and women, some of whom took part in our office's programme of mentoring for new generations – *Mentorat relève*. The idea of such a text received a good reception, which in itself signaled a willingness to do away with hierarchical barriers and shatter glass walls in the university. It proved that if one is open to others, men and women whoever they may be, fruitful intellectual meetings will take place.

Why mention such meetings? Simply to point out that it is very important, even essential, to bring together the forces at work in the observation of society and the relations between men and women, in order to gain a better understanding of the mechanisms of our interactions.

These forces necessarily question certain practices, stereotypes and other prejudices which constrain us and prevent us from functioning together in harmony.

They are in fact working towards beneficial change.

It seemed logical that the Equal Opportunity Office should take part in this exciting adventure since most of the research collected in this volume is resonant with the Office's practice. Indeed, the questions studied occur daily. Gender stereotypes, its catchline for a two-year campaign, as well as studies on women in male hierarchies and in leadership positions, on reconciling one's personal life with a professional life, "queen bees", glass ceilings or vulnerability, are all subjects at the heart of the concerns of the men and women who come to see us at the Office or are themes of conferences and workshops.

The articles presented here should help support our actions, reinforce established policies, and even lead to the adoption of firmer and more coherent measures, in line with our observations concerning womens' and men's behaviour and with findings that very often go unheeded, such as the strange tendency of women to accept and even embrace the injustices they suffer and the equally strange tendency of men to turn a blind eye to the fact that they are often unjustly privileged, the difficulties encountered by other, progressive, men and men of good will in getting their ideas accepted, the traps that are hard to identify and to avoid, and ultimately the fact that often brilliant women researchers are slowed down in their careers but dare not ask uncomfortable questions or take part in support programmes welcomed by the overwhelming majority of their participants. Clichés still hold sway.

Therefore, when studies such as these broach the problem of living or working together, it is essential to link them to practice, in other words to make sure that their results are well publicized, discussed and even applied. Should we not then really examine the questions studied and tackle, at all levels, the problem of stereotypes, of gender bias and of structural checks ? Should we not break down the fences, change the rules and impose parity?

There are infinite possibilities as yet insufficiently explored: to begin with, what of the so-called plasticity of the human brain? And if our brain offers infinite possibilites, why then should we continue to be fettered by the shackles of hierarchy and discipline, and academic constraints versus administrative restraints, when we could, at least in some ways, move forward together?

INDEX